Gender, Authenticity, and the Missive Letter in Eighteenth-Century France

Gender, Authenticity, and the Missive Letter in Eighteenth-Century France

Marie-Anne de La Tour, Rousseau's Real-Life Julie

Mary McAlpin

Lewisburg
Bucknell University Press

Associated University Presses
2010 Eastpark Boulevard
Cranbury, NJ 08512

The paper used in this publication meets the requirements of the American National Standard for Permanence of Paper for Printed Library Materials Z39.48-1984.

Library of Congress Cataloging-in-Publication Data

McAlpin, Mary, 1960–
    Gender, authenticity, and the missive letter in eighteenth-century France : Marie-Anne de La Tour, Rousseau's real-life Julie / Mary McAlpin.
        p.   cm.
    Includes bibliographical references and index.
    ISBN-10: 0-8387-5652-2 (alk. paper)
    ISBN-13: 978-0-8387-5652-2 (alk. paper)
    1. Letter writing, French—History—18th century. 2. French letters—Women authors—History and criticism. 3. La Tour, Marianne Alissan de, 1730–1789—Correspondence—History and criticism. 4. Rousseau, Jean-Jacques, 1712–1778—Correspondence—History and criticism. I. Title.

PQ711.M33 2006
848'.509—dc22

                                                                    2006002570

Contents

Acknowledgments

I AM GRATEFUL TO GITA MAY AND PRISCILLA FERGUSON FOR HELPING THIS project along in its earliest stages, and to the generous readers of Bucknell University Press. I also benefited greatly from a grant awarded by the Columbia University Graduate School of Arts and Sciences, from research leave and funds given by the University of Tennessee Faculty Development Program, and from a Camargo Foundation residency fellowship in Cassis, France. Special thanks to Ray and Celeste for all their support and love.

Gender, Authenticity, and the Missive Letter in Eighteenth-Century France

Introduction: Julie Lives to Love You

R. Let us assume the worst; my Julie. . . .
N. Oh! if she had existed!
R. What then?
N. But surely it is only a fiction.

—Rousseau, "Préface dialoguée,"
Julie, ou La Nouvelle Héloïse

ON SEPTEMBER 28, 1761, SIX MONTHS AFTER THE PUBLICATION OF HIS epistolary novel, *Julie, ou La Nouvelle Héloïse*, Jean-Jacques Rousseau received a letter signed with the pseudonym "Claire," after his heroine's inseparable confidante. Claire had important information, for she wrote to tell Rousseau that the tragic conclusion to his work had been miraculously undone. His virtuous Julie had not died but lived on, in the person of Claire's closest friend: "You will thus not learn, monsieur, who I am: but you will learn that Julie is not in the least dead, and that she lives to love you."[1] Rousseau uncharacteristically allowed himself to be drawn into a correspondence with the two women, although their true identities were unknown to him. While "Claire" (Marie-Madeleine Bernardoni) remained a part of the correspondence for only five months, her friend Marie-Anne de La Tour, the would-be Julie, went on to exchange 175 letters with Rousseau over some fifteen years.

De La Tour prepared a manuscript version of the lengthy exchange as early as 1770, but Rousseau refused to give her permission to publish. She kept her promise never to make the letters public, even after his death in 1778, although she did will her edited copy of the exchange to a Swiss publisher at her own death in 1789. First appearing in print in 1803, the Rousseau–de La Tour exchange has drawn readers for two principal reasons: its novelistic origins, in which fiction and reality seem to blur, and, of course, Rousseau's immense fame. The letters of one of the most influential figures of the French Enlightenment are of obvious interest to scholars, given that they are assumed to reveal a more authentic version of his personality than the works he wrote for publication. Rousseau's attitude toward his devoted female correspondent has driven the varied conclusions reached by critics as to the significance of these particular letters, said to demonstrate, for example, Rousseau's paranoid spitefulness, an interpretation based on his initial encouragement and subsequent dismissal of de La Tour. At the same time, de La Tour's persistence in continuing the exchange despite Rousseau's many attempts to break it off have been cited as evidence of the abuse Rousseau was himself subjected to by the French reading public. This same persistence on de La Tour's part has been read as evidence of the psychosis eighteenth-century readers risked by losing themselves too deeply in a novel.

My goal in this study is to argue for an entirely new perspective on what was at stake in this exchange of letters between a famous author and his most devoted female fan. By analyzing this woman letter writer and her correspondence in their historical context, I demonstrate that Marie-Anne de La Tour constructed herself as an *author*, however careful one must be in applying this term to her. As unlikely as her project might seem to us today, this unknown woman deliberately sought public fame as an *épistolière*, a woman writer of private letters. As I argue in chapters 1 and 2, there is much evidence that de La Tour planned from the beginning to create a publishable private correspondence with Rousseau. She had every reason to believe that this exchange would be a success with the public; Rousseau's novel was the best-selling work of the century, and his fame, along with his controversial reputation, ensured that his private writings were highly valued in the literary marketplace. De La Tour's self-construction as a real-life version of Rousseau's famous heroine, Julie d'Etange, would have made the exchange all the more attractive to readers. Yet another factor contributing to the potential publication value of this exchange, one easily overlooked today, was the heightened status accorded the private missive at the time. In the eighteenth century, de La Tour's chosen genre was at the top of an aesthetic hierarchy in which Truth played a predominant role in determining value. A missive letter was supposed to be a spontaneous expression of personality, characterized by an easy, effortless style that mimicked that of conversation.[2] As such, authentic missive letters easily outranked their less reputable cousin, the epistolary novel, a genre that was in principle—although certainly not in publishing practice—merely a pale imitation of the ideal represented by the true missive letter.

It was unfortunate for de La Tour that she was unable to publish the exchange during her lifetime, for the privileged status of missive letters did not survive long into the nineteenth century. Nor did the public's fascination with all things related to Rousseau. By the time these letters were published in 1803, de La Tour's success in presenting herself as a private correspondent with no literary talents or pretensions whatsoever—as "merely" Rousseau's devoted soul mate, from whose pen the purest of Julie-like sentiments spontaneously flowed—did not bring her the fame and respect she had obviously anticipated. She is at present most often perceived as an annoyingly persistent, and pathetically naive, woman fan. Her letters are treated as data for Rousseau-related research, and considered quite thoroughly mundane as to their value as written documents.

My purpose in arguing for de la Tour's authorial consciousness is not, by any means, to have this exchange placed into the category "literature," as we currently understand this term. While I am indeed arguing that this woman had authorial intentions, I am not attempting to remake her into an "author" along contemporary lines. I am instead arguing for increased sensibility to the publishing potential of eighteenth-century missive letters, and for the consciousness of this potential among eighteenth-century letter writers. We are accustomed to consider publishability as equivalent to "literariness," with the latter notion defined as elevated style and third-person effacement. Given how little we value documents such as letters, we too easily assume that all letters have at all times been written with no thought of publication, unless it is clearly indicated otherwise. In sharp contrast, eighteenth-century considerations of the private letter devote serious attention to the issue of the writer's lack of awareness that his or her letters will one day be published—a clear indication that suspicion of intent to publish was an omnipresent concern. This generalized assumption of the publication value of letters was particularly acute when one of the correspondents was famous. Rousseau himself was certain from the first that de La Tour's aim was to make his letters public; he even suspected that "she" was a man, a "Monsieur Julie" seeking to trick him into sending passionate letters to a chimera, letters that would then be published in order to damage Rousseau's reputation.

The current lack of suspicion of intent to publish in writers of eighteenth-century missive letters is an unfortunate lacuna in the field of epistolary studies, and one I hope to fill with this study. There is, however, one letter writer whose authorial consciousness has been debated at length. Marie de Rabutin-Chantal, marquise de Sévigné, may seem at first an unlikely point of comparison to de La Tour, in that Sévigné is not only the most famous and respected of French letter writers, male or female, but also a seventeenth-century figure (b. 1626, d. 1696). To address the latter point first, it has been argued, notably by Janet Altman, that Sévigné's influence does not begin to be felt until the early to mid eighteenth century.[3] Her reputation as an *épistolière* developed, that is, in the context of an eighteenth-century preference for intimacy and authenticity in letters, a sharp contrast to the seventeenth-century standard of conscious cultivation of epistolary style.[4] But while Sévigné represented "naturalness" and intimacy in the eighteenth century, it was her stylistic mastery that allowed her reputation to survive into the nineteenth century, when concern with form again dominated discussions of the epistolary genre. Sévigné began to be evaluated, that is, according to the "literariness" of her letters, and the positive verdict that was reached has assured her a place to this day in the French canon, alongside such luminaries as Balzac, Flaubert, and Proust.

When the most influential of Sévigné critics, Roger Duchêne, addresses the authorial consciousness of the divine marquise, it is precisely the question of the literariness of her letters that concerns him.[5] Duchêne begins his analysis by carefully distinguishing the *épistolier*, or private letter writer, from the *auteur épistolaire*, or epistolary author, who writes with the intention of publishing. Writing letters for publication was not uncommon in seventeenth-century France, when, again, letters were considered valuable and publishable only when they exhibited cultivated style.[6] That a mere *épistolière* might surpass all the *auteurs épistolaires* of her age, indeed of all ages, would be miraculous, in Duchêne's opinion: "The miracle however took place, and it constitutes the originality of Mme de Sévigné's letters."[7] Duchêne concludes that Sévigné produced a true rara avis, an "involuntary literary masterpiece."

Bernard Bray, with whom Duchêne engaged in an exchange of articles on this topic, counters that because Sévigné routinely showed her letters to a group of acquaintances, these missives were clearly the product of a conscious creative effort to please more than a single correspondent. While far from publication in the current sense of the term, Sévigné's habit of sharing her epistolary writing with cultivated friends does indeed seem to imply consciousness of a public, however limited. This awareness precludes adding the qualifier "involuntary" to Sévigné's epistolary output, in Bray's opinion. To apply Duchêne's terms to Bray's analysis, Sévigné is to be classified as an *auteur épistolaire*, not an *épistolière*, however limited in scope the audience for whom she wrote.

But to what genre would this "voluntary masterpiece" belong? If a letter is "voluntarily" written as a literary masterpiece, does it also maintain its status as a "missive" letter? This question is never posed in the course of the Duchêne-Bray debate because, strangely, these two literary critics are quite unconcerned with the epistolary genre per se, despite their attention to Sévigné, its most esteemed practitioner. Duchêne and Bray are focused on Sévigné's correspondence as literature, not letters. Duchêne may declare Sévigné's letters true private missives, but he does so only to intensify their status as literary masterpiece. To refer to Sévigné as an *épistolière* would be an insult according to the standards of his own analysis, if he were not simultaneously making a claim as to the miraculousness of Sévigné's having produced "literature" by means of this so very negligible of written forms. Both *auteurs* and *auteurs épistolaires* seek to produce Art; the latter has merely chosen a less exalted genre. The difference between an *épistolier* and an *auteur* is, to the contrary, essential: the former is of no interest to us today, unless, as in Sévigné's case, the "miracle" of elevation to literary status occurs.

This obsession with raising correspondences above their status as missive letters is, as I argue in chapter 4, common to current discussions of the epistolary genre. It is alien, however, as I argue in chapter 3, to eighteenth-century considerations of the missive letter, and this difference is essential to my consideration of de La Tour. According to present-day literary-critical standards, Sévigné's and de La Tour's letters belong to two separate genres—literature versus documentation—and the question of their relative value is too ludicrous to consider. In the eighteenth century, however, Sévigné and de La Tour would have been considered side by side, as letter writers. Nor is it clear that de La Tour would always have suffered from such a comparison; despite Sévigné's fame, there were eighteenth-century critics who dismissed her as too "classical," too much of her own time—too "literary," in a word. While most eighteenth-century letter manuals promoted her style, a number of influential commentators declared that Sévigné's letters lacked the expected qualities of a missive letter: naturalness, above all.[8] Her reputation would have suffered greatly, in the eighteenth century, from Bray's conclusion that she was an *auteur épistolaire*; any attribution of "voluntariness" or authorial consciousness to her letters would have excluded them from consideration as valuable. The emotion to be communicated to the reader of private letters was to be immanent—not translated through fiction, not processed through the mind of an "author." It was not fictional, not stylized, not False.

At the same time, there was surprisingly little concern with verifying claims to authenticity in the eighteenth century. Letters presented as authentic are declared in introductory material, including the introduction to the 1803 Rousseau–de La Tour correspondence, to be *manifestly* so; any reader incapable of grasping this authenticity is dismissed as sorely lacking in sensitivity. As a solution to the perennial difficulty of dealing with the pitfalls of authorial intention, this method is as effective as the Death of the Author. In the eighteenth century, one merely passed on the question of a letter's authenticity to the reader, attaching moral opprobrium to anyone willing to doubt, for example, that the letters contained in *La Nouvelle Héloïse* were authentic. When the Author died in contemporary critical theory, the text became the source of all truth concerning meaning, and anyone who questioned its ascendancy by trying to introduce the notion of authorial intention was brushed aside as unsophisticated. The difference in how criticism was countered is again revealing of the obsessions of the two eras: in the first case, the reader is controlled by attacking his morality; in the second, theoretical debate is quashed by an accusation of intellectual naiveté.

If I were to leave de La Tour in the netherworld that the missive letter currently inhabits in discussions of aesthetic value, I would, significantly, not be obliged to enter into the topic of the Death of the Author. The letter writer never died, at least not in the most influential essay on authorship and mortality, Michel Foucault's "What is an Author?" (1969), in which we find a revealing aside: "A private letter may well have a signer—it does not have an author. . . . An anonymous text posted on a wall probably has a writer—but not an author."[9] A "signer" has a more dense ontological status than the discredited "author," albeit barely so; and while Foucault does not pause to develop exactly how the two are to be distinguished, the very marginality of the letter "signer," compared to the unobscure object of Foucault's interest—the author of a literary text, published as such with a title page containing his name and thus misleading readers into accepting his physical presence hovering over the work—allows the signer to escape the implications of the Author's demise. It is unclear whether Foucault is speaking of an autograph letter (probably the case) or of a published private letter;

if one publishes the signer's letters, for example, does this individual acquire, either fully or partially, the exalted status of author, and thus become subject to all the restrictions Foucault places on those who would consider the resulting "work"?

However Foucault himself might have addressed these questions, it is certainly true that in the critical practice of those who embraced the Death of the Author, letter writers remained alive and well. Missive letters, even those by writers with impeccable authorial standing external to their letters, were granted an imprimatur of spontaneous purity that was often used to verify the closed textual readings directed at literary works. As I argue with regard to reader-response theory in chapter 4, and postmodern feminist theory in chapter 5, this too-facile assumption of authenticity, in contrast to the closed-off density accorded the literary text, has allowed a misuse of letters as "pure" data, and in particular of letters by women. While feminist critics, myself included, do not share the condescending attitude toward women characteristic of many of de La Tour's past readers, the search for "authentic" women's voices from the past may at times lead us to rely too heavily on evidence obtained from private writing. The assumption that patriarchy imposes a screen on published writing by women can lead to overreliance on the "purity" of women's private writings. De La Tour's marginal case teaches us, as feminist scholars, to be highly suspicious of a conscious publication project on the part of the writing woman behind the letter.

There are exceptions, of course, to the generalizations I have just made concerning the use of letters. One of the few contemporary studies to consider the unfashionable notion of intentionality and the eighteenth-century missive letter is English Showalter's "Authorial Self-Consciousness in the Familiar Letter: The Case of Madame de Graffigny" (1986). Showalter looks for textual clues pointing to an intent on Graffigny's part to publish her letters to François-Antoine Devaux ("Panpan"), letters made famous (and highly publishable) by Graffigny's descriptions of Voltaire's private life. Showalter finds nothing definitive, and concludes by pointing out that Sévigné's phenomenal success in the early eighteenth century caused every literate French man or woman writing a private letter to be aware of the possibility of publication. This very awareness makes the establishment of authorial self-consciousness in missive letter writers untenable, for Showalter, who notes that any intent to publish on Graffigny's part might well have led to the production of letters that appear to be as "real-seeming" as any incontestably "real" letter. For Showalter, the question of Graffigny's authorial self-consciousness is simply undecidable: "Graffigny's conception of herself as author of familiar letters, 'auteur épistolaire,' need not imply any effort at literariness. The best way to imitate Sévigné would have been to immerse herself so much in the immediacy of her own experience and writing that she felt as free and spontaneous as she did in conversation."[10]

In Showalter's analysis, debate as to any eighteenth-century letter writer's authorial consciousness is a critical dead end, and Mme de Sévigné's shifting reputation is the major source of this impasse. Various solutions exist to avoid the issues raised by Showalter; Janet Altman, for example, declares it necessary to limit one's discussion to the question of which letters were considered publishable at this period in time. This approach also allows Altman to avoid the question of the "literariness" of letters: "I have not found it productive to address the question that has dominated previous critical debates—that is, the question of whether correspondences are—ontologically—literary works. . . . The 'literarity' of letters, I would argue, must be described as the system of values attributed to letters (implicitly or explicitly) in any interpretive act that preserves those letters for posterity."[11] I am following Altman's example, if not her precise terms, by replacing "literariness" with "publishability" in my analysis of the Rousseau–de La Tour exchange. I examine with care the manner in which de La Tour's letters are presented to the public by her various editors, in order to determine the underlying assumptions that guided the editors and readers of her letters at any particular point in the work's history. In contrast to Altman, however, I take one further step, for I believe that the reception history of a letter should not be so easily unlinked from the letter writer's intentions, when these can be either guessed at or, in rare cases, ascertained with some degree of certainty. The heuristic value of raising the issue of intention in letter writers is considerable, for Altman's method ultimately precludes any investigation into the meaning of a letter's style and content at the time that the letter was composed—a not-inconsequential question for any careful reading of a correspondence.[12] Authorial consciousness as to "posterity's interest" at the time of a letter's composition has a profound effect on a letter—if only, as Showalter notes, by making such letters "hypermissive" in quality. If Graffigny imagined future fame as a letter writer, it was as an *épistolière*, not as an *auteur épistolaire*, fame à la Sévigné meant being acknowledged as an "unintentional" epistolary genius, with all that this label implied at the time as to style.

While this type of authorship may remain only suppositional in Graffigny's case, de La Tour's letters provide ample evidence of her efforts to produce "effortless" letters. The difficult circumstances of her exchange with Rousseau were enough in themselves to cause her project to reveal itself. While Graffigny benefited from the friendly complicity that reigned between herself and Panpan, de La Tour had to both provoke and guide Rousseau's responses in order to please the eventual public readers of these letters. Coaxing a recalcitrant correspondent into responding in a publishable manner presents an impossible challenge to verisimilitude, when the correspondence extends over such a prolonged period of time. While occasionally willing to acknowledge de La Tour's devotion, and even to encourage it by playing Saint-Preux to her Julie, Rousseau more often rejected the notion that he had any duty to respond to her letters. At times this denial was part of an effort to end the relationship; at times Rousseau aimed merely for comic effect: "To write to you more often would no doubt be a delightful occupation for me, but I would also lose the pleasure of witnessing the prodigious variety of elegant turns of phrase with which you reproach me for the infrequency of my letters, without ever repeating yourself in your own" (Oct. 21, 1764).

This passage from an early letter raises a serious question: Why did Rousseau respond to de La Tour's letters, and continue to respond for so many years? Understanding Rousseau's role in the creation of this publishable "private" correspondence is essential to understanding its generic status.[13] As one of Europe's most famous and controversial authors, Rousseau was both extremely protective of his public reputation and quite aware of the publication value of his private letters. By interpreting Rousseau's responses to de La Tour in the context of his other works and of his troubled reputation with the European public of his day, I demonstrate that, although as an individual woman his "Julie" seems to have meant little to him, as a paradigm of the French woman reader she played an important symbolic role. He may have often repudiated her and instructed her to cease importuning him, but Rousseau also welcomed and greatly valued her letters. In the short term, these missives provided him with immediate epistolary evidence of his women fans' devotion; in the long term, they represented potential testimony to posterity that a few enlightened souls had remained faithful to his cult, even during his darkest days. Far from an idiosyncratic paranoia, Rousseau's doubts as to the purely private intentions of his correspondent were, again, typical of both the theory and the practice of missive letter writing in his day.

Among the possible objections to my argument that de La Tour sought fame as a writer of private letters is her apparent willingness to accept posthumous recognition. Nor does the epistolary genre, whatever its aesthetic cachet at the time, seem to have been the best choice for a would-be woman writer. Even in an eighteenth-century context, in which women were accorded a special talent for letter writing, this supposed genius did not translate into publication value; as Fritz Nies points out, only 5.2 percent of published *Lettres* in eighteenth-century France were by women.[14] De La Tour's choice of genre is made all the more unlikely by our awareness that there were a number of well-known, successful, and respected women novelists at work in France in the eighteenth century. At the time that de La Tour sent her first anonymous letter to Rousseau, women were indeed poised to explode onto the publishing scene. As Judith P. Stanton demonstrates in her statistical profile of women writers in England, their number increased by about 50 percent per decade from 1760 to the end of the century. The reasons for this increase apply across the Channel as well: increased literacy, increased population, increased leisure time, and improvements in printing technology created a reading public; as for the supply side, Stanton makes the important psychological point that when one woman succeeds, many others are inspired to try their hand, and growth becomes exponential.[15]

And yet it must be kept in mind that Françoise de Graffigny's denial of authorial consciousness extended beyond her letters to Panpan to embrace her best-selling novel, *Lettres d'une Péruvienne*, published anonymously in 1747. Nor was Graffigny at all unusual in her refusal to acknowledge that she deliberately wrote her novel with a public readership in mind; Marie-Jeanne Riccoboni's first novel was rumored to comprise real letters, her own, written to a faithless lover (*Lettres de Mistress Fanni Butlerd*, 1757).[16] To begin with the practical considerations behind such claims, there existed powerful legal incentives for a woman to hide or to attenuate her authorship at this period in French history. Carla Hesse has pointed out that it was not until after separating from their husbands that Riccoboni and Graffigny began to publish their works, and even then it seems likely that they did not have the right by law to sign a contract.[17] Riccoboni soon abandoned the rhetoric of nonauthorship, but Graffigny continued to resist calling herself an author even after she became yet more famous with the success of her play *Cénie* (1750). As Showalter observes in the course of his analysis of Graffigny's letters: "In socioeconomic terms, being an author is primarily a matter of self-definition."[18] To rephrase this statement, the choice to remain a "nonauthor" is governed by a complex socioeconomic equation, especially for women. Riccoboni, a one-time actress, may have felt far freer—had less to lose?—than the more conventional, noble Graffigny, who hid behind the veil of nonauthorship even when anonymity was no longer an option.

Such choices must also be put into historical perspective, for the refusal to acknowledge one's work is a constant thread that runs through the history of women's writing. Faith Beasley points out that seventeenth-century France "witnessed a veritable explosion of women's participation in the literary and intellectual realm," and yet much of this production was anonymous.[19] Far from a humble female withdrawal, however, the refusal to sign their work was for the women of this period primarily a factor of elevated social status. As Joan Landes points out in her important study *Women and the Public Sphere in the Age of the French Revolution* (1988), seventeenth-century noble women were largely unconcerned with the bourgeois norms of domestic propriety so often evoked by de La Tour, despite her own noble status. What concerned women such as Mme de Lafayette, author of the first modern psychological novel in French, the *Princesse de Clèves* (1678), was instead adherence to noble values. By choosing anonymity, but letting it be generally known that they had authored the works in question, women such as Lafayette could achieve fame while avoiding the all-too-bourgeois taint of writing for publication (money).

The solidity of the aristocratic hold on politics and culture in the seventeenth century meant that one's sex was more than trumped by one's social status. As Landes demonstrates, the influence of such powerful noble women began collapsing, along with the Old Regime, well before the French Revolution, as "the older patriarchy gave way to a more pervasive *gendering* of the public sphere."[20] It was at the very period when France witnessed a vast expansion in the production of printed texts, and the simultaneous rise of public opinion as a force to be reckoned with, that women began to be excluded from the public sphere as nobility was replaced with a claim to universalist reason as the basis for participating in debate.

The few who strongly advocated for participation by women at this time were not well received, a point Landes illustrates with the case of Mme de Beaumer, the first female editor of the *Journal des Dames*: "[Beaumer] believed that through useful, constructive activity, women could begin to make a revolution in society. . . . She adopted the feminized form of author and editor, referring to herself as *autrice* and *éditrice*, and dressed in masculine garb, dedicating herself to supporting her sex's 'honor and its rights.'"[21] Beaumer's tenure as editor was, significantly, short-lived; having attracted too much negative attention, she stepped down to save the journal.

One of the most important aspects of this devolution in women's status, in the context of my study of de La Tour, is the commonly held assumption that Rousseau was the central figure behind the move to exclude the "second sex" from the public sphere. His dislike of women who dabbled in writing is justly famous, and becomes an issue at several points in his exchange with his would-be Julie. Nevertheless, writing offered women a career that was in many ways less "public" than others. Martin Hall writes of eighteenth-century women novelists: "Women were successful as novelists partly for negative reasons: the problems of apprenticeship and work opportunities made a career in music, painting or as a playwright a difficult one for a woman."[22] This use of writing as the paradoxical means to avoid going public is reflected in Stanton's analysis of her statistics: "Poetry was the most popular genre [for eighteenth-century women]: though hardly the easiest, it was certainly the most conventional, genteel, and respectable—perhaps, one wants to say, the most sincere."[23] It is thus highly significant that de La Tour began her writing career as a poet, publishing a few poems in her own name before she began her correspondence with Rousseau (a biographical detail she initially hid from her correspondent).[24]

De La Tour's switch from an unpromising career as a poet to that of an *épistolière* was necessarily driven by her particular social and intellectual circumstances, in combination with the greater publishing milieu in which she found herself. What little is known of her life supports the wisdom of her change in approach to achieving fame. She was of the minor aristocracy, well off, but neither terribly wealthy nor well connected. Born Marie-Anne Merlet de Foussomme in Paris in 1730, she married Jean-Baptiste Allissan de La Tour around 1750. The couple had no children, nor did the marriage last long; de La Tour separated from her husband around 1755, before her first contact with Rousseau.[25] She apparently never remarried, although she did change her name, as indicated by a letter to Rousseau of March 1775, signed "Mme de Franqueville, once Mme de La Tour."

There is thus a certain irony to my referring to this woman as "de La Tour," for she obviously expended a great deal of effort to divest herself of her husband and his name, both in her life and in her letters. I am motivated, however, by a desire to distance my discussion from previous treatments in which the use of her first name conveys a certain condescension, or even a conflation of this real woman with the fictional heroines to whom she is often compared. In his reader-response study of the exchange, Claude Labrosse refers to her by her legal first name, "Marie-Anne"; in his 1998 edition of the exchange, Georges May notes his decision to refer to his subject as "Marianne" just as he begins to summarize the very little that is known of her life: "Marie-Anne Merlet de Foussomme—or rather Marianne as she preferred to write it, and as she will be referred to from this point on—was born in Paris on November 7 or 10, 1730, and was thus eighteen years younger than Rousseau."[26] As this explanation reveals, "Jean-Jacques" most often retains his last name, and with it a heightened degree of respect and seriousness.

Commentators have also seized on de La Tour's obviously unsuccessful marriage as the source of her "obsessive" behavior with regard to Rousseau, and the use of her first name aids in the attempt to infantilize her as an out-of-control hysteric. My own proposal that this woman sought fame as a writer seems almost timid, in comparison to such claims to psychological acuity, based as they are on such limited biographical material. The most important detail of de La Tour's life, for my purposes, lies not in her failed marriage but rather in her having been of the nobility, and yet not having belonged to the upper reaches of this exalted class. She was, for example, of a social status below that of such influential intellectual women of her day as the two Emilies, du Châtelet and d'Epinay, whose unusual feminine ambition has been explored by Elisabeth Badinter in *Emilie, Emilie: l'ambition féminine au XVIIIe siècle* (1983). Badinter emphasizes the importance of paternal attention to developing the intellect and self-confidence of these two remarkable women, in addition to their good fortune in having been connected to powerful men who appreciated their talents. If one accepts that de La Tour possessed the "feminine ambition" of which Badinter speaks (and her letters, as I will argue, prove that this drive is present), she may well have been seeking through an association with

Rousseau precisely the type of male encouragement and social support that Voltaire provided du Châtelet, and Grimm provided d'Epinay. Without such support, the obstacles to a woman's achieving fame for her intellect through novel writing or any other arena of publication were considerable, both in the practical and the psychological realms. These obstacles were yet more daunting if she were conservative by character or upbringing, and all the more so if she were noble.

De La Tour's project of recreating herself as a "Julie come to life" becomes, when understood in this perspective, quite reasonable, however little it conforms to current notions of literary fame, not to mention current feminist notions of what constitutes a strong woman writer. And yet, I have, overall, little interest in the obstacles faced by de La Tour; what interests me is that she did in fact choose to make a name for herself, actively, not passively, by fashioning herself as a real-life Julie. I am also fascinated by what de La Tour's authorial status—that of a self-fashioned *épistolière*, an intentionally constructed "nonauthor"—reveals about the history of women's writing. My project thus takes its place in a new wave of feminist criticism, a new attitude with regard to women writers in the early modern period. As Sonya Stephens describes this trend in the introduction to a recent history of women's writing in France: "Not all women seek to assert their difference as women and most strive rather to establish their difference as writers, often in a way that is inclusive of their gender (if only, sometimes, because it cannot be exclusive of it). The convergence of literary trends and constraints with social ones, and women's creative engagement with these trends and constraints, brings to the fore the question of established literary forms and feminine experimentation and the highly complex relationship between gender and genre."[27]

I am not seeking, in other words, to diagnose de La Tour as a victim of patriarchy, nor to place her unusual authorial project within a tradition of feminine resistance to dominant generic values. Nor am I seeking a "lost" woman's voice, a lost literary talent that was unfortunately channeled into letters instead of more exalted forms of writing. I do not view de La Tour's voice as "lost"; she speaks, loudly and clearly, to anyone who is willing to listen. The message her writing conveys is simple, yet revealing: she wants fame, and is willing to manipulate generic conventions and accept her correspondent's at times misogynist pronouncements, as well as her culture's, in order to get it. She chose a genre that in her time carried considerable cachet, the private letter, and ensured the publication value of her own missives by cultivating a correspondence with one of the most famous men of her day. She heightened this publishability by identifying herself with a fictional character, and using fictional devices to strengthen her position. For example, the taboo value of sending a letter to a man was far worse in fiction than in reality, yet de La Tour frequently evokes her "fear" of being discovered corresponding with Rousseau to add to the believability of her desire to remain "unknown"—and thus to the impeccable authenticity of her "private" letters.[28]

In order to place de La Tour in a wider perspective, I end my study with a consideration of other eighteenth-century women letter writers who may have consciously sought to create a reputation for themselves as *épistolières*: Suzanne Necker, Marie-Jeanne Roland, and Julie de Lespinasse, in particular. While there can ultimately be no fixed method for determining authorial consciousness in eighteenth-century missive letter writers, I do definitively demonstrate the need for greater awareness of the publication value of such documents. I also examine other letter writers who sought and gained the attention of Jean-Jacques Rousseau, with, I argue, the same intention to publish as de La Tour. The most important of these correspondents is the (still) anonymous "Henriette ***," who wrote to Rousseau for permission to think and act like a man. She argued that because her status as an impoverished, genteel spinster made her a social exile, Rousseau should exempt her from his general standards of feminine conduct. Critics have been far gentler in dealing with Henriette than with de La Tour, viewing the former as a naive although potentially gifted writer whose spirits were too easily dashed by Rousseau's discouragement. These same critics have not, however—significantly—read the carefully edited version of this exchange prepared by Henriette and enlarged with her considerable commentary as a published "work" in its own right. I argue that, like de La Tour, Henriette was engaged in a clearly authorial project from the time she drafted her first letter to Rousseau.

Men's private letters must also be viewed with suspicion, of course, although the desire for fame has been more readily assumed in men, as I demonstrate through the example of that most famous of all literary sycophants, James Boswell. While on a sort of Grand European Tour of literary greats (his next stop was Voltaire), Boswell set himself the task of demonstrating that his epistolary prowess could gain him access even to the famously reclusive Jean-Jacques

Rousseau. Like de La Tour, Boswell flatteringly addressed Rousseau as Saint-Preux incarnate ("O dear S[t] Preux! enlightened mentor! eloquent and lovable Rousseau!," *CC*, 22:3694 bis), but while de La Tour adopted the role of Rousseau's allegorically perfect, fictional Julie, Boswell employed a seductive rhetoric of masculine honesty in keeping with Rousseau's published views on the ideal male character. Both correspondences involve careful self-presentation according to the terms of Rousseau's own philosophy, but while Boswell's tactics have been read critically, as a creative, deliberate process, de La Tour has been consistently and symptomatically misinterpreted—until the present study—as a prime representative of the overly emotional, "authentic" female novel reader, whose unformed reactions to a literary masterpiece spontaneously overflowed into her private letters.[29]

1

Claire and Julie Write Saint-Preux

In the midst of so many humiliations, I had the sweet consolation of receiving news from time to time from the two charming friends. I have always found the female sex to possess a great consoling power, and nothing softened my afflictions during my disgrace so much as to feel that a charming female person was taking an interest in my situation.

—Rousseau, on Mlles de Graffenried and Galley; *Confessions*

Rousseau was enjoying a period of relative freedom from "afflictions and disgrace" when he received his first anonymous letter from Marie-Madeleine Bernardoni. He had led an eventful, peripatetic youth, working as a musician, composer, and tutor, among other unsuccessful attempts to earn a living. By September 1761, in his late forties, Rousseau had at last achieved both financial stability and fame. The key to his success was his association with the philosophes, especially Diderot, his closest friend, and d'Alembert, who engaged him to write articles on music for the *Encyclopédie.* At Diderot's instigation, Rousseau composed his first *Discours* (1750), an essay that not only won him a prize from the Academy of Dijon but also became much disputed, and thus famous, after its publication. With his *Discours sur l'inégalité* (1755), Rousseau was established as one of the major voices of his day, a position solidified when Voltaire composed one of his own most influential works, *Candide* (1759), in response to an essay by Rousseau on Providence.

As his fame grew, Rousseau's relationships, both professional and personal, began to disintegrate. Although never a friend, Voltaire developed an undying enmity for Rousseau that would have serious consequences in the years to come. More immediately, Diderot began to view Rousseau as professionally dangerous in his opposition to many of the values dear to the philosophes. Joined by others, Diderot also came to attack Rousseau as an ingrate in his personal relations, particularly with regard to Mme d'Epinay, who had arranged for him to live on her country estate in 1755. Whether one faults Rousseau for ingratitude or pities him as the victim of a concerted attack by the philosophes depends on which version of events one accepts, that recounted in the *Confessions,* or d'Epinay's version, known as the *Contre-Confessions.*[1] In either case, in December 1757 Rousseau was obliged to find a new place to stay.

When he received Bernardoni's first letter, announcing that Julie lived, most of these stormy proceedings were well behind Rousseau. He had been living for some time in Montmorency, where he enjoyed the more tranquil patronage of the influential maréchal and maréchale de Luxembourg. Two of his most important works, the *Contrat social* and *Emile,* had just been finished and were heading for the printers. The success of *La Nouvelle Héloïse,* published in January 1761, had been immediate and almost overwhelming, as manifested by the flood of fan letters he had been receiving. Neither the influence of the maréchal de Luxembourg nor Rousseau's popularity with the French public would suffice to save him from exile less than a year later, following the publication of *Emile,* but in September 1761 his living situation approximated the ideal of peaceful retreat to which he so often claimed to aspire in his writings.

This stability gave Rousseau the time and the energy to engage in a lengthy epistolary flirtation with the two "charming friends" who identified themselves only as Claire and Julie. The women no doubt also benefited from Rousseau's positive relationship with readers at this period in his life. According to the letters he was receiving, his novel was actively working to change lives for the better. Readers wrote to tell Rousseau that he had inspired them to seek out a mode of existence such as Julie and her husband Wolmar enjoyed at Clarens, or to tell him that he had saved them from a life of dissipation, or, worse yet, a bad marriage.[2] Not all readers were positive, although even Rousseau's worst critics acknowledged the power of his novel. Emphasizing Julie's premarital affair with Saint-Preux, they expressed concern over the effect on readers of a heroine who continued to impress with the quality of her virtue, despite the serious consequences of her indiscretion: a miscarriage followed by the death of her mother.

Rousseau anticipates these detractors with an editorial preface in which he declares that he has given these "letters by two lovers" a title suggestive enough of its contents to frighten off virtuous young girls. As for more seasoned readers, they are to be repulsed by the letters' style and content. Fashionable types (*les gens de goût*) will find these missives too gauche; the overly severe reader will be alarmed by the letters' content; libertines and philosophes need read no further, for "all the sentiments expressed will appear unnatural to those who do not believe in virtue" (*OC*, 2:5). The "very few readers" capable of appreciating these letters will be those select souls possessed of extreme sensibility to the truth in a world obsessed with appearance.

Rousseau offered discerning fans other indications of the type of response he desired from his readers. While he was clearly following tradition in claiming that these "letters by two lovers living in the foothills of the Alps" were authentic, he added his own idiomatic, moralizing twist to this claim: "Did I write it all, and is the entire correspondence thus a fiction? Men of the world, what do you care? It is surely a fiction for you" (*OC*, 2:5). A reader desiring to enter into contact with this author was thus well advised to adopt an open attitude toward the possibility that the novel was based on real events. Even those readers who rejected the authenticity of the letters as such often expressed eagerness for biographical details pointing to a true story, declaring themselves convinced by the intensity of the emotion inspired in them by these letters that Rousseau had modeled his heroine on a woman whom he had loved as Saint-Preux loved Julie.

It fell to de La Tour, with the help of Bernardoni, to capitalize most completely on the metafictional implications of Rousseau's novel by presenting him with his own Julie come-to-life. De La Tour not only identified with the ethos of his novel, she claimed to embody it; she not only accepted the novel's "truthfulness," her very existence seemed to corroborate it. In this chapter, I consider the letters exchanged among these three correspondents between September 1761 and January 1762. I begin by examining the self-positioning of the three letter writers as they establish ground rules for the exchange. I demonstrate in particular how sensitive all three letter writers were from the beginning to the publication potential of their "private" missives. I emphasize as well the determining role played by "Claire," for Bernardoni has been rather neglected in previous studies of these letters. De La Tour is in some part responsible for this neglect, for she took care to efface Bernardoni's name when editing the exchange for publication. She had good reason to do so. Playing Claire to de La Tour's Julie meant that Bernardoni was destined to be a secondary figure, for Claire is merely the heroine's confidante, virtuous of course, but somewhat flighty; essentially a foil for her extraordinary friend. But while Saint-Preux is irresistibly drawn to Julie's superior qualities, in real life Rousseau found Bernardoni's teasing far more appealing than the somber tone de La Tour adopted in imitation of Julie. When life failed to imitate art, de La Tour apparently turned on her friend. The second part of this chapter focuses on the break up of the two women's friendship as their initial complicity in presenting de La Tour as Rousseau's ideal woman met the reality of their correspondent's preference for Claire.

While in this first chapter I consider only five months' production of letters, in the next I treat the fourteen-year period that ends with de La Tour's last letter to Rousseau in November 1776. This quantitative disparity reflects previous scholarly practice, for critics have been most fascinated by the initial letters in which the fictional world of *La Nouvelle Héloïse* is evoked by the correspondents. This five-month period also produced the most creative and complex portion of the correspondence, that is, the letters in which one sees most clearly that de La Tour was not merely a loving and simple woman expressing her admiration for her favorite author. Neither was she a slightly psychotic and overly sentimental fan unable to separate reality from fiction. Marie-Anne de La Tour was first and foremost a writer, and her adoption of a role based on Rousseau's novel was part and parcel of the complex negotiations in which all three participants consciously engaged as to the status of their letters: literary or private, sincere or mocking, seductive, or all of the above?

As a Parisian, and a rich and noble one at that, Marie-Anne de La Tour faced some daunting obstacles in offering herself to Rousseau as the double of his humble Swiss heroine. Parisian women and their wanton ways appear as a predictable subject of scorn in Rousseau's novel. In a letter to Julie sent during his Parisian exile, Saint-Preux observes that women in the French capital cultivate false appearances, both literal and linguistic: "They saw that the common people have a horror of rouge, which they persist in coarsely calling paint, and they applied four-fingers worth, not of paint, but of rouge; for the word being changed, the thing is no longer the same" (*OC*, 2:267). In contrast, Julie d'Etange is modest before men and obedient to her father and mother. Taking a lover hardly fits this paradigm, and so Rousseau has his heroine meet Saint-Preux in a manner that does not call into question Julie's antique Swiss virtue:

the respectable if classically dangerous circumstances evoked by the title's medieval reference. Mme d'Etange hires Saint-Preux to tutor her daughter as a welcome-home surprise for Julie's father, conveniently away on an extended trip and thus unable to exercise his considerable paternal authority.

The need to present de La Tour in the right light while capturing the attention of a famous author besieged by readers' letters is evident in Bernardoni's enticing opening paragraph:

> Ah! such is the inconstancy of women! While reading *La Nouvelle Héloïse*, I had promised never to write again; I said it to everyone, determined never to change my mind.
>
> Projects vanished as soon as they were formed, here I am writing, and to whom? To Monsieur Rousseau himself. I can preserve my pride only by remaining anonymous: a sad creature who scarcely knows how to assemble the twenty-four letters of the alphabet, daring to enter into the lists, face uncovered, against the most famous pen of past, present, and no doubt future centuries, that would be an insufferable audacity. You will thus not learn, monsieur, who I am: but you will learn that Julie is not in the least dead, and that she lives to love you. (Sept. 28, 1761)

The most important themes of the first months of the correspondence are already present in the above quotation: the implication that a sexual encounter is in the offing; the difference between writing for the public and writing a private letter; and lastly, the competition between the two would-be *inséparables,* as Julie and Claire are known in the novel. This last is only subtly present in Claire's opening, but Bernardoni does delay mentioning the existence of her friend until she has herself made an impression.

Bernardoni goes on in her opening letter to establish that her friend is not one of those Parisian women who move from man to man. At the same time, she hints that for an exceptional man, her Julie might succumb: "I have told my divine friend that Julie's soul breathes in her, with the exception of her mistake; all who know how to appreciate her agree with me; she disputes this claim out of excessive modesty, and assures us, with that lovely candor that only demonstrates her to be all the more that which she will not admit to being, that she would like even at the price of Julie's fall to resemble her in every way; and that she is only sure of not committing this sin, because she is sure of never finding a Saint-Preux (supposing of course that she is not married)." The turns and twists of this long sentence hardly obscure the offer of this virtuous Julie for more then merely epistolary flirtation. Rousseau is informed that although the soul and spirit of Julie live on in Claire's divine friend, this real-life Julie has of course never had an extramarital love affair. So great is her virtue, however, that she would be willing to commit such a carnal sin, if the act would bring her closer to resembling Rousseau's perfect heroine; an admission Claire makes "secure" in the knowledge that there is no real-life Saint-Preux to take her up on her offer.

The fictional Julie's affair—her famous "mistake," "fall," or "sin," as I have variously translated the French *faute*—of course takes place before her marriage to Wolmar. Such an act becomes unthinkable once she swears fidelity to a husband and settles into the well-ordered universe of Clarens. In the real world of eighteenth-century France, however, there were intermediary stages between the status of single or married, and de La Tour inhabited one of those ambiguous positions. Claire's initial, if parenthetical reference to her friend's marital status is clarified later in her letter when she informs Rousseau that this Julie is indeed married, although to a man unworthy of her. This claim is true to what little is now known of de La Tour's life; Jean-Baptiste, a man whose family, like de La Tour's own, belonged to the least impressive of noble classes (*la petite noblesse de robe*), proved himself a less-than-ideal husband. He was so financially and morally irresponsible that he lost a lucrative official position, and by 1761, when Bernardoni wrote to Rousseau, the couple had separated. De La Tour presumably had control of her own money, however damaged her social standing may have been by her marital difficulties.

Rousseau was given no such details, nor did he ever seek to learn them, although Claire's air of sexually charged mystery concerning Julie's availability does seem to have appealed to him. He responded immediately with a clever missive of his own, in which he did not leave unexplored the possibility of a liaison with the charming Claire herself: "To the editor of one Julie, you announce the existence of another, one who really exists and whose Claire you are, I am charmed for your sex and even for my own, for whatever your friend may say, as soon as there exist Julies and Claires, Saint-Preux will not be lacking; warn her of that, I beg you, so that she may be on her guard; and you yourself, should you be, which I do not presume, as mad as your model, do not believe that her example suffices to protect you from folly" (Sept. 29, 1761). Claire is "mad" in the best sense of this term: laughing, teasing, flirtatious, somewhat empty-headed, yet loyal and sexually virtuous, if only by lack of deep sensibility. The fictional Claire never succumbs to seduction, unlike her serious and profound friend Julie, yet Rousseau warns this real-life Claire that she should not count on such flighty protection from sin. He goes on to admit that what he has just said may strike his correspondent as forward, for which she has only herself to blame: "What to say to those whom one would like to believe very likable and very virtuous, but whom one does not at all know? Charming friends, if you are such as my heart supposes, may you for the honor of your sex and the happiness of your life never find Saint-Preux; but if you are like the rest, may you find only Saint-Preux!"

By this point, "finding Saint-Preux" has taken on connotations far removed from the spirit of the novel. While the unmarried Julie d'Etange indeed succumbs to adultery, albeit under the considerable pressure of circumstances, the virtuous Mme Julie de Wolmar represses her feelings for Saint-Preux until the point of death. To the contrary, Bernardoni's real-life married Julie is presented as able to resist adulterous liaisons only until she finds a worthy suitor. Rousseau's "warning" conveys that if the two women are worthy of comparison to his heroines he may offer himself as this Saint-Preux, not only to Julie but to Claire as well. On the other hand, he hopes that if they are indeed worthy of a Saint-Preux they not find suitable lovers, for that would be an offense to their virtue, unless of course they are misrepresenting themselves, in which case he damns them to a stream of inconsequential affairs. The contradictory and playful nature of these various scenarios attenuates their seriousness, as does Rousseau's emphasis on his bad health; yet he does declare himself curious, and makes several suggestive remarks as to the disruption the two friends might pose to his solitary existence: "A solitary man must not expose himself to the sight of Julies and Claires when he wishes to retain his tranquility" (Thérèse Levasseur—Rousseau's companion and future wife, and the mother of his five abandoned children—obviously does not count in this equation, although she will play a role much later in his relationship with de La Tour).

How seriously any of the three correspondents took the possibility of a physical affair is of course impossible to determine. Rousseau later blamed the women for obliging him to write in a manner not natural to him: "I never thought that I had enough wit to abuse it; and I do not care enough about it to want to do so. But it is true that the type of correspondence that it has pleased you to establish with me may have caused me to have recourse to bad jokes that do not suit me and that I cannot make work" (Oct. 30, 1761). That Rousseau took a certain authorial pleasure in receiving seductive letters such as Bernardoni's is quite evident in book 11 of the *Confessions*, in which he writes that following the publication of *La Nouvelle Héloïse* he might have had his choice of any number of such well-born women fans. He tells the reader that he will not reveal any supporting evidence for this claim, but gives no reason for this reticence. We are to imagine that his sense of gallantry has come into play concerning some rather explicit offers: "Sentiment was divided among men of letters, but in the world there was only one opinion, and women in particular were mad for the both the book and the author, to the point where there were few women, even of the highest rank, whose conquest I could not have made had I undertaken it. I have proof of this that I do not want to expose here, and that, without my having followed through, proves my assertion" (*OC*, 1:545).[3] No specific reference is made here or elsewhere in the autobiography to Bernardoni and de La Tour, although their initial letters surely occupied pride of place among the proofs to which Rousseau alludes. Later, in the same book of the *Confessions*, he reveals that he considers readers' letters in response to *La Nouvelle Héloïse* worthy of publication, if only to demonstrate the capricious nature of public opinion: "I gathered most of the letters written to me about this work in a package that is in the hands of Madame de Nadaillac. If this collection were ever to appear, one would see quite singular things in it, and contrary judgments that demonstrate what it is to be involved with the public" (*OC*, 1:546).

Rousseau makes it quite clear in his first letter to Bernardoni that he has no intention of allowing his letters to her to be published. He begins with a firmly worded rebuke: "I hope, madame, that despite the beginning of your letter you are not at all an author, that you have no intention of becoming one, and that you are not provoking me into a battle of wits." He then points out the dual sense of "to write" in Bernardoni's claim that her letter violates her vow "never again to write," a position inspired by her reading of *La Nouvelle Héloïse*: "Nevertheless you promised yourself, you say, never to write again in your life; I promised myself the same thing, madame, and surely I will keep that promise; but this engagement is relative only to the public, and does not extend to the exchange of letters, which is a good thing no doubt, for your own letter would, I greatly fear, cost me an infidelity." Rousseau makes quite clear a distinction Bernardoni leaves unexplored, that between writing for the public and the private exchange of letters. Bernardoni is by rights to be counted among the members of the public to which Rousseau refers, as she is unknown to Rousseau and announces herself only as a reader of *La Nouvelle Héloïse*; by reinforcing the "private" nature of their exchange, Rousseau seeks to remove the possibility of publication while simultaneously appealing to her vanity. While he is willing to enter into a written exchange with Claire on the level of flirtation, any authorial pretensions, marked by both content ("battle of wits") and by the habit of publishing must remain thoroughly suppressed.

Bernardoni beats a hasty retreat in the opening to her second letter: "No, monsieur, I am not at all an author; and have never had, as you so very well put it, the intention of becoming one: I have only the precise amount of wit necessary, to feel all my insignificance in this regard" (Oct. 5, 1761). She had been quite sure, she claims, that Rousseau would misunderstand the motives behind her attempt to enter into contact with him, but had decided not to change her first letter; for a nonauthor such as herself, rewriting simply leads to more confusion, not less. This explanation seems hardly sufficient to erase her first letter's reference to entering into the competitive lists with Rousseau, writer to writer ("a sad creature who scarcely knows how to assemble the twenty-four letters of the alphabet, daring to enter into the lists, face uncovered, against the most famous pen of past, present and no doubt future centuries"). Her reference to Rousseau as "a famous pen" is telling, for it signifies metonymically his entitlement to what Claire so vehemently denies she wants: the status of author. Somehow, according to the logic of her second letter, her lack of wit or intelligence (*esprit*) is to block the transformation of her pen into an instrument of literary warfare. It is indeed this very lack that accounts for such an inappropriate metaphor in the writing of a woman so manifestly not an author.

Having absolved herself of the charges raised by her first letter, Bernardoni goes on in her second to establish the terms on which the two women will themselves accept a continuing correspondence. These terms aspire to place the seal of privacy on the exchange, compensation perhaps for the authorial tendencies Bernardoni had previously displayed by denying them. She informs Rousseau that she and her Julie will not reveal their real names and that the exchange must remain a closely guarded secret. Rousseau is not to show their letters to anyone, for fear that someone might recognize their handwriting. Bernardoni also assures her correspondent that Claire and Julie will write their letters separately, with each reading the other's letters only just before they are sent off. She is assuring Rousseau, in other words, that their letters will be strictly missive, that is, strictly personal in composition (however studiedly so).

Bernardoni explains these terms in a letter dated October 5, her second letter, accompanied by de La Tour's first, in which the latter predictably denies that she has the right to claim Julie's identity. De La Tour declares herself but a pale imitation of Julie, "that admirable woman," explaining that Claire has allowed herself to be carried away by her characteristic enthusiasm: "It is my model that she has sketched in her letter, and not my portrait" (Oct. 5, 1761). She tells Rousseau that she had not dared hope for a response when agreeing to allow Claire to send a letter—although it is difficult to imagine anyone resisting Claire's considerable epistolary charms, and certainly not a man such as Rousseau announces himself to be in his writings. She herself, in contrast, offers few charms as a correspondent, as she is painfully aware, for her friend's light and frivolous tone is impossible for such a serious (sincere?) person as herself: "I have only one manner of being, thinking, feeling, speaking." Her letters will no doubt bore Rousseau; why then bother him at all? "But . . . but why am I writing to you then, since I do not have the talent to amuse you; and I do not claim to interest you? Why? Because I never said that I would not write again, because Julie wrote, and Claire writes much better than I; and because I have many things to tell you." De La Tour is obliged to write to Rousseau, she tells him, because of the great concern she feels for his welfare. Foremost among her worries is the need to persuade Rousseau to take care of his health: "You should not have published *La Nouvelle Héloïse*; or, you should devote all of your care to curing a disease you make incurable by persuading yourself that it is."

Inquiring as to the health of one's correspondent is a well-worn epistolary device linked to physical affection, as Mireille Bossis remarks: "The other's physical troubles seem to provide a privileged if not unique way for the writer to show attention to and affection for the other's body. The status of illness is thus called into question. There is indeed a strategy to be examined in letters which verbalize illness."[4] Something strategic is indeed going on in de La Tour's letter, for in addition to their being strangers, the particulars of Rousseau's medical history make her verbalization a bit odder than the average show of affection through reference to illness. His well-known sufferings were caused by urinary troubles that he attributed to an incurable internal deformation. De La Tour's accusation that his health problems were psychosomatic was founded on public opinion, and therefore all the more stinging to a man who consistently believed himself to be near death. Rousseau had not long before asked Mme de Luxembourg to take care of Thérèse following his imminent demise, so that while de La Tour's expression of concern for his health can be read as a rather transparent strategic ploy, it is also the first of her many faux pas. She is quite explicitly calling into question the status of Rousseau's illness. At the same time, her need to justify her boldness in writing to a man she has never met supports her status as a Julie, who would have certainly hesitated to do so. When she cites a poem by Ariosto, she again works to justify her identification with Rousseau's heroine. The verses are inserted to illustrate her declaration that she has no desire to meet Rousseau in person, out of fear that he will be disappointed, but these lines of poetry have a greater message to send as well. All of the many fragments of poetry cited in *La Nouvelle Héloïse* are in Italian, beginning with the epigraph from Petrarch that equates Julie to Laura. Rousseau was to recognize the truth of "Julie lives" not only in de La Tour's concern for him, but also in her style. He was to recognize his two *inséparables* come to life in the matched pair formed by de La Tour and Bernardoni. Their Saint-Preux had only to respond in kind.

Things did not go quite as planned. The women received no response to their carefully composed letters, Claire's explaining that she was no author, Julie's that she was no Julie. Assuming the worst, they sent another set of letters on October 16. A postscript to Bernardoni's letter reveals that she had initially written on her own to berate Rousseau for having offended Julie's delicate sensibilities, had indeed been in the very act of sealing this indignant missive ("What! monsieur, you who are so familiar with the science of the heart . . ."), when she was handed a letter—from Julie! Within this letter was yet another (sealed) letter addressed to Rousseau, that Bernardoni was asked to forward or to throw into the fire, as she saw fit. Given de La Tour–Julie's exalted nature and epistolary talent, the latter option would of course constitute a heinous act; Bernardoni thus encloses de La Tour's suspiciously well-timed missive with her own. The letter from the bereaved de La Tour ends on a plaintive note of self-accusation: "Goodbye, monsieur, pardon me for allowing myself the satisfaction of sharing with you the pain you are causing me." In this second letter, de La Tour's model seems to be less the dignified Julie than the pathetically abandoned nun of the seventeenth-century *Lettres portugaises,* or her precursors in Ovid's *Heroides.*

This time, the two women do receive a response, in which Rousseau declares that he never received the letters he stands accused of ignoring. He declares himself amazed by the intensity of the two women's reaction. While he again seems charmed by Bernardoni's flirtatiously aggressive remonstrations, he is far from taken with the sensibility behind de La Tour's plaintive, literary adieu. Based on the evidence of this one sad missive—the first of her letters that he has received—Rousseau decides that de La Tour is a man hiding behind a female pseudonym. He christens this man "Monsieur Julie" in a letter to Bernardoni: "I am unable to imagine your tête-à-tête with M. Julie collaborating on your letters and all the mockery addressed to the poor dupe, without feelings of anger" (Oct. 19, 1761). As R. A. Leigh notes, Voltaire had been the target of a similar ruse, entering into a correspondence with a Mlle Malcrais de La Vigne who turned out to be one Paul Desforges-Maillard.[5] Rousseau, as the male creator of a famous female letter writer, was all the more likely to be the target of such a trick, meant perhaps to embarrass him as much as to exalt the reputation of the letter writer in question. Rousseau had enemies among the most talented writers of the day, as he knew only too well. His definitive break with the philosophes had taken place not long before he received these anonymous letters, and it had been precipitated, significantly, by his involvement with the original "real-life Julie," Sophie d'Houdetot, sister-in-law to Mme d'Epinay.[6]

The version of this (probably platonic) affair we find in the *Confessions* is important to any reading of Rousseau's epistolary relationship with de La Tour. This passage helps to explain, for example, why he believed de La Tour's to be those of a man, for in the course of recounting this rather shameful episode in his life, Rousseau expounds at length on both women (fictional and real) and letters (fictional and real). When he first met Sophie d'Houdetot, Rousseau tells us, he was quite unimpressed, finding her "not at all beautiful." Later, in January 1757, hard at work on his novel, Rousseau reacted quite differently to the sight of Mme d'Houdetot arriving at his cottage on the d'Epinay estate: "She came, I saw her, I was drunk with love without an object, this drunkenness charmed my eyes, the object became fixed in her, I saw my Julie in Madame d'Houdetot, and I soon saw only Madame d'Houdetot, but adorned with all the perfection that I had just accorded to the idol of my heart" (*OC,*

1:440). It is important to note that, at least in hindsight, Rousseau ascribes d'Houdetot's apotheosis to his own desperate need for a love object. More importantly, he tells us that he fell not for Sophie d'Houdetot but for his own fictional creation; Julie, not Sophie, is "the idol of his heart."

This subtle denigration may be in part inspired by spite, for unlike Julie d'Etange, and despite ample opportunity to do so, d'Houdetot never fully succumbed to seduction, at least according to the *Confessions*. This first real-life Julie was not equally willing to view in Rousseau the incarnation of her own male ideal, perhaps because she was at the time not only married but also already possessed of a "Saint-Preux" in the person of Rousseau's friend Saint-Lambert. Rousseau tells us that the resulting physical deprivation provoked a potentially fatal hernia, "that I will carry or that will carry me to the grave" (*OC*, 1:446). A less dramatic but more important detail of this account, for my purposes, is Rousseau's revelation in the *Confessions* that his physical torments were also the source of an interesting variation on the *billet doux*. Waiting for d'Houdetot on "a pleasant terrace," Rousseau tells us, he would scribble effusive letters in an effort to alleviate his excitation. These notes, by their very unreadability, were to testify mutely to Sophie that her would-be lover was at least sincere in his physical passion: "To distract myself I would write notes with my pencil, notes that I might have written with the purest of my blood: I never was able to finish one that was legible. When she found a letter in the agreed-upon niche, she could see only the state in which I had been while writing it" (*OC*, 1:445–46).

Rousseau did write letters to d'Houdetot in a calmer state, letters that are again offered to the reader as so many proofs of the intensity of his love for his friend's mistress.[7] Unfortunately, Rousseau cannot reproduce these letters for our delectation, and his own defense, any more than he can transcribe his illegible efforts on the terrace, for when at the end of his misbegotten interlude with d'Houdetot he handed over her letters as instructed, she told him that she could not return the favor, having already burned his. Rousseau doubts the truth of her assertion, in the process valuing his letters to d'Houdetot over his best-selling novel: "No, one does not put such letters into the fire. Julie's letters were found to be fiery. Oh God! what would they have then said of these? No, no, a woman who could inspire such a passion would never have the courage to burn the proof of it" (*OC*, 1:463). "Courage" is required, we assume, because the morally appropriate act would be to burn such letters; it is lacking, we assume, because any woman would glory in the pride of having inspired such "fire" in a man, especially a man capable of writing such letters.

Despite their "fire," these letters did not succeed in physically seducing their recipient. However little credit Rousseau may have been able to take for the nonconsummation of his affair with d'Houdetot, he stresses this fact when determining the amount of culpability he bears. In a process familiar to readers of the *Confessions*, Rousseau relies on internal sentiment when excusing himself for having attempted to seduce his friend's mistress, although the guilt he assumes in this particular instance of confession is strikingly stronger than elsewhere in the autobiography. He explores his guilt most fully in an interesting passage that describes his first meeting with Saint-Lambert after the affair, a meeting that includes the reading of a letter. Like his mistress, Saint-Lambert seems to have been singularly unaffected by Rousseau's epistolary powers:

> Although I knew in my heart that I had acted honorably, there was so much external evidence against me, that the invincible shame that always dominated me gave me a guilty air in [Saint-Lambert's] presence, and he took advantage of this in order to humiliate me. One example suffices to illustrate our situations vis-à-vis each other. I was reading to him after dinner from the letter that I had written to Voltaire the previous year . . . he fell asleep during the reading, and I, once so proud, now so foolish, did not dare to interrupt my reading, and continued to read while he continued to snore. (*OC*, 1:462–63)[8]

Rousseau's assessment of his love letters to d'Houdetot reflects a typically eighteenth-century epistolary hierarchy of central importance to my study as a whole. While I will explore the eighteenth-century view in general in chapter 3, it is necessary to understand Rousseau's assumptions about letters, their value, and their characteristics, before going on any further with an examination of the de La Tour–Rousseau correspondence. First, as we see in the *Confessions*, it is important to Rousseau that his authentic private letters to d'Houdetot exceed his fictional creations in one crucial aspect: the level of *obviously authentic* passion they contain.[9] It is, significantly, the reader who verifies this innate difference, or rather two sets of readers: first d'Houdetot, the recipient of the letters, who could "never" have destroyed them; second, the readers of *La Nouvelle Héloïse*, who, had they access to the missives Rousseau wrote to d'Houdetot, would recognize the real passion that inspired these authentic letters, and thus their superiority over the "merely" fictional missives.

There is one idiosyncratic aspect of Rousseau's views on letters that is left unspoken in this passage from the *Confessions*, although it is implicitly present. This detail is also all-important to de La Tour's relationship to her correspondent, for it denies her, by virtue of her sex alone, the ability to write passionate letters that express true emotion. By the time Rousseau published *La Nouvelle Héloïse*, his views on women and letters were well known, for in a famous note to the *Lettre à d'Alembert* (1758), Rousseau had gone against the perceived wisdom of his day concerning the authenticity of the nun Mariane's despairing letters to her faithless French lover: "I would bet the world that the *Lettres portugaises* was written by a man." The note continues at length, with a contrarian attack on his era's clichéd assumption that women possess an innate talent for letter writing: "Women, in general, love none of the arts, know nothing of them, and possess no genius. They may succeed with small works that require only lightness of wit, taste, grace, sometimes even some philosophy and reasoning . . . but that celestial fire that warms and inflames the soul, that genius that consumes and devours . . . will always be lacking in women's writings: they are always cold and pretty like women themselves."[10]

Rousseau was right concerning the *Lettres portugaises*; it was demonstrated some two hundred years later that the work was an epistolary novel, written by a French man, Gabriel Joseph de Lavergne, vicomte de Guilleragues.[11] However, this fact somewhat undermines Rousseau's own argument, for he leaves unmentioned that if the *Lettres portugaises* had indeed been written by a man, the emotion expressed in this work would be necessarily inauthentic, for the letters would be fictional, just like those of his Julie. Rousseau similarly leaves unexplored in the *Confessions* the possibility that his own passionate letters to d'Houdetot were in some measure written not to her but to a fantasy of his own making. If we follow Rousseau's arguments more closely than he perhaps intended, the fire with which the letters in his novel burned must be seen as *identical* to the passion behind his letters to d'Houdetot. The two sets of letters were written by the same man under the sway of the same illusionistic fantasy. While one can argue that by the time he wrote these letters to d'Houdetot, he no longer confused her with Julie but rather lusted for the real woman, one can equally well respond that in its early stages, the novel was written to a woman as real to Rousseau as d'Houdetot would become. Earlier in book 9, Rousseau claims to have written his novel in a sort of dream state: "The impossibility of communicating with real beings forced me into the land of fantasy, and seeing nothing in existence worthy of my frenzied dream, I nourished it in an ideal world that my creative imagination had soon peopled with beings suitable to my heart" (*OC*, 1:427). Adding that he wrote the letters with no thought of publication, he stresses his lack of artistic purpose by describing the difficulty he had in making a "novel" of these spontaneous missives: "I first jotted down on the paper a few letters with no connecting narrative, and when I decided to link them together I often had great difficulty doing so" (*OC*, 1:431).

In his introduction to *La Nouvelle Héloïse*, the editor Bernard Guyon ascribes this genesis to creative considerations: "Rousseau had to choose a mode of expression that for many reasons was in conformity with his genius. . . . It seems that Jean-Jacques was able to believe true only that which he *understood*; that in order to reach his mind and heart it was necessary that a word, or preferably a song, first move his ear. A great number of the letters in this novel are songs" (*OC*, 2:xxxvi). I would add that this passage of the *Confessions* accords the letters that would become *La Nouvelle Héloïse*—that is, the letters in their initial, unedited form—the same imprimatur of authentic emotion that Rousseau claims for his letters to d'Houdetot. They were written in a similar state of heightened passion, with the same intent of relieving frustration and excitement that had no object on which to spend itself; their very unreadability testifies to their authenticity.

There are of course important distinctions between the Rousseau–d'Houdetot and the Rousseau–de La Tour episodes. Most obviously, Rousseau knew and spent time with Sophie d'Houdetot, while de La Tour was an unknown correspondent. Equally important, however, is the reversal of sex roles in the de La Tour correspondence. Rousseau actively pursued d'Houdetot, who resisted his advances; de La Tour pursued him, and in not-so-subtle terms offered herself to him. It is revealing that Rousseau seemed at first quite pleased to adopt a passive role in his letters, at times going so far as to express "fear" of the consequences of her visit, given his "vulnerable state." However attractive to Rousseau this passive, victimized role may have been in practice (and there is ample evidence for such an attraction in the *Confessions*), this reversal of the standard male and female roles went against his theoretical stance—a point he made to de La Tour when-

ever it suited his purposes to do so. Rousseau viewed sexually aggressive women as unnatural creatures; it is perhaps for this very reason
that he declared women quite incapable of writing burningly effective love letters. Sexually aggressive women are clearly an affront to
nature in Rousseau's writings, and as such are found only in such
"unnatural" environments as Paris. It follows that when Rousseau
claims to have had his pick of well-born Frenchwomen following the
publication of *La Nouvelle Héloïse*, the letters sent by these women
are presented as merely laughable curiosities, "pretty cold things"
striking for their effrontery, not for their passion.

Despite Rousseau's suspicions concerning Monsieur Julie, he continued to respond to Claire, for, he tells her, in the process of closely
examining Monsieur Julie's missive he has discovered a clue that
allows him to dismiss the possibility of a tête-à-tête, the most dreadful aspect of the conspiracy he had conjured up: "While reading this
distressing letter, while examining its every fold in an attempt to find
that chimerical Julie whom I could not stop myself from regretting
to the point of tears, I happened to discover that the postal stamp
had pressed through the envelope to the paper, from which I concluded that the author of this letter had not written it in your room;
this discovery immediately disarmed my fury." Rousseau nevertheless vows to end the exchange, adding his own Adieu: "My decision
is made, I do not like dispute. . . . Farewell, madame; here will probably end our short correspondence" (Oct. 19, 1761).

Bernardoni takes up this *probably* as the challenge it appears to be,
responding on October 24 with her own interesting twist on sex and
letter writing in the form of an unexpected revelation: "What delights me is that you take women for men, and men for women. . . .
My third letter, that is the second that you received, was written entirely by my husband." The letter was of her husband's composition,
although copied out by her hand; she had been unable to compose
the letter herself, for she had vowed not to write to Rousseau again
until he promised to take better care of his health (the implication
that he was a hypochondriac having been quickly abandoned by the
two women). By this point, Bernardoni's vow "not to write" excludes only writing at its most literal, the forming of letters on a
page. Pride in epistolary authorship is now deflected onto others:
"Admire my husband's fine character; he is no less humiliated at
being taken for a woman, than Julie is vain for having been taken
for a man."

Antoine Bernardoni had appeared once before, in a postscript to

Bernardoni's first letter to Rousseau: "My husband knows and approves of what I am doing" (Sept. 28, 1761). But while there was no jealous husband waiting in the wings, there was an interested party eager to put a stop to the goings-on between Bernardoni and Rousseau: Marie-Anne de La Tour. Sensing that she was being pushed to the periphery of an exchange that by rights should have guaranteed her a starring role, Julie responded to her doubting Saint-Preux with a letter dated October 25. Taking no chances, she sent this letter by a messenger with orders to await Rousseau's response. The messenger also carried copies of the two lost letters, copies the existence of which de La Tour is careful to justify. She reminds Rousseau of the epistolary contract established by Bernardoni according to which the two friends sent copies of their letters to each other after composing them, stressing that "this is the only agreement between us, with regard to our letters." De La Tour offers Rousseau many reasons to respond in addition to the waiting messenger. His very honor as a man is at stake, for she declares his attack on her womanhood to be merely an unchivalrous pretext: "You pretend to doubt that I am a woman, in order to dispense in my case with the regard that your sex owes my own." She adds one last self-pitying comment to the effect that she knows Rousseau will not abandon communication with Claire, whose letters he appears to like so much—indeed, so much more than her own.

Rousseau answers both women with a single letter dated October 26, addressed "To the *inséparables*, men or women." He declares himself still too distrusting to respond directly (*nommément*) to Julie, although he has come to believe that this letter writer might be a woman. If his correspondent is a woman, then he must write to her "properly" (*comme il faudrait*); if a man, this man is to be congratulated, for he "has a great deal of wit, but intelligence is like power, one always abuses it when one has too much." Given how intense (*vif*) the exchange has now become, Rousseau ends by demanding that the women reveal their true names, adding: "This is my last word."

De La Tour responds on October 28, but not with a revelation of her true identity. She instead insists that Rousseau write to her directly (*nommément*) as Julie, or Claire will cease writing to him, a drastic strategy to which she says her friend has agreed. She informs Rousseau that Claire, as befits the character on whom she is modeled, is more than willing to give up Rousseau for Julie's benefit. De La Tour takes great pains at this point to establish the hierarchy of her relationship with Bernardoni, pointing out to Rousseau that the friendship between the real women is as unequal as the relationship between Julie and Claire in the novel: "In our relationship, as with your heroines, it is Claire who is useful to Julie." She adds that she has only her own lack of finesse to blame for his refusal to respond to her letters, but then goes on to attack Rousseau's character. He may be ill, yet "even when suffering, one has a duty to be just." Especially when one has presented oneself to the public as the very soul of sensibility: "The soul that shows itself in your works, is it not your own? Have I accorded my truest esteem only to false appearances? Was my cult only an idolatry?" De La Tour declares that she and her friend will reveal their names only if he will agree to consult their surgeon about his latest health crisis (the soft end of a catheter had become stuck in his urethral canal, an event about which the two women were apparently well informed).

At this point in the exchange, Rousseau had sent a grand total of two letters, one addressed to Claire and one addressed to both women. De La Tour's desire for a personalized response is evident in her first letter, written before Rousseau suspected her of epistolary perfidy: "But I passionately desire to have one of your letters; and I will no longer write to you. May the cessation of an exchange that I should never have begun, leave you with no *anxiety*" (Oct. 5, 1761). As indicated by the italics, de La Tour is already citing the one letter Claire has received at this point from Rousseau ("if our exchange finishes here it will not leave me without some anxiety" [Sept. 29, 1761]); in the future, her counting of letters and constant citation of past letters will be a source of continuing annoyance to her correspondent. De La Tour's hunger for a letter of her own explains a reference to her "famished" state in a letter of October 26 addressed only to Bernardoni: "I do like your warning not to steal anything from you. Lack does not make me a thief . . . your treasure is in its entirety in the envelope that contains my *widow's mite*." This letter from de La Tour to Bernardoni contained three others: Rousseau's first letter to Bernardoni, considered her possession; the short second letter from Rousseau to both women, accorded to de La Tour as her "widow's mite"; and de La Tour's letter of October 28, her third to Rousseau. De La Tour instructs Bernardoni's husband to copy the latter two and send back the originals.

The most revealing aspect of de La Tour's letter to Bernardoni of October 26 is her pleasure at how well she and her friend are succeeding in imitating the styles of their fictional counterparts: "I am sending you our oracle's letter, and my sad response. He will laugh well at your epistle, if he laughs as much as I did. It is original, *miraculously* well written, and will contrast marvelously with the mournful tone of my own." Their letters are literary efforts to be appreciated as such not only by each other, but also by their "oracular" correspondent. Rousseau is referred to sarcastically as "the sage of Montmorency," whose words the women breathlessly anticipate, but it is important to note that de La Tour assumes that Rousseau as well is conscious that they are playing an epistolary game.

To de La Tour's plaintive and hyperfeminine letter of October 28, Rousseau responds at last with a missive addressed "To Julie" (Oct. 30, 1761). Any continuation of the exchange, he states, will depend on knowing the identity of his correspondents. He agrees to see the doctor Julie has in mind, although he is certain that nothing will come of the interview.[12] After revealing that the surgeon is Sarbourg, de La Tour requests that Rousseau reveal to her in return why he mistook her for a Monsieur Julie: "You will oblige me infinitely by telling me by what signs, flattering or not, you took me to be a man" (Nov. 5, 1761).

Rousseau's explanation is based primarily on technical details rather than epistolary style. He rather unconvincingly claims that he had never thought Julie's letter had been *composed* by a man; he suspected that it had been copied out by a man's hand. Not only are de La Tour's written characters too regular to be a woman's, her punctuation is worthy of a printer's shop. She has the particularly damning habit of ending her letters with a mark (./.) that Rousseau refers to as:

> A certain little character bracketed by two dots at the end of all your letters, the most decisive factor, in spite of my particular doubts. Where for goodness sake did you dig up that damned character produced only in offices, and that caused me such despair? Charming Claire, carefully examine your friend's pretty hand; I bet that her fingers could not make such a character without getting a callus. But that is not all; you wish to know why I was afraid that your letter was not written by a man. It is because Claire had given you life, and this man had killed you. (Nov. 10, 1761)

This explanation seems in part to be a response to Bernardoni's earlier "what delights me is that you take women for men, and men for women," for if Rousseau had not noticed the male mind behind the letter composed by Bernardoni's husband and copied out by her, this lack can now be explained by his exquisite sensitivity to gendered penmanship. As for the content of de La Tour's letter, Rousseau points on that no woman of their day knows Italian poetry: "The era of women such as Bouillon, La Suze, and La Fayette is over."

Flattery aside, it is revealing that, far from connecting de La Tour to Julie's Swiss simplicity, the use of Italian quotations links her in Rousseau's mind to three great French epistolary stylists of the seventeenth century. The comparison is nevertheless meant as a compliment, for Rousseau had a decided taste for such antiquated writing and for the women who produced it, however cold he might find such "pretty" letters. As a young man he had worked briefly for the aged comtesse de Vercellis, of whom he writes in the *Confessions*: "Her letters had the style and almost the grace of those of Mme de Sévigné; one might have mistaken some of them for hers. My principal task, and one that did not displease me, was to write from her dictation" (*OC*, 1:81).

Rousseau goes on to declare that he is now certain that de La Tour is a woman: "I believe you to be a woman, I have no doubt." Despite her professional punctuation, every other aspect of her first letter indicates that she is indeed female, especially its evident *délicatesse*. In literary terms, *délicatesse* implies a sweet finesse, a delicate refinement, but Rousseau leaves unclear exactly how *délicatesse* expresses itself in de La Tour's letters. We do seem to be rather far from the fiery male tone he associates with the *Lettres portugaises* and with his own love letters to Sophie d'Houdetot. What Rousseau appreciates most in de La Tour's letters, again, seems to be the manner in which she manifests the essential qualities of a well-bred seventeenth-century salon hostess and letter writer. Nor should she take his attentions any more seriously than one should take salon badinage, for while flattering his correspondent, Rousseau's letter of November 10 also cautions her that he will never be her faithful friend. To his Julie who so carefully copies, counts, and quotes from his previous letters, he sends a clear and early warning: "I wish to conserve my freedom even in my close relationships."

Rousseau ends his letter of November 10 by forbidding de La Tour to send him letters for which the postal charges have already been paid. Although at the time postage was commonly paid by the recipient, it was not uncommon for unsolicited mail to be prepaid by the sender.[13] De La Tour had asked permission to prepay her letters, claiming that this step would assure their arrival. Rousseau asserts that prepayment leads to more rather than fewer lost letters, as it removes the financial incentive to deliver. He points out as well that he is in any case in no need of largesse. In a highly unusual claim to financial stability, Rousseau declares that *La Nouvelle Héloïse* has brought him more significant returns than mere fan letters: "I am at present very rich and will be so, I hope, for a long time." More compelling still may have been his refusal to become indebted to de La Tour, a common theme in his relationships with wealthy admirers, even those from whom he accepted a great deal. With de La Tour as with others, Rousseau insists on guarding his freedom, financial as well as emotional; it is doubtful that he imagined the degree to which his Julie would ignore the restrictions he attempted to place on their correspondence, for years to come.

La Nouvelle Héloïse of course records no such restrictions on Saint-Preux's feelings for Julie, nor does Rousseau's heroine need to plead for epistolary tokens of affection from her lover. At the very heart of Rousseau's novel lies the unquestioned power of Julie's peculiar charisma.[14] If, as Paul de Man has argued, the characters peopling *La Nouvelle Héloïse* are best read as abstract allegorical figures, Julie is surely the personification of Sensibility and Virtue combined.[15] Claire's devotion to her best friend is an enigma to Claire herself, who acknowledges Julie's reign but cannot grasp the source of her friend's ascendancy over all who meet her. The two are equal in talent and looks: "We each love virtue; honesty is equally dear to us; our talents are the same; I have almost as much intelligence as you, and am scarcely prettier. I know all of that; and in spite of it all you dominate me, you subjugate me, you confound me, your spirit crushes my own, and I am nothing before you. . . . Explain, if you can, this enigma; as for me, I understand nothing of it" (*OC*, II:409). While Claire herself personifies a light and amusing feminine touch in the novel, Julie is more serious, more inclined to profound thoughts, and more sensitive to love, beauty, and duty. Claire's "I have almost as much intelligence as you" indicates the only point unrelated to pure charisma on which she accords Julie ascendancy: quality of mind. And yet, ultimately, her native intelligence is irrelevant to Julie's gentle reign; as Claire tells us, Julie's "genius" is in the nature of a companion spirit. Her power is a mystical enigma.

Rousseau's admission that de La Tour was no man out to trap him into writing amorous *billets doux* was far from an acceptance of his correspondent's ineffable charm and mystical ascendancy over all other women. As his letters clearly indicate, what he most admired in de La Tour was the cleverness of her feminine mind, expressed in the *délicatesse* of her epistolary style. Quite sensitive to this discrepancy between herself and the fictional Julie, de La Tour attempted to reestablish the terms of her relationship with Rousseau following his all-important acceptance of her femaleness. In a letter of November 24, she first admits to having impressive orthographic skills and penmanship, then declares that in her case these technical skills go hand in hand with a fundamental ignorance: "I forget everything, as soon as there is talk of teaching me. One can be a woman, understand Italian, know how to spell, punctuate correctly, and write coherently; and be ignorant of a great many things: no one knows this better than I." So singularly devoid of *esprit* is this real-life Julie that in asking for his advice as to what ridiculous tics she should remove from her epistolary style, she specifies: "It is necessary to speak clearly to me; I warned you of that; I possess no cleverness, and I always hesitate when interpretation is required."

De La Tour had read Rousseau's letter to Bernardoni warning that he had no intention of engaging in a battle of wits with a would-be "woman author." The women's awareness of the importance of demonstrating their lack of *esprit* to Rousseau is most evident in what develops into a veritable battle over which of the two is the more deprived of this elusive quality.[16] The sparring begins with Bernardoni's first letter, in which she makes a disparaging reference to her relative lack of epistolary talent: "This Julie is not myself, you can see that by my style; I am no more than her cousin, or rather her friend, just as was Claire; if I do not possess the merit of the latter, I do at least have the same feelings and zeal" (Sept. 28, 1761). De La Tour's own first letter includes a similarly novelesque reference that exalts Bernardoni's light, Claire-like *esprit* over her own seriousness: "You will find in my style neither the lightness nor the gaiety that embellishes that of my dear Claire. I possess infinitely less wit than she: I have only one manner of being, thinking, feeling, speaking; and I do not know how to choose, as she does, among all possible tones, the one that best fits the circumstances" (Oct. 5, 1761).

The women's claims to lack a cultivated style quickly become more combative. Several letters into the exchange, de La Tour again makes a reference to "Claire, who is able to win forgiveness for possessing infinite wit" (Nov. 5, 1761). Bernardoni does not let this charge go unanswered. She writes to Rousseau: "[Julie] was wrong nevertheless to tell you that I am able to win forgiveness for possessing infinite wit: I would have been more flattered if she had said, as she should have said, that I am able to forgive her for having infinitely more than myself." Bernardoni then further insists on her own lack of subtlety by declaring herself incapable of interpreting hidden motivations. She must be spoken to without stylistic embellishment, a point she makes clear through a reliance on the etymological relationship between "French" and "frankness" or "clarity": "Speak to me clearly, in French, and I will answer the same way" (Nov. 14, 1761).

Rousseau meanwhile insists that both women recognize and admit to their *esprit* as it so clearly manifests itself in their letters. While he declares himself far more eager to receive letters composed in Claire's light tone than in Julie's tone of melancholic seriousness, he does find one telling fault in Claire's letters: "And the other who just stupidly wrote to me that she has no intelligence! I am thus a fool, I who find her to possess as much as you? Is that not obliging? Lovable Claire, pardon my frankness; I cannot stop myself from telling you that men of wit always admit their talents, and that modesty is in them always falseness" (Nov. 24, 1761). As in the novel, Claire is accorded "almost as much intelligence as Julie," but Bernardoni receives a lesson in false modesty as well. She is driven into a corner, obliged either to admit that she does possess *esprit* or to bear the accusation of hypocrisy. Claire responds heatedly by projecting the blame onto Julie: "Read, monsieur, read, I say to you, and you will see that it is she who so *stupidly* in all of her letters say that she possesses no *wit*; and that finally disgusted with all that, I said in one or two of mine that she has infinitely more than myself" (Nov. 28, 1761).

The lack of playfulness in this one aspect of the women's letters reflects the centrality of the condemnation of *esprit* to Rousseau's overall philosophy. Bernardoni and de La Tour, careful readers of Rousseau's oeuvre, knew that they must carefully fend off the accusation of possessing this quality of mind, however clearly it might manifest itself in their letters and however much it might in practice please Rousseau. The ideal of the author-intellectual in Rousseau's philosophy is that of a solitary man struggling to express truth. Attempts at clever turns of phrase in published works are condemned as fame-seeking tactics; in missive letters, such stylistic tricks indicate authorial intent. Rousseau expressed his opinion on this matter quite clearly less than a year after receiving Bernardoni's first letter, when he published the following announcement in the *Mercure de France*: "Jean-Jacques Rousseau, Citizen of Geneva, asks . . . that the

Beaux Esprits no longer send him letters of compliment, even prepaid; not being able to pay so much postage, nor respond to so many letters" (March 1762).[17] The *Beaux Esprits* of this appeal would by implication have both the money and the time that Rousseau lacked. They might also be seeking his eventual support for their literary works (Rousseau had recently complained to his publisher, Marc Michel Rey, of receiving unsolicited manuscripts [*CC*, 10: 1664]).[18]

A far more nuanced approach to the definition of *bel esprit* is to be found in Voltaire's 1755 *Encyclopédie* entry *Esprit* (*Philos. & Belles-Lettr.*).[19] Asking why *homme d'esprit* is never used ironically, while *bel esprit*, not in itself an ironic term, may become so, Voltaire explains: "It is because *homme d'esprit* does not signify *superior wit, marked talent*, while *bel esprit* does. The expression *homme d'esprit* does not announce pretension, and *bel esprit* is a signpost; it is an art that demands cultivation, it is a sort of profession, exposing one to envy and ridicule." It follows that for Voltaire, while the *bel esprit* runs the risk of bringing ridicule down upon himself, it is only through running such a risk that he achieves stylistic greatness. The ability to master original and striking turns of phrase is both a gift and a hard-won talent. Voltaire points out that this observation has held true since ancient times: "Aristotle taught us perfectly the manner in which to say things with *esprit*." Paraphrasing the *Rhetoric* on this point, Voltaire goes on to explain the need to use metaphor in expressing oneself, as well as the need for constant renewal of the metaphors one uses: "[Aristotle] says that this art consists of not simply using the proper term, which relates nothing new; but that one must rather employ a metaphor, a figure with a clear meaning energetically expressed. . . . Aristotle was right to say that *there must be something new.*"

For Rousseau, such creative turning of language constitutes the deliberate perversion of an already untrustworthy medium.[20] In *Emile*, the tutor argues that while all languages fall far short of the ideal of intuitive communication, French is the one language so corrupt that it is impossible for a writer to prevent this obscene medium from becoming the message. The passage in question comes just as Emile reaches a long-delayed puberty, a transformation deliberately deferred by the tutor in consonance with the "natural" apathy of the male libido.[21] By rights, at long last, the tutor's pedagogical narration should now turn to the subject of sexual development, yet he hesitates: "The French language, they say, is the most chaste of languages; I myself believe it to be the most obscene; for it seems to me that the chastity of a language consists not in carefully avoiding unchaste turns of phrase, but rather in not possessing them. In effect, in order to avoid them, one must think of them, and there is no language in which it is harder to think purely in every sense than French. The reader, always better at finding obscene meanings than is the author at avoiding them, is scandalized and alarmed by everything" (*OC*, 4:649).

Due to this unique tropological penchant, the French language is unsuited to the transparent expression of morally pure thoughts or feelings. Despite his best efforts, any chaste individual employing this unchaste tongue produces a discourse hopelessly contaminated by a purely linguistic obscenity. The contamination begins with the writer, who is forced to think of the obscene thing in order to avoid its insidious capacity to achieve expression in French. The writer's intentions are then misinterpreted by the reader, who sees only the (idiolectical) manifestation of the writer's individual impurity. Rousseau is not proposing an anarchic theory of linguistic reception; the reader is responding to something that is there, on the page, but this obscene thing was not placed there by the author. In this theory of language, the author's unintended obscenity resembles an early avatar of Freudian parapraxis, although Rousseau places any onus solidly on the *vehicle* of expression: the French language.

Only ignorance of the "thing"—the vice in question—can prevent its penetration into one's discourse. So it is that the French used by Rousseau's "letters by two lovers living in the foothills of the Alps" escapes the general rule, in their case thanks to geographical coincidence. The preface to *La Nouvelle Héloïse* stresses that the central characters are not *beaux esprits,* living as they do far from Paris, with its high degree of corruption. So it is inevitable, the (pseudo-) editor explains, that their plain letters appear suspect to fashionable people by virtue of their monotonous sameness—that is, their lack of rhetorical invention. Saint-Preux does at one point in the novel come dangerously close to succumbing to Parisian *bel esprit,* as he will later fully succumb to one of the *belles Parisiennes.*[22] When he does so, Julie sends him a critique of his style in which she points out that Paris has begun to pollute his stylistic purity: "There is effort and gamesmanship in your letters. I am not speaking of that lively tone and animated expression born of strong feeling; I am speaking of the amiable style that, not being natural, arises naturally in no one, and indicates pretension on the part of those who use it. Oh God! pretension with what one loves!" (*OC*, 2:238).[23]

As close readers of *La Nouvelle Héloïse*, Bernardoni and de La Tour knew that if expert manipulation of language is the mark of *bel esprit*, maladroitness and animation mark sincerity. The two real women, however, faced an extralinguistic obstacle from which the fictionally ideal Julie was immune. As women, they had little defense against the charge of hypocrisy, according to their correspondent's general views on the female sex. In "Sophie or Woman," book 5 of *Emile* and Rousseau's most deterministic essay on female character, he stresses that in the moral realm as in the physical women may at times appear to constitute a separate race from men. Hypocrisy is an innate character trait for women, for the cultivation of appearance over reality is an essential feminine trait. While such apparent falsity violates Rousseau's prime directive for any upright man (*honnête homme*), it is true to the nature of woman, as he explains to his (obviously male) reader: "You repeat incessantly: women have such or such a fault that we do not have. Your pride fools you; they would be faults for you, but are qualities for them . . . their honor is not only in their conduct, but also in their reputation, and it is not possible for a woman who consents to pass for infamous ever to be honest. Man, in doing well, relies only on himself, and is able to brave public judgment" (*OC*, 4:695).[24] Little wonder that in the *Lettre à d'Alembert* and elsewhere, Rousseau declares *délicatesse* to be characteristic of women's letters, rather than the manly, heartfelt emotion of the missives contained in the *Lettres portugaises*.

Rousseau did admit of exceptions to such biological determinism, among both men and women. In a letter of October 1762, he admiringly describes Julie Bondeli as the ideal androgynous union of opposites. For Rousseau, this Julie combines "judgment and attractiveness, the reason of a man and the wit of a woman, Voltaire's pen and Leibniz's mind."[25] According to the subtle chiasmus present in the last pair of attributes (male/female, male/female, female/male), Voltaire's graceful style places him in a less-than-masculine position. Attractiveness and wit are evident in the writing of one who lets himself be guided by stylistic concerns (*la plume*); in seeking to please, Voltaire abandons the reasoned search for Truth.

That Rousseau did not view sex as a universal determinant of style is also apparent in his *Lettre à d'Alembert*. After praising Françoise de Graffigny's *Cénie* (1750), Rousseau notes: "It is not out of thoughtlessness that I am citing *Cénie* here, even though that charming play is the work of a woman: for, in seeking the truth in good faith, I am incapable of hiding that which is counter to my feelings; and it is not to one woman, but to women that I refuse to attribute the talents of men."[26] He makes two similar exceptions in the note in which he condemns women's letters as "cold and pretty": "Sappho alone, to my knowledge, and one other woman, merit exception."[27]

Rousseau's admiration for Voltaire's work in general, as well as for the writing of Mmes de Sévigné, de Graffigny, and other *femmes d'esprit*, demonstrates that he was not insensitive to the charms of the fully "feminine" intellect, even when expressed in epistolary form. When in January 1763, he compliments de La Tour on her letters, he insists on the quality of her mind: "I would love, madame, to converse with you at my leisure; your mind is clear and luminous, and all that comes from you attaches and attracts me, with one little exception" (Jan. 4, 1763).[28] As indicated by "clear and luminous," for Rousseau *esprit* in its best sense carries overtones of an appealing lightness of touch and clarity of mind that is particularly attractive in its penetration. The highest level of achievement of this outdated style is to be found, of course, in the undisputed stylistic mastery of Voltaire, but Rousseau refuses to accord any moral value to such writing, and this refusal damns de La Tour, along with Voltaire and the vast majority of women writers, to insignificance. While enjoying his correspondence with her, Rousseau repeatedly insists that he feels no responsibility toward her as an intimate friend.

It thus comes as no surprise when we learn that de La Tour avoided revealing to Rousseau that she was a published author. As R. A. Leigh notes: "Mme de La Tour had not judged it wise to reveal to JJ that she was an author in her idle hours. In fact, I have discovered in Hébrail and La Porte, i. 162, under the rubric 'Alissant de La Tour, wife of the Payer of Rents of the Hôtel de Ville,' the following two little works: 'Epistle to M. Jeliotte,' and 'Epistle to Mademoiselle Dumesnil.'"[29] De La Tour's publications advertised themselves by their very titles as the product of her *esprit*, for by the eighteenth century *épître* had evolved from its original meaning of missive letter to constitute a popular form of published letters in verse addressing a wide range of topics.[30] The *Encyclopédie* distinguishes epistle from letter as follows: "This term is now used almost only for letters written in verse, and for the dedication to books. . . . Today one associates *épître* with the notion of reflection and work, and it is not permitted the same casualness as the letter. The letter's style is free, simple, familiar."[31] When in her letter of October 28, 1761, de La

Tour praises Mme Bernardoni's clever missive ("he will laugh well at your epistle, if he laughs as much as I did"), *épître* is shorthand for "your supposedly sincere and personal letter to Rousseau, in fact so well-crafted." The women's "epistles" are clearly understood to be the product of their *esprit,* or stylistic cleverness.

Rousseau is not privy to this letter, of course; as an epistolary seduction technique, the composition of an *épître* violates the sentimental ethos of *La Nouvelle Héloïse.* Julie comments early on to Saint-Preux that she had recognized his love in his constraint when tutoring her; she then wonders: "Who knows if, aware of my sensibility, you are not employing a more subtle means of seducing me? But no, I am unjust, you are not capable of using artifice with me" (*OC,* 2:14). She later writes: "If in your lessons you had bent philosophy to your own ends, if you had tried to establish maxims favorable to your own interests, in trying to fool me you would have quickly learned your own lesson; but the most dangerous of your seductions is to employ none at all" (*OC,* 2:62).[32]

Skill in argumentation and metaphorical innovation may be markers of insincerity for Julie, but they are for de La Tour a necessary component of her letters. Her style had to both seduce Rousseau and interest future readers, and yet be somehow convincing as expressions of emotion written down by a woman with no literary pretensions. De La Tour addressed this contradiction in a typically Rousseauvian fashion. Whenever Rousseau referred to her *esprit,* she simply countered with a declaration of her ignorance and guilelessness; better yet, she appealed to her inner sentiment, evidence whose authority Rousseau could not question. As this technique demonstrates, and despite the obvious difficulties de La Tour faced in passing herself off as a Julie, her position was much stronger than it might at first appear. While it is impossible to understand this exchange adequately without examining Rousseau's views on women and letters, his was not the only voice at work in establishing the complex relationship that developed over the years between himself and his persistent fan. De La Tour was far from a meek victim; from the beginning, she countered her correspondent's views on women. She laid claim to an exceptional, if typically feminine, talent for grasping complex situations intuitively. If she admired Rousseau's work, it was because he was intellectually capable of expressing truths that she already possessed deep within herself. She writes that while she anticipates the appearance of *Emile,* "It is however true that I have never found anything in your writings (your music ex-

cepted) that did not seem to me to have always been in my soul"
(Jan. 9, 1762). She also appeals to his societal duty to be kind to
her, in spite of, or rather because of, her relative lack of developed
intellect: "Let us see by comparing our advantages if it would be a
crime to claim to establish a perfect equality in our communication:
those advantages that society accords to my sex will serve, for better
or worse, as compensation for those that nature gives to yours; and
we will speak of this no more" (Mar. 31, 1764).

While not above open resistance to those aspects of Rousseau's
views on women that did not suit her purposes, de La Tour wisely
refrained from engaging in an open philosophical debate on wom-
en's sincerity. Had she "won" such an argument, after all, her very
victory would have illustrated her *esprit*, rather than the integrity of
her feelings. Instead, she merely persists in claiming the transparency of her love for Rousseau. She appeals to her inner sentiment
as proof of the nature of their relationship, positing Rousseau's desire to end the exchange as an unfortunate deviation from the ideal
relationship that he himself had set in motion by publishing *La Nouvelle Héloïse*. Relegating Rousseau to the role of "faithless lover"
(*amant inconséquent*), she judges him according to the ethos of his
novel, apostrophizing his fictional double: "Saint-Preux, Saint-
Preux, how little your author resembles you!" (Nov. 27, 1761). Having once accepted the role of Saint-Preux to de La Tour's Julie,
Rousseau was never again immune to the charge that, despite having written the chef d'oeuvre of sensibility, he himself lacked feeling. The fictional Saint-Preux cries out: "O Julie, what a fatal gift of
heaven is a sensitive soul!" (*OC*, 2:89); de La Tour lashes out: "O
sensibility! pernicious faculty, of which I above all others feel the in-
conveniences, who could suspend your power over a man born for
you; whose soul is your sanctuary; whose genius you inflame; whose
pen you lead, and who paints you so well!" (Aug. 10, 1762). Rousseau was not above engaging in such remonstrances himself, as
when he berates de La Tour for not having detected that he was ill
by the style of his previous letter: "You hear that I have been quite
sick and still am; that is news for you; you noticed nothing of it in
my letter; because, madame, your heart does not possess as much
understanding as your mind" (Jan. 31, 1762).

Rousseau's most powerful tool in combating de La Tour's claims
to his attention, however, was the true nature of the two correspondents' relationship. Not only had they never met, their living situations were entirely different. In a particularly dismissive letter of

January 11, 1762, Rousseau refers with unguarded disdain to the re-ality of their situations. He depicts himself as the persecuted con-verse of Saint-Preux (metamorphosed for the occasion into a carefree hedonist), while de La Tour is recast as the persecuting neg-ative of Julie: "Saint-Preux was thirty years old, healthy, and con-cerned only with his pleasures; nothing less resembles Saint-Preux than J.-J. Rousseau. On receiving a letter like my last, Julie would be less offended by my silence than alarmed by my state; she would not in such a case entertain herself with counting letters and underlin-ing words; nothing resembles Julie less than Mme de La Tour. You have much intelligence, madame, and you are pleased to show it, and you want only letters from me. You are more the product of your neighborhood than I believed."

This letter was the beginning of the end of the three-way ex-change. As indicated by Rousseau's officious "Madame de La Tour," at this point in the correspondence the pleasures and dangers of the women's anonymity no longer existed for Rousseau. He knew the women's names and had learned some of the details of their lives, such as the significant fact that Bernardoni was of inferior social status to de La Tour (although both were noble by birth).[33] In a por-trait in words of de La Tour by Bernardoni, the latter stresses her own, simpler life, pointing out that she lives in a far less affluent part of Paris: "One lives in the neighborhood of the Palais-Royal, the other in the Marais: you well understand that it is I who am the Lady of the Marais" (Nov. 18, 1761).

The implications of de La Tour's residence in the Palais-Royal have been the subject of some debate. While the Palais-Royal was infamous for its prostitutes, it was also a neighborhood inhabited by those newly wealthy through business ventures, as Georges May points out in rectifying Sainte-Beuve's reaction to this letter: "Sainte-Beuve qualifies as a 'gross insult' . . . the allusion that he sees here to the gardens of the Palais-Royal, the capital at the time of Parisian prostitution. I prefer to interpret 'neighborhood' as new and rich neighborhood of finance and business. . . . JJR, who de-spised riches and often also those who possessed them, seems by this allusion to the neighborhood of the Palais-Royal to be reproaching his correspondent for her capriciousness and pretensions, charac-teristic of a rich woman."[34] Rousseau's "you are more the product of your neighborhood than I believed" of January 11, 1762, no doubt refers, as May argues, to the coin-counting parvenus of this area, and by analogy identifies de La Tour as their avaricious epistolary counterpart. She stands accused of wanting only letters; Rousseau senses no genuine feeling behind her claims to selfless love for him. She is, in his estimation, damningly insincere.

The connotations of the Palais-Royal have nothing to do with de La Tour's actual social condition, for she lived in the Montmartre neighborhood, at the other end of the rue de Richelieu.[35] The point mattered much less to the correspondents than to subsequent readers of the letters; although Rousseau twice made reference to the Palais-Royal, as in his hyperbolic: "Immortal Providence! there is thus still virtue on this earth? in women? in France, in Paris, in the neighborhood of the Palais-Royal?" (Nov. 24, 1761), de La Tour did not bother to correct him. She did however take care when editing the letters for publication to suppress the most enticing portion of Bernardoni's written portrait of her, that now reads: "My heroine is.............. such are the characteristics of my divine friend" (Nov. 21, 1761).

Leigh responds to this suppression with annoyance, lamenting "the details that constituted all the interest of this letter" (*CC*, n. to 9:1557). The missing passage is indeed to be lamented if we believe Rousseau himself. He tells de La Tour that she will be little surprised and perhaps less flattered to learn that Bernardoni's portrait of her friend has moved him to tears. While he found Claire to be charming when speaking of herself, "how much praise does she not wring from me by speaking of you? . . . Twenty times while reading her last letter I would have kissed at least her hand, if we had been at the harpsichord" (Nov. 24, 1761). Casting himself as the adoring Saint-Preux stealing kisses, he evokes a famous scene from the novel, often portrayed in prints. In this rewriting, Saint-Preux's attention is shifted from Julie to Claire; acknowledging this change, Rousseau remarks on how sad he finds it that he must follow the template of his novel or provoke jealousy between the two women: "The worst of it is that I must admit this to you as if it were a crime."

Why did de La Tour suppress this gem of a portrait—of herself? Georges May offers the explanation that Bernardoni's description of de La Tour "might have offended her sense of modesty. The suppressed passage equally erased her anonymity."[36] I would counter that de La Tour's sense of modesty was a rhetorical ploy. What the suppression reveals is rather authorial jealously, masquerading under the guise of personal modesty. The anonymity that de La Tour did indeed ultimately seek was not for herself, but for her friend, Marie-Madeleine Bernardoni. If de La Tour did seek to take revenge upon Bernardoni through editing, she succeeded, for Bernardoni's identity was a mystery until recently. Pierre-Paul Plan first found her name in a list made up by Rousseau in 1762 indicating those who were to receive a complimentary copy of *Emile*; R. A. Leigh then provided for the first time what little is known of Bernardoni's life.[37] There are no extant originals of Bernardoni's letters; there are two sets of copies of these lost autographs, the first made by de La Tour at the time the letters were written (the originals would have been returned to Bernardoni), the second (copies of these copies) made in 1770, as de La Tour prepared the exchange for publication.[38] De La Tour was quite faithful to her own autograph originals and to Rousseau's when copying them for publication, even when Rousseau's letters did not portray her in the most favorable light; there is thus little reason to believe that de La Tour seriously altered her ex-friend's original letters, other than to excise the portrait in question.

Despite Rousseau's obvious preference for her letters, Bernardoni's last contribution to the correspondence is dated January 15, 1762, and is addressed to de La Tour, not Rousseau. She is writing to comment on de La Tour's response to a recent and especially nasty missive from their "oracle" (Jan. 11, 1762). Bernardoni has herself had enough of Rousseau's letters: "I find them overall to be inconsequential, false, impertinent, etc." She regrets having started the exchange, and reiterates her esteem for her more tolerant friend. The beginning of her letter indicates that she does not anticipate the same degree of esteem in return: "It is, no doubt, my Julie, because Molière consulted his servant, that you wish to have my opinion of your letter to Jean-Jacques. Well then! Here it is: it is delicious, with as much dignity as delicacy, and as much wit. I would rather have written it than the Héloïse novel."

This passage reflects no small resentment on Bernardoni's part at having been consistently relegated to the secondary role of faithful confidante, despite her success in attracting Rousseau's attention. This resentment does not prevent her from reacting as a friend—a "Claire"—should to de La Tour's request for a literary critique, providing that the praise given, with its effusive nature and casual addition of "and as much *esprit*," is not meant to be sarcastically offensive. Bernardoni follows up her resentment at playing servant to de La Tour's Molière with a vitriolic rejection of Rousseau that might serve as an epitaph to her short career as one of his numerous female admirers: "My husband, who will be visiting you on Thurs-

day, claims that Jean-Jacques should be buried alongside his dog"
(the dog in question is the recently deceased Turc, whose health was
apparently followed by the public as closely as Rousseau's urethral
events). De La Tour profits from the need to inform Rousseau that
Bernardoni no longer wants to write him by again insisting on her
friend's overabundance of *esprit*: "Claire, who is more capable than
any other of feeling the pleasure of communication with you, but
whose mind is engaged more willingly than her heart, is quite
piqued by the indifference you have shown me" (Apr. 21, 1762).
Rousseau responds that he had guessed the reason for Claire's silence, adding that Julie might do well to follow her lead: "Furthermore, this pride does not displease me, and I believe it sets a good
example" (Apr. 24, 1762).

The disintegration of the epistolary triangle is a major turning
point in the correspondence. It marks the end of what de La Tour
will in the future reconstruct as an edenic period during which
Rousseau was willing to accept her as Julie to his Saint-Preux. The
absent Claire becomes an easy object of blame, recast as a *femme d'esprit* who led de La Tour astray by involving her in a correspondence
she would otherwise never have begun: "Why did Mme de B . . .
push me to seek your friendship? Without her encouragement, I
would never have dared to do it: my natural timidity would have
held me back, rather than any prudence" (July 23, 1762). In reality,
the pattern of the correspondence was set from the first: plaintive
letters in the Portuguese manner from de La Tour, followed by a
return of Rousseau's interest, an interest that soon wanes, to be followed by reproachful letters from de La Tour, answered by nasty in-
vectives from Rousseau, then silence on his part; then once again,
plaintive, accusatory missives from the abandoned Julie.

2

Going Public: "Mme de ***,
Amie de Jean-Jacques"

Jean-Jacques is dead; the news was announced to me yesterday
at dinner, I immediately felt my appetite disappear, my stomach
contracted involuntarily and I felt nauseated.

> —5 a.m.; July 7, 1778; Marie-Jeanne Phlipon
> (later Mme Roland), to Marie-Henriette Cannet

RAYMOND TROUSSON APTLY DESCRIBES THE ROUSSEAU–DE LA TOUR
exchange as a predictable series of events: "Honeymoon, dispute,
reconciliation, such is their cycle."[1] Rousseau was invariably the in-
stigator of breaks in the correspondence, although de La Tour often
provoked him into calling for an end to the exchange when she had
not received a response for some months. A letter of rupture was a
letter, after all; better yet, it required a lengthy refutation on her
part. As Rousseau himself pointed out early on, his correspondent
possessed a genius for garnering responses from him after he had
vowed never again to write her: "You always obstinately insist on an
answer, and you possess the art of making one always necessary"
(Oct. 15, 1762). Rousseau finally did break off contact with de La
Tour in 1772, although this definitive rejection did not dissuade her
from sending him letters until his death in 1778. The demise of her
correspondent was, ironically, a liberating event for de La Tour, who
immediately launched a publishing career as the *Amie de Jean-Jacques*,
avenger of all slights against her hero. She published her defenses
first in a journal, the *Année littéraire*, then in a self-published work
entitled *Jean Jaques Rousseau Vangé* [*sic*] (1779). The work was considered important enough to be republished, corrected, and revised
under the title *La Vertu vengée*, in a 1782 edition of Rousseau's collected works.

In this chapter, I begin with an analysis of the exchange between de La Tour and Rousseau after Bernardoni's abrupt departure, with particular attention to de La Tour's role in the Rousseau-Hume affair of 1766. I then argue that de La Tour's letters in defense of Rousseau's posthumous reputation were designed, at least in great part, to prepare the reception of the publication of their correspondence after her own death.[2] She engaged in an elaborate game within these letters, signing them with various pseudonyms who referred to each other, and included cryptic references to her real identity, as well as to the cache of letters by Rousseau that she possessed, edited and ready for the presses. De La Tour's pursuit of a man who so often demonstrated little regard for her has been cited as irrefutable evidence that she was merely an emotionally disturbed fanatic; her public defenses of Rousseau's reputation after his death become, in such analyses, merely the continued ravings of a purblind fan. Any "normal" woman, it is assumed, with a life of her own (such as Bernardoni, well equipped with a husband and child), would surely have lost interest. As I argue here, these carefully and cleverly written letters demonstrate that until her own death in 1789, de La Tour never ceased sculpting her reputation as a Julie worthy of the name—a "humble," self-effacing Julie, willing to wait for posthumous glory, if necessary.

By early June of 1762, five months after Bernardoni's defection, de La Tour had good reason to congratulate herself on having repaired her epistolary relationship with Rousseau. She had succeeded in reconciling her Saint-Preux to an ongoing dialogue, and the "nothing resembles Julie less than Madame de La Tour" that had ended the three-way exchange seemed forgotten. Their letters had become effusively flirtatious once again; of a proposed face-to-face meeting with his Julie, Rousseau wrote: "Your trip is something to meditate on; for I admit that in spite of my state, I am quite afraid of you" (June 1, 1762).[3] Three days later, he reiterated: "No, I have never feared a woman as much as I fear you" (June 4, 1762).

The emotion attached to this meeting echoes the famous scene from *La Nouvelle Héloïse* in which Julie and Saint-Preux exchange their first, mortally decisive kiss. Although arranged by Julie, this kiss was a reward for good behavior on the part of Saint-Preux; her own reaction to the kiss (she all but faints) came as a surprise. In the real-life scenario, Rousseau reverses the roles, casting himself as the vulnerable male object of de La Tour's passionate advances, who may give in, but may also live to regret his "weakness" in doing so.

His vulnerability is to a great degree physical, of course ("in spite of my state"), but his representation of an amorous woman in pursuit of her favorite author, rather than of a man pursuing his beloved, is a crucial distinction between their relationship and that of the novel's protagonists, just as it contrasts with Rousseau's passionate pursuit of Sophie d'Houdetot.

There are signs that Rousseau was quite serious about a potential relationship with de La Tour. He had requested permission to reveal her name to Mme de Luxembourg, to whom he had already spoken of his "Julie." Evoking the need for secrecy, de La Tour begs him not to do so, adding: "Ah! monsieur, it is to me that you must speak of me" (June 5, 1762). He responds in a letter of June 7 that he respects her desire to remain anonymous, and that although loath to burn her letters unless she orders him to do so (she does not), he will destroy her seal and other signs of her identity. She does the same, as Leigh notes: "In fact, the seals have been torn off of the letters Mme de La Tour had received up until this point from JJ, leaving only traces of wax" (*CC*, n. to 11:1836). More than de La Tour's own desire to remain anonymous, this precaution reflected the seriousness of Rousseau's situation following the publication of *Emile*. He had far better reasons than the redoubtable Mme de La Tour to fear for his safety. Having heard rumors that she describes as quite disturbing, de La Tour begs him in a letter of June 7 to inform her fully of the dangers he faces, arguing: "You owe this mark of confidence to my extraordinary interest in you."

Rousseau did not have the time to respond, for on June 9, 1762, the Paris Parlement ordered his arrest. He had been forewarned in time to flee France for Switzerland, where, ordered to leave Berne, he settled in Môtiers in Neuchâtel, having been granted asylum by Frederick II. Rousseau's stay in Môtiers constitutes the two correspondents' most considerable honeymoon period. At one point, Rousseau apologizes for not having sat down to reread de La Tour's letters, and hints that he plans to gather them into a sort of private letter book for his own renewable enjoyment: "I am anticipating the pleasure that I will experience in rereading your letters and arranging things so that I may reread them often" (May 14, 1762). He even helps de La Tour in her attempt to buy land nearby, a project she abandons when he is again forced to flee in 1765.

Counting on Rousseau's apparent openness to a relationship with her during this period, de La Tour takes the calculated risk of sending him one of her poems for a critique. Her creation is now lost, but, judging from Rousseau's response, de La Tour's poem was written to sing the praises of her favorite author (Oct. 15, 1762). She had read the clear warning issued to her ex-friend Bernardoni in Rousseau's first letter ("I hope, madame, that despite the beginning of your letter you are not at all an author"); she was also aware of Rousseau's negative opinion of women writers; and yet, while she does carefully place her elegiac poem with regard to the public and her own lack of intentional authorship, the reason she ultimately gives for daring to send Rousseau her poetry is shockingly inadvisable in its potential to annoy:

> Addressing verses to you is a singular manner in which to attempt to please you (a goal of which I never lose sight), when one is a woman; and one has read your writings. That is why the verses I am attaching to this letter were written some time ago; I dared not send them to you, the tone of our correspondence did not seem to justify this act of temerity: it seems to me that it has taken on another tone, better suited to gaining me your indulgence; and what most convinces me is that it is now claimed that you are no longer as rigid concerning the analogy that one's occupations should have with the faculties attached to one's sex. They tell me that you are learning to make *lacets* [decorative braids]. (Aug. 31, 1762)

In other words, while Rousseau occupies himself with womanly pursuits, she will take over as writer. With exquisite misjudgment, or perhaps out of the desire to inspire more interesting responses from her correspondent, who was at the time quite preoccupied with his general affairs, de La Tour paints a portrait of a feminized Rousseau. Her description has him almost literally *tombé en quenouille*, to use the French expression for a man who takes the subordinate, female role.

Rousseau had indeed changed considerably since his flight from France, but as one might anticipate, and as is confirmed in book 12 of the *Confessions*, he himself did not view this process as a "feminization." In his autobiography, Rousseau is careful to justify his notorious adoption of apparently "feminine" attire, declaring that he had begun wearing what he refers to as his Armenian costume out of strictly practical concerns connected to a very male organ (he was trying to accommodate his frequent use of probes or catheters to alleviate his urinary troubles). He had, it is true, taken to creating the *lacets* to which de La Tour refers: flat braids worked or knotted, usually, by women. In further support of her letter, Rousseau explains in the *Confessions* that his adoption of this hobby was the result of his decision to have nothing more to do with writing or publishing. Nevertheless, this change in occupation clearly did not indicate any androgynous softening in his views on the distinction between the sexes—quite to the contrary. Forced into the company of women by his inactivity once he arrived in Neuchâtel, Rousseau tells us, he needed to occupy his hands and distract his mind in order to endure their mindless blatherings. "Having completely abandoned literature," he writes in the *Confessions*, "I decided that to avoid living like a savage I should learn to make braids. I carried my cushion with me on my visits, going like a woman from door to door and conversing with passersby. That helped me to endure without boredom the inane babbling of the female neighbors I visited, several of whom were quite likable and not lacking in intelligence."[4] Rousseau assigns a didactic value even to this seemingly insignificant hobby, adding: "In order to make my braids useful, I presented them to my young women friends when they married, on the condition that they nurse their children." De La Tour, childless and separated from her husband, was hardly a candidate for the role of nursing mother, and thus ineligible for one of Rousseau's braids; she later despairingly notes his infidelity in sending not only a *lacet* but also a letter to a certain young Parisian woman, who showed off her two treasures to everyone.[5]

The protofeminist note to de La Tour's analysis of her new relationship to Rousseau reveals both resentment and the hope that he may now accept her as a writer. When she informs him "it is now claimed that you are no longer as rigid concerning the analogy that one's occupations should have with the faculties attached to one's sex," she implies that male and female characteristics may well be only loosely "attached" to biological imperatives. Specific talents have perhaps been somewhat artificially grafted on to each sex; at the very least, in exceptional cases they can be "detached" and assigned to a representative of the opposite sex. The latter argument had, again, been presented by Rousseau himself in the *Lettre à d'Alembert* concerning women writers; perhaps de La Tour hoped that he would recognize in her a "new Sappho," as well as a "nouvelle Héloïse."

Despite the daring tone of her letter, de La Tour takes great care not to go too far in qualifying herself as an exceptional woman, that is, a bluestocking. She stresses that her writing has not caused her to suspend strictly feminine activities: "This amusement [writing verse] did not cause me to disdain those particularly suited to my sex."

Among these suitable tasks she lists sewing, embroidery, knitting, playing music, and the proper running of a household. Nor does *esprit* enter into her poetical compositions, for her description of her writing practice resembles a *furor poeticus* in which poetry flows spontaneously from her pen: "In addition, you must forgive me for thinking in verse, when I am strongly affected: (for that is what I do)." As a last insurance against accusations of authorial intention, and even though she is asking Rousseau for a critique of her verses, she denies any literary ambition and blames her husband for having previously publicized her talents: "You think perhaps that vanity, that produces nothing good, has made me a poet? Not at all: I fear nothing more than being known as a poet: it was against my will that my husband gave me this reputation: I neither praise nor pass around my verses" (Aug. 31, 1762).

Far from impressed by her claims to hide her verse—she is after all sending him her poetry—Rousseau writes back referring to her poem as an *épître*: "I received in good time, madame, the letter that you sent to me by M. du Terreau and the *épître* attached to it." He would not know how to praise praises directed at himself, nor to comment on poetry written expressly for him; furthermore, he is "overwhelmed by letters, testimonies, poems, praise, and criticisms." In his view, clearly, de La Tour's role as a correspondent is to provide consolation and distraction through her feminine *délicatesse* and *esprit*. She is the epistolary equivalent of the several Swiss women whose unlikely wit made the babbling of the others bearable, while he distracted himself with his braiding.

In other words, Rousseau's abandonment of authorship has not left a spot open for de La Tour to fill. Throughout their relationship, he had little trouble accepting that de La Tour's admiration for him was genuine (leaving aside several paranoid accusations), but he was quite unwilling to accept her as a writer, even a "writer" veiled by the rhetoric of instinctive creation to which she insistently adhered. He also resisted the notion that her devotion to him implied a reciprocal emotion. Just as he only occasionally acquiesced to the conceit that de La Tour was Julie, he only occasionally accepted the existence of a real emotional tie between them. Nor did he hesitate to withdraw his affection at a moment's notice.[6] Rousseau was willing to accept de La Tour as simply an admiring woman fan with no claim to talent of her own, and no claim to his devoted attention to either her or her letters. Even during the honeymoon of his stay in Môtiers, Rousseau responds to one of her efforts to reanimate herself as Julie as follows: "Be content, trust me, to be Marianne; and if that Marianne is such as I imagine her, she has little reason to lament her fate" (May 29, 1762).[7]

In order to "imagine" her in greater detail, Rousseau later asks for and receives a physical description of de La Tour. She goes into exquisite detail: brown hair, blue eyes with "small pupils," "as much roundness as one should have," an agreeable profile with a somewhat prominent nose, an oval face, a high forehead, teeth that are "healthy, white, and well placed," a well-made chin. Perhaps the most important physical detail she provides is that her face—like that of the Julie of the novel—is "a bit marked by smallpox." Her real opportunity to shine comes as she begins a description of her physiognomy, of which she declares: "Thank heaven, I have one." She means that through her physical features one perceives an attractive soul, "more contented, than gay; more good, than sweet; more vivacious, than malicious; more soul, than mind." She ends on her all-important "sincere smile," before beginning a description of her modest dress (Jan. 13, 1763).

Some months later, de La Tour offers Rousseau a chance to see her portrait in paint, as soon as Mlle de Briancourt, the *peintresse* working on the piece, has finished. De La Tour's use of *peintresse* is a neologism with, once again, protofeminist undertones.[8] She comments explicitly on her choice of a woman painter, assuring Rousseau that he will receive a faithful portrait of herself, for Mlle de Briancourt is quite skillful, and less likely to flatter her than a man. De La Tour then cites Ariosto: "I would rather deal with women than with men; and as for talent, I agree with Ariosto that 'Women have achieved a degree of excellence / In all the arts to which they have applied themselves'" (Oct. 8, 1763; the quote is from *Orlando Furioso*).

Rousseau does not respond to this obvious provocation. When the painting finally arrives at his door, he remarks not upon its quality but rather upon the striking similarities between his own situation and a scene in his novel in which Saint-Preux receives a long-awaited miniature of his beloved Julie during his stay in London. Like Saint-Preux, Rousseau is distracted by the presence of visitors from enjoying the portrait of his dear Marianne at the moment it arrives. He laments this missed opportunity, adding: "And that is not the only way in which I resemble Saint-Preux at this moment" (Oct. 16, 1763). This last reference is a flattering analogy to his hero's adoration of his lover's beauty, but while Rousseau's lovelorn fictional hero flees his importunate visitor to contemplate his idol and to transcribe his reaction in a long letter to her, Rousseau merely glances at the painting and rushes off a short note before returning to his affairs. He will study it later, he tells de La Tour, then return it by the next post.

As promised, he soon returns the portrait with a brief note of apology for how little time he has to write. This note is short, charming, and utterly unsatisfying to de La Tour. Rousseau compares the portrait to her previous self-portrait in words, remarking that the two do not resemble each other, which increases his pleasure: "It is like having two mistresses at once, passing deliciously from one to the other, tasting the pleasures of infidelity while remaining faithful" (Oct. 23, 1763). He may keep the first while he must return the latter, so he prefers the first, of which he had written: "Medea would have needed no other magic to rejuvenate old Eson, and if dawn had been made as you are, the decrepit Titon's age and sufferings would have disappeared in seeing her, although he remained still sick. As for me, so far from you, I gain only regrets and ridicule from all this, a rejuvenated heart is only a new cause of suffering alongside so many others, and nothing is as ridiculous as an old man of twenty years" (Jan. 27, 1763).

De La Tour had no doubt anticipated a yet more dramatic response to her portrait in paint and was quite disappointed with the short, gallant response to Mlle de Briancourt's work. She writes back to demand exactly what differences he has noted between the two portraits, written and painted, and to complain that what she seeks from her correspondent is not flattery but *immediacy*, that hallmark of truth of sentiment. Why did he not immediately sit down, as did Saint-Preux, to contemplate his beloved's portrait and to convey his impressions to his *amie*? De La Tour closes her letter with an anecdote designed to take the sting out of her demands, in which she quotes the peasants of Montmorency gathered together to bemoan Rousseau's flight: " 'We are so unhappy that he was taken away from us: he was so charitable! He was a father to us all!' " (Nov. 1, 1763).

Unimpressed, Rousseau responds quite viciously to de La Tour's complaint that he should have made time for an immediate epistolary response to her portrait. Repeating his previous negative references to her residence in a wealthy neighborhood, he emphasizes her characteristic lack of consideration for his real-life travails: "But I laugh at my simplicity in thinking that I could explain such a different situation to a Parisian woman, whose social standing makes her idle, and who has no other occupation than that of writing and receiving letters, and believes that her friends are exclusively occupied with the same goal" (Dec. 25, 1763). He had, after all, specified quite clearly that he was suffering; his rejuvenated Titon "remained still sick." At least, in her case, all this practice at writing letters has been rewarded by skill, for Rousseau ends his letter on a reconciliatory note in which he makes the astonishing claim that he knows no one who writes letters better than de La Tour: "You are, madame, a very likable woman; I know no one who writes letters better than yourself. I believe that you have a good heart and an agreeable mind, and your friendship is precious to me; but, in my present state my tranquility is yet more precious, and because I can only sustain a stormy correspondence with you, I prefer to sustain none at all."

Even before the portrait episode, de La Tour had been pleading with her *ami* to send her a letter the emotional purity of which would be guaranteed by the timing of its composition: "I beg you to respond to one of my letters, this one, or another, as you please, at the moment that you receive it; even if your answer is mailed eight days later. The first emotions of a heart such as yours must be delicious to observe; especially for the object that excites those emotions" (Oct. 8, 1763). She most particularly regrets that Rousseau did not develop his response to a letter that had moved him by "the precious marks" that enriched it (her tears, of course). When he responds that he had had neither the time nor the requisite good health to develop his reaction to these marks any further, de La Tour laments: "You who express yourself with such delicacy, how much would you not have put into giving the details of the impressions made upon you by those *marks* of which you remind me, so that I know, at least that you noticed them!" (Aug. 25, 1763). His having to "remind" her of the tears she had shed on her stationery indicates that she had "forgotten" them; she perhaps had been aware of crying, but had sealed her letter unaware of the "precious" gift it contained.

However hypersentimental in tone, de La Tour's request for an immediate response to her letters and her portrait indicate an awareness of epistolary aesthetics. When citing the superiority of the third-person narrator for the novel form, critics often observe that the epistolary novel suffers to a degree from the impossibility of rendering the immediacy of emotional response to events. Letters are written, of necessity, after the fact; the letter writer recalls some previous event in relative tranquility, pen in hand. Efforts to surmount this structural difficulty in an epistolary novel can be at times somewhat comical, as in a letter from the beginning of *La Nouvelle Héloïse* written while Saint-Preux hides in Julie's dressing room just before making love to her. This "before-the-fact" account is as close to a real-time description of lovemaking as a reader could possibly enjoy, in an epistolary novel. Like Rousseau awaiting d'Houdetot on the terrace, Saint-Preux is writing to relieve himself of an excess of sexual excitement, as he declares in a passage that also serves, however awkwardly, to establish verisimilitude: "How fortunate that I found ink and paper! I express what I feel in order to temper the excess."

While Saint-Preux clearly tells us that he has relieved this "excess" by writing and not in some less seemly manner, the reader has just been treated to a scene of metonymical intercourse. As he pens his reactions, Saint-Preux visually examines various articles of Julie's clothing until, arriving at her *corps,* or inner supporting garment, his letter collapses into ellipses: "In front two slight bulges...... O voluptuous spectacle.... the whalebone has ceded to the force of the pressure..... delicious traces, may I kiss you a thousand times!.... gods! gods!" Saint-Preux functions in this imagined encounter with Julie as a strangely passive object of desire rather than as an active male lover, his more usual role. It would appear that Julie, or rather her disembodied breath, has her/its way with Saint-Preux: "Julie! my charming Julie! I see you, I feel you everywhere, I breathe you in with the air that you breathed, you penetrate my substance; your presence is burning and painful to me!" (*OC,* 2:147). De La Tour no doubt sought something similar from her "Saint-Preux," imagining Rousseau writing with eyes fixed upon her portrait, or her tears. That this spontaneous letter would also exhibit a strong sexual component, however sublimated, goes without saying.

Saint-Preux's suggestive account is far less explicit than Rousseau's description of the famous masturbatory "supplement" he practiced on the road to d'Houdetot's residence, as an alternative to scribbling illegible notes to the object of his desire. In book 9 of the *Confessions,* Rousseau tells us of d'Houdetot's habit of greeting him with a welcoming embrace, a "fatal kiss" that would make his blood boil and bring him to the point of fainting: "Aware of the danger, I tried upon leaving to distract myself and think of something else . . . no matter what I tried, I do not believe that I ever arrived having made the journey with impunity." He would arrive, he tells us, "weak, worn out, exhausted, barely standing" (*OC,* 1:445).

Obviously, and despite his oft-cited pre-Romanticism, Rousseau was not one to mask the raw truths of human physicality, even in his novel. When Saint-Preux writes to Julie from the mountains, he is no Byronic hero whose exalted spirit seeks out its ideal geographical environment on the uppermost isolated peaks. Rousseau's hero, instead, treats his lover to a disquisition on the varied effects of different altitudes on the psyche. He discovers that his self-pity is strongest at a medium height, while the thin pure air of the higher peaks instead restores him to calm equilibrium.[9] Rousseau's realism exhibits itself equally in his dismissals of de La Tour's attempts at sentimental excess in her letters. He frequently appeals to the reality of their relationship in order to temper her rhetoric, pointing out how little they know of each other. He does at rare intervals accept her as a true intimate: "Believe me, madame, I beg you, I tenderly include you in my small group of friends. . . . I will tell you only that among the mass of letters I continually receive, I place to the side those that are dear to me, and yours certainly do not occupy the least rank of these" (May 14, 1763). Far more often, he rejects the notion that he has any binding duty to respond to her letters: "I have always believed that nothing was more free than the ties of friendship. Especially purely epistolary relationships, and I believed that it was always permissible to break them off when they ceased to suit us" (Feb. 13, 1763). Nor does Rousseau allow de La Tour to manipulate his responses to her through appeals to the vagaries of the postal system. These excuses often appear as suspect to Rousseau as any pseudoeditor's claim in an eighteenth-century epistolary novel to have found a packet of private letters in some secret attic cache: "Another lost letter, madame? This is becoming frequent, and it is bizarre that this misfortune happens to me only with you" (Nov. 29, 1761). Although he here points to a lack of verisimilitude, he later responds unquestioningly, after a long silence, to inform her that she had mistakenly placed a charming letter to someone else in an envelope addressed to him: "Madame, you have made a small blunder" (May 21, 1762).

One of de La Tour's most serious offenses against Rousseau seems to have stemmed from a less innocent manner of soliciting a letter. By February of 1765, Rousseau was somewhat neglectful of de La Tour, although the short letters he sent were full of admiration. The latest had ended with a reminder as to the private nature of their correspondence: "In letters written to be shown, I hold up better; but I never hide my weaknesses in writing to you; you will know what that means" (Feb. 10, 1765). Perhaps hoping to stir him to a longer response, she answers this declaration as to the private nature of the exchange by striking at the heart of Rousseau's self-image. She casts aspersions on the truth of Rousseau's many claims to abhor public fame:

> For a long time I have suffered from my reserve, and from your own. . . . I am going to speak to you openly. I respect your weakness, dear Jean-Jacques: but I do not understand it. By consecrating your pen to the truth, did you not prepare your soul to remain constant? You who seem to know men so well, how could you have thought that they would welcome a man who condemned their morals by his own example; and thundered against their prejudices in his writings? The road that you have taken was not destined to lead you to repose, but rather to fame; you were surely aware of this. (Feb. 25, 1765)

De La Tour "sincerely hopes" that her letter will in no way shake Rousseau's sense of self, that is, his vision of himself as a seeker after truth who rejects earthly fame. God forbid that he should question his own motives (she leaves unsaid: as he has so often questioned hers): "Such is my way of thinking about everything that has happened to you since I came to know you. God forbid that in revealing all this to you, I mean to attack the internal satisfaction that must console you for everything; God forbid that I believe myself to have this pernicious power over you, or to want it! You would be too unhappy, if you began to doubt the soundness of the reasons that caused you to combat so many received opinions; for without entirely sacrificing your self-image, you would be unable to go back."

Rousseau answers on March 10. He has read her letter, he says, with great attention, given the seriousness of the charges at hand. He does not counter her accusations; instead, castigating her abuse of the truth as a weapon to attack the weak, he implies that her reading of his relationship to publicity is quite correct. He declares that in her place, he would have simply lied: "You were flattering during my prosperity; you become frank during my time of suffering. . . . I love the truth, of that there is no doubt: but if I should ever have the misfortune of seeing a friend in the state in which I find myself, and if I should have no consoling truth to tell him; I will lie."

Despite the severity of de La Tour's charges, the two went on to reconcile. She first withdraws her accusation that Rousseau sought glory through his published writings: "I was wrong: I am more persuaded of that than ever before" (July 3, 1765). Then, in a wonderful twist, she transforms her own false statements about Rousseau into an argument for the necessity of his writing her more letters. If he does not break his silence with her he will demonstrate the truth of the accusation that she has (so falsely!) thrown at him, for as there is no public glory to be gained by writing private letters to her, the only result of his act will be to break her sentimental heart: "Humanity itself, if I did not carry it in my heart, would seem only a vain word to me, if you forced me to believe that the famous pen from which I thought it flowed, was guided only by a thirst for fame."

De La Tour's accusations had been particularly ill timed, for as Rousseau points out in his letter of March 10, 1765, they came at a most difficult period in his life. He had attracted the wrath of the Swiss pastors by publishing his *Lettres écrites de la Montagne* in 1764, and had been declared un-Christian. Soon after, in December 1764, Voltaire anonymously published the *Sentiment des citoyens*, in which he revealed to the world that Rousseau had abandoned his five children at a foundling hospital. Although Frederick II had, in response to the Swiss pastors, declared his protection of Rousseau to be unwavering, Rousseau remained under attack, at times literally, as when on the evening of September 6, 1765, stones were thrown at his house. Having then fled Môtiers for an idyllic month on the Ile de Saint-Pierre, celebrated in the fifth "Promenade," Rousseau was again ordered to leave his place of asylum on October 16. In what seemed at the time a fortunate turn of events, he received on October 22 a letter from the famous British philosopher David Hume offering him a place of refuge at his home in England.

Rousseau's journey to England was something of a triumphal march that included visits to Berlin and Strasburg, as well as a short stay in Paris, during which he received a large number of visitors. Among these—at long last—was his Julie-come-to-life. The interview that took place on December 28, 1765, seems to have gone well, for on January 2, 1766, Rousseau wrote to express his regret that he would not be able to see this particular visitor again: "I am leaving, dear Marianne, with the regret of not having seen you again. I have no more forgotten my promise than I have forgotten you. . . . I will write to you, I will give you my address. I greatly desire that you love me, that you do not reproach me any longer, and even more that I not merit your reproaches. But it is too late to correct myself of anything. I will remain as I am, and it is no more possible for me to be likable than for me to cease loving you."

While Hume greeted Rousseau in mid-January with open arms, relations between the two famous men disintegrated with alarming speed, in a manner that brought delight to Rousseau's opponents back in France. What became known as the "Hume-Rousseau affair" began officially in July 1766, when Rousseau sent a long accusatory letter to Hume from Wootton, to which he had withdrawn with Thérèse Levasseur. Hume's supporters decided that a public response was in order. They prepared a "justification" of Hume that included Rousseau's letter along with other letters, followed by an account of the imbroglio written by Hume himself. Two versions were prepared, one in English and one in French. As befitted a quarrel more French than English in its public interest, there appeared first, on October 20, 1766, the translated French version, *Exposé succinct de la contestation qui s'est élévée entre M. Hume et M. Rousseau avec les pièces justificatives* (A Concise Account of the Dispute That Arose between M. Hume and M. Rousseau, with Documents).

The resulting uproar took place on a European scale, and has attracted a great deal of critical attention.[10] It also led to de La Tour's greatest moment of glory as Rousseau's friend and public defender, and is thus worthy of lengthy discussion here, particularly given the role played by private letters in this messy "affair." The editor of the first public shot fired, that is, the French version of the *Concise Account,* is careful to justify the publication of Rousseau's private letters to Hume, while assuring us that we are reading "exact copies of the originals." The publication of Rousseau's letters without his permission is justified by placing them under the rubric of legal evidence (*pièces justificatives*), as well as by reference to yet another defamatory letter that Rousseau had supposedly sent to a Parisian publisher— and had thus, it is implied, written with the intention to publish. In this second letter, we are told, Rousseau "demands" that Hume himself violate the ban on publishing private letters: "M. Rousseau wrote a letter to a Parisian bookseller in which he accused M. Hume of being in league with his enemies in an effort to betray and defame him, and in which he openly defied him to print the evidence that he had in his hands."[11] It was only when informed of this (potential) publication, we are told, that Hume was reluctantly convinced to write an account of the events leading up to the rupture, and to allow the publication of Rousseau's letters to him.

In a lovely rhetorical flourish, the editor then concludes by advising the reader to toss the book aside. This dispute as a whole is a private affair of little interest to the public, just as "private" letters should not concern other, third-party readers: "This pamphlet will present rather strange examples of bizarre behavior to those who take the trouble of reading it; but those who do not bother will do better; that is how little its contents concern those not involved."[12] Hume and his supporters are, to rephrase the preface, lobbing the first public salvo in this battle from a defensive position. Their only desire is to see the debate quietly fade away.

The response to this would-be last word on the subject was an extraordinary outpouring of pamphlets and published letters that included de La Tour's anonymous "Lettre à l'auteur de *la justification de M. Rousseau*" of November 1766. The previously published work referred to in de La Tour's title had appeared in London under the full title: *Justification de J.-J. Rousseau, dans la contestation qui lui est survenue avec M. Hume* (Justification of J.-J. Rousseau, in His Recent Quarrel with M. Hume). Among the many attacks and counterattacks that make up this famous "affair," de La Tour's defense of Rousseau stands out as a strikingly self-conscious jewel of feminine epistolary rhetoric in the public realm. While it is true that bringing attention to oneself as a supporter of Rousseau at this time would have been unwise, given his disfavor with the French authorities, de La Tour's defense of her anonymity instead turns obsessively about the issue of publishing a private letter. Identifying herself only as "Mme de ***," she declares to the author of the *Justification* that she is making her letter public only because she has no choice. If only she were able to send a *private* missive to this person: "Monsieur, this letter is written only for you; and I would not have made it public, if I had had another means of getting it to you. But I could not resist the desire to communicate to you a few of my thoughts."[13] These "few thoughts" run some twenty-five pages and take the form of carefully argued suggested additions to the anonymous writer's justification of Rousseau, additions that he would no doubt have included himself had he not been pressed for time ("You would have said that . . . You would have added, monsieur . . . Finally, monsieur, you would have said . . ."). De La Tour further justifies her audacity in presuming to edit this man's letter with a lavish layer of self-effacement in which lack of *esprit* plays an important role: "I do not have enough *esprit* to satisfy your self-esteem by applauding your style, monsieur; so I will not speak of it. But, I have enough good sense, and a good enough heart, that you may be flattered by the admiration that I have conceived for your character" (2).

De La Tour ends her letter by berating her correspondent for remaining anonymous. She addresses the obvious contradiction: "If I were not a woman, I would myself take the advice that I am daring to offer you, monsieur; I would give my name. But it would draw too much attention to me, if I openly declared myself in favor of a man who, they say, heaps insults on my sex" (30). Rousseau's antiwoman stance, referred to here as commonly accepted by the public, is more or less accepted by contemporary feminist scholars.[14] The most convincing evidence in favor of Rousseau's misogyny is found in book 5 of *Emile,* in which, as I have mentioned in chapter 1, woman's biology is said to make her a necessarily deceitful creature concerned above all with protecting her reputation, while man (at least, the ideal man) seeks truth and justice. What interests me here, of course, is not Rousseau's stand on women per se, but rather the manner in which de La Tour manipulates his reputation for misogyny in her public letter. This particular argument for anonymity is absurd, and meant to be taken as ironic. The notion that the negative public reputation of the man she is defending in public—a reputation she goes on to refute—requires her to remain nameless is obviously contradictory. Its true purpose is to allow de La Tour to go on to defend Rousseau's views on women. She declares that by requiring more of women, Rousseau merely proves his high opinion of them, and further points out that he only rarely criticizes women: "He does us precise justice in saying much good of us, and a little that is not" (31). De La Tour is, in other words, already moving beyond the affair at hand to defend Rousseau more generally, preparing herself for what will become after Rousseau's death something of a career for her.

De La Tour's "timid" letter attracted attention from the pro-Hume faction. On December 28, 1766, Marie de Vichy de Chamrond, marquise Du Deffand, wrote to Louise-Honorine Crozat Du Châtel, duchesse de Choiseul: "I am sending you an excerpt of that impertinent little pamphlet entitled: 'Lettre à l'auteur de *la justification de M. Rousseau.*' You will see how our friend [Horace Walpole] is treated in it. I do not know if this should be allowed." Of this imperious missive, R. A. Leigh comments: "That same day, Mme de Choiseul answered, from Versailles: 'I am not at all of the opinion that M. de Choiseul should speak to M. de Sartine about this pamphlet in which M. Walpole is treated so ridiculously and injuriously. The excerpt that you sent me makes me judge that we can leave to the author the care of her own destruction and that of her works. Her impertinent absurdities are redeemed by nothing. To forbid the pamphlet would be to make it known'" (*CC,* n. to 31:5646). While the duchesse de Choiseul's lack of appreciation for de La Tour's letter would have no doubt hurt the latter's authorial sensibilities, she did have the honor of seeing her piece appear in print again in 1767, as part of a larger work entitled: *Précis pour M. J. J. Rousseau, en réponse à 'l'exposé succinct de M. Hume': suivi d'une lettre de Madame de *** à l'auteur de la justification de M. Rousseau* (Brief for M. J.-J. Rousseau, in Response to the Concise Account by M. Hume: Followed by a Letter by Madame de *** to the Author of the Justification of M. Rousseau).[15] De La Tour had become acquainted with the publisher of this work, Pierre Guy, some months previously, when in September 1766 she had asked him to forward a letter to Rousseau. As Rousseau's publisher of choice, Guy was an obvious choice as a contact with Rousseau during this eventful period of his life. Recognizing her name from having previously sent her one of Rousseau's works at the author's request, Guy agreed to send her letter to Rousseau in England. De La Tour was already aware of the developing scandal, although the *Concise and Genuine Account* would not appear until October. She nevertheless castigates Rousseau for leaving her in the dark: "You are aware, my friend, of the many reasons for the public's interest in you; and you are surely aware that your argument with M. H. has received a great deal of attention here: but what you cannot know, is how disagreeable it is for someone who loves you to be obliged to have recourse to these vague, varied, even contradictory rumors, that is, to believe nothing of what is said of your affairs" (Sept. 4, 1766). Her lack of information concerning the details of the affair did not, of course, prevent her from writing the "Lettre à l'auteur de *la justification de M. Rousseau*," for hers was a false claim to ignorance. By stating to Rousseau that she "believes nothing" of what she hears, de La Tour is guarding herself against the accusation that she is capable of accepting the truth of false rumors about her correspondent; she is also, as always, begging for more, and more detailed, letters.[16]

It was in 1767, in the form of Guy's *Précis pour M. J. J. Rousseau,* that "Mme de ***'s" letter reached the one reader most capable of appreciating it—indeed, the one reader for whom it may well have been intended from the start: Rousseau himself. Still living in Wootton, Rousseau wrote to Guy—in the Bastille at the time for having published the *Précis*—and asked him to forward an enclosed letter to "Mme de ***." Rousseau wrote that if he did not fear for her safety, he would send his letter to this woman himself, for he had instantly divined her name: "I do not possess enough friends capable of such zeal and talent to be mistaken about its author" (*CC,*

31:5713). He declares as well that he is quite certain that the author of the *Précis* is unknown to him, or he would have recognized his style with as much facility. Rousseau was, as mentioned previously, proud of his talent for discerning authorship through epistolary style; in a 1766 letter to F. H. d'Ivernois concerning the authorship of the *Lettre au docteur Pansophe,* he writes: "You must have a low opinion of my discernment in matters of style if you imagine that I could be fooled by that of M. de Voltaire" (*CC,* 30:5394; while right about this particular letter, Rousseau never accepted Voltaire's authorship of the far more injurious *Sentiment des citoyens*).[17]

Rousseau's letter to Mme de *** is short, but overflowing with emotion: "I have just received in one pamphlet two works by authors whose identities are being kept from me. Reading the first made me cherish its author without recognizing him. As for the second, while reading it, my heart began to beat quickly, and I recognized my dear Marianne. I hope that she knows me as well" (Feb. 7, 1767). As R. A. Leigh notes dryly of the circuitous route this letter took before reaching de La Tour, it "suffered a certain delay. By February 15, Mme de La Tour had still not received it" (*CC,* n. to 32:5712). Leigh's supposition is based on a letter sent between times to Rousseau by de La Tour in which, with exquisitely bad timing, she berates him for not having written her. Despite this faux pas, Rousseau did his best in the months that followed to express his appreciation to de La Tour. This period of the exchange includes his most respectful letters, in which he treats her almost as an equal, and certainly as a player in public debate. Even when, four years later, he breaks off all friendly contact with her and accuses her of possible complicity with his enemies, he adds: "You defended me against the schemes of my persecutors during my stay in England. This generosity transported me; you must have seen how much it meant to me" (Apr. 14, 1771).

De La Tour insists that Rousseau's recognition of her letter means recognition of the purity of her sentiments for him. He could not have recognized her style, for she had, after all, been writing under a pseudonym. That is to say, she had adopted a style for the occasion, taking on the persona of a woman who writes letters for publication: "It is thus proven that you know my heart! For it could not have been from my style that you recognized me" (July 29, 1767). De La Tour need not have worried about justifying her public epistolary act, for it was exclusively the public nature of her defense that impressed Rousseau. He is sublimely unconcerned with the difference between de La Tour's public and private styles; for his purposes, de La Tour's anonymous letter is exclusively a sign of her devotion to him, and it is solely on that count that he imagines her garnering future fame: "It is with tenderness that I imagine my dear Marianne one day receiving the honors due her as the first among the small number of those who had the courage to defend me while I was alive" (Jan. 20, 1768).

That de La Tour understood these terms is clear in a long letter to Rousseau dated March 31, 1764. This letter contains the most revealing of her statements concerning the nature of their relationship, addressing as it does the distinction between men and women in general, with a particular emphasis on the proper roles of the Great Man and his admiring, devoted female fan. The two correspondents' respective positions vis-à-vis publicity are addressed in a highly nuanced, at times even contradictory, manner. De La Tour notes that while Rousseau's public celebrity certainly eclipses her own, in the eyes of "good people" (*honnêtes gens*) their merit is equal: "It seems to me, my illustrious friend, that judged by the different points of view appropriate to each of us, we have an equal right to the esteem of good people; and as that is all that matters to me, I lay claim to privileges equivalent to those that I accord to you." He is notable for his mind, she for her heart; his role is public, hers private: "You are the most brilliant genius of the century; as for me, I have the best heart in the world: your manner of judging is sure; my ability to feel never fails me . . . you enjoy well-merited fame; my own merit lies in being completely unknown."

The clearest manner in which de La Tour's womanhood and her letters come together in this examination lies in her claims to an exalted level of *sensibilité*, that elusive quality so important to the period. Women were said to possess it in excess; letters that did not exhibit it were worthless, for the letter was by definition an expression of personal feeling. Both letters and women were relegated, in principle, to the private sphere; and both were made all the more enticing for this reason, when "exposed" in public. As a superior woman, de La Tour's sensibility necessarily trumps Rousseau's own: "You are the most sensitive of men; myself, without being perhaps the most sensitive of women, I am more sensitive than you." She points out, perhaps as an example of her superior *sensibilité*, that he is incapable of truly seeing her. What Rousseau loves in her is the reflection of his own glory: "You received my praise without disdain; I offered it without pride: it is you whom you love in me; myself, I love only you in yourself; and we are both right." While Rousseau is active, at work in the world, changing it for the better ("settling its long uncertain opinions"), de La Tour, with her infallible sensitivity, is uniquely able to recognize his worth: "You are worthy of statues; as for myself, I am worthy of raising statues of you."

De La Tour leaves unsaid that raising statues of famous men can of course lead to fame for oneself, even if those "statues" take the form of private documents that express the writer's own superiority. After all, when a third-party reader finds such expressions of esteem and love in a private letter, the document's very private nature gives them the guarantee of sincerity. De La Tour is hinting at the sort of secondhand fame that may be allotted to her as Rousseau's *amie*, and is also implying that such secondhand participation in the public sphere may be all that her society will allow her. These considerations become clear when she establishes the ground rules for her side-by-side comparison of herself and her correspondent: "Let us see by comparing our assets if it would be wrong to claim to establish perfect equality in our relationship: those advantages society accords to my sex will serve, for better or worse, as compensation for those nature grants your own." Nature, in other words, may not enter into the *restrictions* placed on women, a point she had made two years earlier with regard to Rousseau's *lacets*.

To rephrase this point in more contemporary terms, the "advantages society accords my sex" may be, for de La Tour, only culturally constructed compensations for an inferior position, a position that is not—at least in every case—based on natural difference. And while she may be excluded from the creative role she at times sought through her poetry, she is willing to capitalize quite fully on the "advantages" she does have, especially the right to judge men's hearts. Her letter thus does not, in the end, allot her to an entirely passive role. Her promotion of Rousseau's public reputation is ultimately as essential to his fame as is his own active engagement with the world, for only the recognition of a superior woman, endowed with an infallible ability to "sense" the superior man's merit, establishes the true worth of that Great Man in the eyes of his contemporaries, and of posterity.

In his response to de La Tour's manifesto, Rousseau laments that she is incapable of acknowledging the extent of his consideration for her, and offers to send her several of his works that she has been wanting to obtain *in-octavo*. Without telling her, he also has the publisher Duchesne send separately a copy of an anonymous letter from

1764. Rousseau had published the letter to prove that a previously published letter signed "Rousseau," the "Lettre à M. l'archevêque d'Auch," was not his own. Upon receiving a copy of this anonymous letter, de La Tour writes to thank Rousseau, although his name was nowhere on the package or the letter. Little need for such information; she has recognized his style: "Imagine with what pleasure I recognized my friend, as much by his attention to me, as by his style!" (June 7, 1764). She adds that in her case, Rousseau might have spared himself the trouble of writing this anonymous self-defense, for de La Tour had easily established on her own that the letter to Auch was not of his composition. She had even anticipated all of Rousseau's self-defensive arguments, with two small exceptions: "The use of the formal *vous* with God, and of *your humble servant.*" Her emotional reaction when she realizes that Rousseau had asked his publisher to furnish her with a copy of this letter takes the form of an almost painful desire for public glory, reflected, as always, through the fame of another: "My soul was moved, my heart swelled, my eyes filled; and I sighed at being unable to share with the universe such a flattering distinction" (June 7, 1764).

Her public response to the Hume affair ensured de La Tour of such recognition in the future, at least in Rousseau's opinion, at the same time that it momentarily raised her to the status of a true friend. Rousseau went so far as to suggest a reversal in their sentimental situation, referring to "the bonds of a friendship now as dear to my heart as it once was to your own" (Mar. 23, 1769). This phrase is somewhat undermined by its context, for Rousseau is explaining that for health reasons de La Tour should expect only short, infrequent letters from him. Her subsequent efforts to inspire longer missives brought on the inevitable fall from grace. The worst of many such efforts came when she wrote in July 1769 to communicate her enthusiasm for a portrait of Rousseau she had recently acquired: "I have procured from London your engraved portrait after the original by Kamsay [*sic*]; and I have placed it on the table that serves as my writing desk, just as a worshipper places over her shrine the image of the saint to whom she is the most fervently devoted" (July 9, 1769).

The famous work in question, "Jean-Jacques Rousseau in Armenian Costume," was actually painted in 1766 by Allan Ramsay (1713–84), official painter to King George III.[18] De La Tour's iconization of this engraving precipitated a coldness on Rousseau's part that never entirely disappeared, for he had taken a violent aversion to the engraving, as well as to the original portrait. He considered the image a deliberate pictorial distortion of his features, and therefore an implicit attack on his character, all part of a greater plot to destroy his reputation. The painting had been made at the request of David Hume, a detail that is enough in itself to explain Rousseau's paranoia concerning Ramsay's motives. It did not seem to matter that in 1764 de La Tour had been instrumental in forwarding another portrait to Rousseau, the Quentin de La Tour that was his favorite; her misjudgment concerning the Ramsay portrait was a blow from which she never quite recovered.[19]

De La Tour of course tried valiantly to reinstate herself as a true friend of Jean-Jacques. In July of 1770, she attempted to rekindle the initial atmosphere of the exchange by returning to *La Nouvelle Héloïse*. Her letter begins: "I must share my enchantment with you: I am reading *La Nouvelle Héloïse* for the seventh or eighth time: it moves me more than the first" (July 25, 1770). After regretting that her right to the name of "the tender Julie" has been withdrawn by her correspondent, she gives a critique of the work's originality as an epistolary masterpiece, mentioning in the process Montesquieu's *Lettres persanes*, Richardson's *Clarissa*, and Riccoboni's *Lettres de milady Juliette Catesby*. She declares herself, once again, the consummate reader of Rousseau's work: "Do you wish me to tell you, my friend, what make me most proud, when my sufferings allow me the courage to feel so? It is to possess the soul most capable of seizing the beautiful things that Jean-Jacques spreads throughout his works: I would dispute this claim with the whole world." Such praise is not enough to break through Rousseau's continuing glacial silence; only when she threatens to visit him (he is again in Paris) does she receive a short note barring her entry to his residence. The note is coldly insulting: "I do not accept, madame, the honor that you wish to do me. I am not housed in a manner that allows me to receive the visits of ladies, and your own could not fail to be as bothersome to my wife and myself, as it would be boring for you. . . . Please accept, madame, my greetings and my respect" (Sept. 4, 1770; Rousseau had married Thérèse Levasseur in 1768).[20]

De La Tour responds by inviting Rousseau to her own house, although she had declared such an invitation impossible in the letter of September 2 in which she had asked permission to visit him: "You know that I have always kept secret from my acquaintances the correspondence with which you have honored me; it is my secret: more sensitive than vain, I prefer enjoying it to vaunting it." Six days later, she has dropped coquetry for manly honesty: "If someone sees you there, if they are surprised, I owe no one an account of my conduct" (Sept. 8, 1770). She then adds, in a lightly menacing tone: "Furthermore, I have so thoroughly given up on keeping our correspondence a secret that I am violently tempted to make it public. I have carefully preserved all the letters I received from you, and copies of all those I sent to you: I am going to the country to busy myself with putting them in order: on my return, I will be ready to hand them over for printing."

Placed in context, de La Tour's "violent temptation" to publish these letters is a clear threat intended to force Rousseau to treat her as the honored friend she aspires to be. If not, she will go public with letters that prove both his past protestations of eternal friendship and his present perfidious treatment of her. She refuses, she tells Rousseau, to be placed "by your verse, your hieroglyphic date, your epithet of *madame*," into what she refers to as "the general class." As a taste of things to come, she fires a telling citation at him from one of his own letters: "Are you not that sensitive man who wrote to me on January 3, 1769: 'My heart will never cease to be full of you. I cherished you for all the amiable qualities that you demonstrated to me; but one service born of true friendship [the letter of Mme D***] will forever cause me to feel a stronger attachment to you than to any other, a feeling that absence and time will never overcome, and should I have a short or a long life ahead of me, you will be as respected, as dear to me, until my last breath'?"[21]

This letter contradicts her previous and constant insistence that her own circumstances forced her to keep the correspondence a closely guarded secret, and as such constitutes something of a manifesto of her power as a correspondent, just as her letter of March 31, 1764, constitutes, if not a "feminist" manifesto, a declaration of her power as a woman. Negative public opinion is now recast as of little concern to de La Tour, coming as it will only from fools: "This endeavor will make me look ridiculous in the eyes of fools (one must learn to be above unfortunate gossip), but it will also assure the success of some of my efforts: While I have been unable to prolong the friendship that united us, I will at least succeed in immortalizing the evidence of it: I do not fear that a work in part written by you, and otherwise about you, will fall into oblivion." She will ensure her own fame, and is even thinking of joining a "little work" to the letters, that is, her second contribution to the Hume affair that Pierre Guy was prevented from publishing by his six-month stay in the Bastille.

She gives this work the title "Réflexions sur ce qui s'est passé au sujet de la rupture de J. J. Rousseau & de M. Hume" (Reflections on the Events Surrounding the Break between J. J. Rousseau & M. Hume). Surely the public will be interested in yet another letter by Mme D***, not to mention interested in learning her true identity, the intensity of her connection to Rousseau, and his harsh abandonment of this worthy Julie?

Rousseau, somewhat surprisingly, did not respond. While de La Tour kept her promise to retire to her country estate and edit the letters, almost a year passed before she next wrote to Rousseau. She reported the completion of her project, her return from the country, and her unilateral decision not to publish their exchange, "as long as the two of us exist" (Apr. 14, 1771). Six letters in particular of the 158 that had recently "passed under her eyes" must be kept secret, namely those in which Rousseau speaks candidly of his plans, his enemies, and his friends, in a manner that is now said to impose a sacred duty of nonpublication on his correspondent. The worst "secret" of the letters, however, at least in de La Tour's opinion, is Rousseau's unconscionable treatment of his faultless correspondent. She paints a truly alarming picture of potential public reaction to this aspect of their correspondence. Readers would be shocked and disillusioned, for whoever could otherwise imagine, she asks, that the most loving of men, Jean-Jacques Rousseau, was capable of plunging a poisonous knife into the heart of an allegory of Friendship? That he was capable of rejecting a woman whom he once feared to love too much, and who now stands before him with outstretched arms? The choice of Friendship rather than Love is significant, given de La Tour's hypothesis that Rousseau is refusing to respond to her letters only because his wife has become unfairly jealous: "Can it be Mme Rousseau who is against it. . . . But how could our relationship injure her rights?" (Apr. 14, 1771).

Rousseau responded to this letter immediately, with a resoundingly negative missive. De La Tour's promise not to publish until after their deaths has not impressed him. He insists that he had always responded frankly and openly to her letters: "Without foreseeing that my letters would one day be exposed in print, I freely expressed the diverse impressions that your own letters made upon me." As for her public defense of his character, he may have been impressed at one time, but has since learned to trust only those he knows well. He points out that they have met face-to-face only once, briefly. Judging her as one among his many correspondents, he places her at the bottom of the list: "Of all my correspondents you were at one and the same time the most demanding, the one I knew the least well, and the one who revealed the least to me about things I needed to know and of which you were not unaware. I have thus decided to cease a correspondence that has become onerous to me and for which your true motive may be hidden from me" (Apr. 14, 1771). Trousson remarks: "Poor Marianne, who quite simply loved him."[22] Pitiable or not, loving "simply" or not, de La Tour responds by promising that their letters will never be printed (Apr. 26, 1771). She also attaches her "Réflexions sur ce qui s'est passé au sujet de la rupture de J. J. Rousseau & de M. Hume," the unpublished piece she had intended to make public along with their letters.

By renouncing her publication plans, de La Tour seems to have hoped to regain Rousseau's epistolary attentions, but when he finally returned the "Réflexions" after her repeated requests, it was in the coldest of terms: "Here is the manuscript for which Mme de La Tour appeared so eager and that I only delayed in sending to her because she had asked me to keep it. I found it worthy of her pen, and of a heart that loves justice. I was however more touched, I must admit, by the piece read by the entire world than by the piece seen only by myself" (July 7, 1771). Nor did Rousseau respond to the most blatant attempt to garner interest in the letter that had accompanied this manuscript: "Adieu my dear Jean-Jacques; adieu for always. What a word! How much it costs me to conceal from you. . . . Never mind, you will be satisfied: you will hear of me again only after my death."

Following the failure of her claim to be teetering on the brink of death to elicit anything other than abuse, de La Tour made yet another dramatic attempt to restart their relationship. She visited Rousseau *incognito*; he failed to recognize her (Apr. 7, 1772). She had come to him under the pretext of asking Rousseau to copy some music for her, a common tactic for gaining admission to his residence.[23] His fame guaranteed him a profitable stream of curiosity seekers masquerading as clients for his copying business. Such clients certainly did not come for his alacrity in completing the work, for he tells de La Tour that it will take him three months to copy four pages of music (she had chosen, following his own musical preference, "an Italian air").

Their third and final meeting is recounted in Rousseau's last letter to de La Tour, dated June 24, 1772. She had brought with her "La Reine Fantasque," a tale written by Rousseau that had been clan-

destinely published.[24] She apparently offered to publish an authorized version herself, for in Rousseau's letter he asks pardon for not
having recognized her (once again), thanks her for the piece, but
sends it back. He also declines a far more generous editorial project
de La Tour had volunteered to undertake, that of comparing all of
Rousseau's approved publications with fraudulent editions. He rejects this offer on the grounds that it will be too costly and time-
consuming, then politely declares that their third meeting has not
changed his resolution to break with her. De La Tour counters that
despite his opposition she will indeed undertake a comparison of
"the correct editions" of his works with an unauthorized edition
said to be underway (she will undertake, that is, an unauthorized
rebuttal of Rousseau's unauthorized publications). She notes that
"an involuntary movement that you made as I was leaving you" is
proof that he still has feelings for her. Her relationship with Thérèse
has apparently improved, for she laments: "If only you shared Mme
Rousseau's opinion of me! I would not have believed anyone could
be more clairvoyant than yourself!" (June 24, 1772).

Although Rousseau never again wrote to de La Tour, she continued to send him letters and even managed one final epistolary faux
pas, perhaps her most spectacular. In December 1773, she wrote to
inform Rousseau of a truly vicious rumor making the rounds concerning his family situation, referring with disapproval to a letter
sent to her by an unidentified "woman of condition." De La Tour
cites the offending sentence from this woman's letter: " 'I have been
told of the odious conduct of our friend Jean-Jacques: if it is true,
you will cease to admire him, as have I. They assure me that he abandoned all of his children at the foundling hospital' " (Dec. 1773).
May notes that the woman in question is undoubtedly Mme d'Epinay, and points out as well that the scandal was quite stale at this
point: "If the affair resurfaced after such a long period, the reason
is no doubt the counteroffensive of JJR's enemies, alarmed by the
readings he gave of the *Confessions* in various Parisian salons in
1771."[25] De La Tour could not have been learning of this rumor for
the first time, for she had already made reference to the *Sentiment
des citoyens* in a letter of February 25, 1765.[26] Perhaps she meant this
belated "warning" to Rousseau as proof that she was not in league
with Mme d'Epinay, who had contacted Sartine of the Paris police.
In any case, de La Tour takes her effort to the extreme, emphasizing
her shock that anyone would attribute such an immoral practice to
Rousseau. She, however, can be counted on to let him know what

his enemies are saying: "And so! do you still care about public rumor! . . . As for the rest, you see how I keep my word" (Dec. 1773).

Unfortunately for de La Tour, the rumor was of course true. As old news, the resurfacing of the abandonment of his children had little effect on Rousseau's reputation, but it no doubt hardened him all the more against his correspondent to see a reference to it in her letter. De La Tour's letter-writing career was at this point effectively brought to a halt, to be revived only when Rousseau died at the estate of the marquis de Girardin on July 2, 1778. At that point, with her correspondent safely dead, de La Tour was able to reactivate her status as his *amie.* As R. A. Leigh (somewhat disparagingly) describes de La Tour's next step: "Soon after Rousseau's death, madame de Franqueville assumed the role of her idol's champion. From 1778 to 1781, she gave birth to an entire series of letters and pamphlets, some anonymous, others signed with diverse pseudonyms" (*CC,* n. to 42:7343).

De La Tour had already experienced some success writing a public letter in defense of Rousseau, of course, but there is one quite dramatic difference between the "Lettre à l'auteur de *la justification de M. Rousseau*" of 1766 and the letters she began writing in 1778. In 1766, the editor of de La Tour's letter was arrested. In 1778, no such danger existed. In an article revealingly entitled "Burn Diderot," Bronislaw Baczko notes that Rousseau had, in death, definitively won over popular opinion: "Since the night of July 2 or 3, 1778, when the marquis de Girardin chose the Ile de Peupliers as the lasting resting place of Jean-Jacques, Ermenonville had become the capital of the cult of the 'great man.' Of a surprising form and size, the pilgrimages to Ermenonville represent an extraordinary phenomenon that testifies to the sensibilities of the period." Rousseau worship was not an entirely isolated phenomenon, for other "great men," such as Voltaire, who died the same year as Rousseau, were treated to a similar deification. Baczko nevertheless notes a specificity to Rousseau's fans: "In this cult choice of place went to Rousseau. The enthusiasm he inspired in his admirers was of a kind with the exaltation of his virtue, with the conformity between his life and his works and principles, and with the glory accrued by his exile and persecutions."[27]

De La Tour's moment, in other words, had come; yet, she was unable to publish her private correspondence, the exchange that would have demonstrated to the public that she had some claim to have received Rousseau's imprimatur as the embodiment of Julie.

Her promise to Rousseau that the letters would never be made public until both of the correspondents were dead was recorded in a letter to him that she did not possess. Leigh attributes de La Tour's prolixity as a letter-writing defender of Jean-Jacques to "her natural disposition and her combativity that did not permit her to neglect any detail" (*CC*, n. to 42:7343); it is obvious to me, however, even in her first pseudonymous letter of 1778, that de La Tour was embarking on a new enterprise designed to prepare the way for the posthumous reception of her private correspondence with Rousseau.

This letter is signed "Mme du Riez-Genest," and addressed to Louis Stanislas Fréron (1754–1802), editor of the *Année littéraire*, a well-known journal founded by his father, Elie Fréron.[28] As was the case with Mme D***'s "Lettre à l'auteur de *la justification de M. Rousseau*," du Riez-Genest is writing "merely" to fortify a previous defense of Rousseau that she views as too weak. Her letter is designed to add to a rebuttal by M. Olivier de Corancez of the "Jugement de Jean-François de La Harpe sur J.-J. Rousseau," in which La Harpe had surveyed Rousseau's publications and declared that the same overheated imagination that made the man so childish in his conduct also raised his creative work to new heights.[29] Corancez, not himself an author, had defended Rousseau's character based on personal acquaintance with him.

Mme du Riez-Genest's letter appeared in the *Année littéraire* in November, prefaced by a remarkably flattering piece in which Fréron describes its writer as "a lady yet more to be commended for her social virtues than for her talents; she joins charity and sensitivity to the gift of intellect; and she is worthy of appreciating the value of *Jean-Jacques Rousseau*."[30] He has garnered these impressions from a brief exchange of letters with du Riez-Genest, in which "she did me the honor of writing to me on the topic of the little work you are about to read." Predictably, rather than immediately asking that her letter be published, the worthy "du Riez-Genest" had first written to ask that Fréron himself defend Rousseau. She had, however, included in this request a list of the points that Fréron should make, and the editor had recognized in her remarks a style so "noble, pure, elegant" that he had been sure that her writing would please his readers.

Despite Fréron's praise for the "nobility and elegance" of her writing, du Riez-Genest is not at all nuanced in her attack on La Harpe's motives and reputation. She points out that M. de La Harpe displays much temerity in attacking other writers, when his own literary productions have been such dismal failures. What most distresses her is La Harpe's accusation that Rousseau, "a philosopher who took as his motto, *Vitam impendere vero*," might have abandoned "the prize of virtue in order to pursue that of eloquence." This theme runs throughout the public debate about Rousseau's personal and literary merit that erupted after his death. By taking as his personal motto the claim to uphold the truth at all times, he had opened himself up to an examination of his motives. De La Tour had of course herself accused Rousseau of seeking fame by deliberately attacking the reading public's fondest beliefs, in her letter of February 25, 1765; as Rousseau's public defender, however, she is unequivocal in her stand that no man ever lived and wrote in a more fully straightforward manner than Jean-Jacques. She takes Corancez to task on just this point. He had been quite familiar with Rousseau, and had affirmed in his own article that "[Rousseau] viewed everything through the veil of modesty." Mme du Riez-Genest, who has "never met" Rousseau, declares on the basis of his writings alone that moderation, not modesty, was Rousseau's greatest virtue. He was too sincere to be modest: "*Jean Jacques* was not at all modest, he was more than that, he was truthful. *Men of wit* [esprit], he would say, *always acknowledge their status, modesty in them is always falseness.*"

Readers of the *Année littéraire* curious about the source of this citation would have looked in vain in Rousseau's published works, for du Riez-Genest was quoting a private letter written by Jean-Jacques Rousseau on November 24, 1761, to one Marie-Anne de La Tour. Rousseau was speaking of Claire, who had just written to him, quite "stupidly" in his estimation, "that she possessed no *esprit!*" (Nov. 24, 1761). In yet another echo of the private correspondence, de La Tour, or rather du Riez-Genest, ends her letter with a postscript in which she asks that Fréron include in his publication the following poetic celebration of Rousseau, in the form of an epitaph:

> Under this tomb consecrated to the virtues,
> The sacred remains of *Jean-Jacques Rousseau,*
> Thanks to the cares of a friend, brave the efforts of time;
> And his ever-revered memory,
> Will carry the fame of the name *Gérardin* [*sic*]
> > Beyond the limits of time.

Fréron does indeed see fit to publish this piece that, in its author's estimation, is by its very simplicity "worthy to be offered to the public." We are not specifically told that these verses are by "du Riez-Genest," but we are told that the epitaph was written in the first few days of July, written, that is, immediately after Rousseau's death, with all that this timing implies of tender hearted grief and poetic spontaneity.

De La Tour's celebration of the marquis de Girardin as the *ami de Jean-Jacques* who by his acts of friendship will gain eternal fame is quite significant. In addition to her own pendant role as the *amie de Jean-Jacques*, de La Tour was dependant on Girardin's good will, for in November of 1778 he was rumored to have control over Rousseau's papers. This collection included de La Tour's letters to Rousseau, those precious documents that, as he had informed her several times, he had carefully preserved apart from his general correspondence. By the time her letter appeared in the *Année littéraire*, de La Tour had already written to Girardin concerning the disposition of Rousseau's will. Girardin had reacted quite coldly to her inquiry; Leigh conjectures that Girardin's guilty conscience caused him to overreact, given that he had in fact misappropriated Rousseau's papers: "No doubt, by innocently raising the issue of JJ's testamentary dispositions, poor Marianne had cut the marquis to the quick."[31] But perhaps "poor Marianne" herself had less-than-innocent concerns in mind in inquiring as to how Rousseau had settled his literary affairs; not only was the preservation of her original letters in question, she herself possessed a considerable number of autograph letters from Rousseau, and was thus not an insignificant player in any posthumous edition of his complete writings. As Leigh himself hypothesizes: "It is clear from this text that Girardin was ignorant of the epistolary relationship that had existed between JJ and Mme de Franqueville, and of her cult-like adoration for her hero. If he had known that she possessed more than 150 letters by the *promeneur solitaire*, he would no doubt have overcome his first reaction" (*CC*, n. to 41:7196).

De La Tour followed up on her success as Mme du Riez-Genest by sending Fréron a second defense of Rousseau under a different pseudonym, "Mme de La Motte."[32] In his introductory remarks to this letter, published in December 1778, Fréron declares that Rousseau's cause has become the common cause of the gentler sex, citing his previous publication of du Riez-Genest's letter. Mme de La Motte's tactics are different from those of her predecessor, for she declares that she is writing with a simple request for Fréron's "help" in resolving a dilemma she is facing. She has recently read a notice in the *Mercure de France* informing the public that Rousseau's widow is soliciting subscriptions to a volume; does Fréron believe that this notice was written by Rousseau's friends, or by his enemies? De La Motte must of course then detail why she suspects that the author of the notice is not the marquis de Girardin, the possessor of Rousseau's documents. A long and detailed diatribe follows, after which de La Motte closes by adding that if Fréron publishes her letter, it will prove to the public that "Madame *du Riez-Genest* is not the only woman capable of appreciating you." In direct contradiction to the authoritative tone of the body of her letter, de La Motte then declares herself incapable of resolving such great issues on her own. She limits herself to "sensing" Rousseau's superiority: "I believed that the role of *amie de Jean-Jacques* did me the most honor, and fit me best, and that I should limit myself to filling it." Fréron appends a response to de La Motte's letter in which he declares her perfectly justified in suspecting that the notice is not by Girardin. Fréron unfortunately cannot tell de La Motte the name of its real author, not being admitted into the circle of confidence of the "gods of the *Encyclopédie*" (the *Année littéraire* was known for its antiphilosophe tendencies, making it the perfect vehicle for de La Tour's pro-Rousseau offensive).

De La Tour then sent her third letter in as many months to Fréron, signed with yet a third pseudonym, "Mme de St. G***." Fréron did not see fit to publish Mme de St. G***'s letter, written to "correct" a previous review in the *Journal de Paris* of a *Supplément aux Oeuvres de J. J. Rousseau.*[33] In response to this failure, de La Tour sent yet another letter signed Mme de La Motte, a letter that Fréron again chose not to print. He did print one additional letter by de La Tour, unsigned, and dated July 17, 1779.[34] The letter is an anonymous critique of one point of an otherwise positive entry on Rousseau in the *Nouveau dictionnaire historique.* Fréron had just favorably reviewed the *Dictionnaire*, but de La Tour will not stand for the entry's suggestion that Rousseau had carefully cultivated a public image as an eccentric. The wording of her defense of Rousseau has the undesirable effect of representing him as something of a naive idiot concerning the motives of others: "*Art* was never a factor in his conduct; his lack of talent for detecting it in others is the proof: no one was easier to fool than he." The anonymous letter writer ends by declaring that she is in a position to know of what she speaks: "Even if I had not been honored by a relationship with *J. J. Rousseau,* I would believe it no less of a duty to make him better known to these Gentlemen, in order to inspire in them a greater esteem for him than he already enjoys."

Whether or not Fréron suspected that one woman was responsible for the many vehement letters he had been receiving, letters that went beyond attacking Rousseau's enemies to criticize the lukewarm character of Rousseau's supporters, he appended a "Reflections in the Guise of a Response" to de La Tour's last contribution to the *Année littéraire*. Fréron advised Rousseau's many defenders to desist from raining letters upon him, however well written: "I beg those respectable persons who continually send me apologias of *Jean-Jacques* to consider that the public knows how to judge his character, and will become tired of so many explanations, should they be as well written as the one I have just published."

De La Tour's pseudonymous publishing career was now in full swing, however, and she had little intention of allowing Fréron to stop her. She had gone beyond her limited role in the Hume affair by participating in public debate in an ongoing fashion. In doing so, de La Tour became part of a process described by Dena Goodman as typical of the Enlightenment, in which "readers" were deliberately drawn into the production of public letters: "This vibrant epistolary network was a two-way street, as readers responded to writers, becoming writers themselves in pamphlets and in the columns of an emerging periodical press that was itself an institutional extension of the epistolary network."[35] De La Tour was a special case, however, given her long private relationship with one of the most famous men of the time. Well aware of her particular status, she was unwilling to remain merely another "reader-turned-writer" participating infrequently in the periodicals of her day. Even before Fréron put a stop to her brief career with the *Année littéraire*, she was arranging to have her various letters published in a brochure entitled *Jean Jaques Rousseau vangé* [*sic*] *par son amie, ou morale practico-philosophico-encyclopédique des coryphées de la secte* (Jean Jaques Rousseau Avanged [*sic*] by His Woman Friend or Practical-Philosophical-Encyclopedic Morality of the Leaders of the Sect, 1779). As the mistakes in the title alone indicate, de La Tour encountered many difficulties in preparing and publishing her work. She explains in a "public notice" that these problems were due to the censorship imposed on her by Rousseau's enemies. "The Temple of Truth," given as the publishing locale of the work, is apparently not to be found in France: "Should [Rousseau's friends] wish to raise their voices against imposture? They are barred on all sides; all the presses are forbidden them. It is thus necessary, in order to make the truth heard, the truth that impudence outrages and intrigue would reduce to silence, to have recourse to foreign presses, at the risk of compromising the exactitude of dates, so essential to evidentiary proofs, but the holder of these originals is known, everyone is free to verify them with him; thus the typographical errors offer little support to the efforts of the spiteful."[36]

The mistakes in the *Jean Jaques Rousseau Vangé* render it rather unimpressive as a legal document, but while lamenting any errors, de La Tour in her role of anonymous editor points out that the holder of the original documents it contains is known: M. Fréron of *L'Année littéraire*, to whom de La Tour would have her readers go *en masse* to consult her autograph letters. She also wrongly informs us that the one letter and four excerpted pieces that follow have already appeared in print, but are provided in that they will probably not have been available to those living outside of France. Apparently, de La Tour had anticipated publication of both the letter from Mme de St. G*** and de La Motte's second letter; an asterisk following the title "Lettre de Madame de Saint G*** à M. Fréron" leads to a note in which we are told: "When M. Fréron refused to insert this letter in the *Année littéraire*, we decided to print it separately" (53). A similar note is appended to the letter signed Mme de La Motte. The need to publish "abroad" is accompanied by a general veiling of identities, as in the "Lettre d'une anonyme à un anonyme" (Letter from an Anonymous Woman to an Anonymous Man), a refutation of d'Alembert's *Eloge de Milord Maréchale* (Praise of Milord Maréchale). Some of the work's *pièces justificatives*, or accompanying documents, do carry names, such as the letters by Du Peyrou, Rousseau's friend and benefactor. De La Tour had received these papers from Du Peyrou along with a letter of May 9, 1779, in which he gave her permission to publish them, adding "you may name me in good conscience." He promised to provide further documentation on demand to the public at large: "I am ready to send the originals to those who want them, or authentic copies, and I defy J.J.'s accusers to produce the equivalent" (*CC*, 43:7532).

Du Peyrou's relationship with Rousseau was in some ways quite similar to de La Tour's, as Rousseau himself recognized. In November 1767, he began a letter to de La Tour, never finished, that he intended to have Du Peyrou deliver to her. Rousseau stressed that he wanted his two most devoted supporters to meet: "Dear Marianne, my heart is attached to you by the sweetest and strongest bonds. Those that attach me to Du Peyrou are no less true" (Nov. 8,

1767). The two "friends of Jean-Jacques" did eventually come to know each other, and this relationship would be vital to de La Tour's future publishing career. Du Peyrou would be involved in the publication of her private exchange with Rousseau, as described in the following chapter; he also saw fit to include the *Rousseau vangé* in his 1782 edition of the *Collection des oeuvres de J.-J. Rousseau* (Collected Works of J.-J. Rousseau).[37] Considerably cleaned up, and now entitled *La Vertu vengée par l'amitié ou Recueil de lettres sur J. J. Rousseau par Madame de **** (Virtue Avenged by Friendship, or Collection of Letters on J. J. Rousseau by Madame de ***), this work includes new prefatory material by de La Tour (or "Mme de ***," as she now "signs" her work). She explains once again that the *Encyclopédistes* ("the sect") had been working to stop her, although she carefully exculpates Fréron, despite his refusal to continue printing her material: "When he refused, a refusal above suspicion, I took the part of printing it separately, and of distributing it, not as I would have liked, but as it pleased MM. the Encyclopédistes to allow me to do so (*note b*: You will understand that I refer to the obstacles they place before all efforts to unmask them)" (5).

This grandiose reference to the problems de La Tour faced in publishing her letters is somewhat pathetic; the greatest threat to the printing of the *Rousseau Vangé* may well have been public indifference, as reflected in Fréron's plea to her various pseudonyms to stop sending him letters. R. A. Leigh expresses a frustration similar to Fréron's concerning the length of de La Tour's journalistic endeavors, explaining that he has chosen to include only the most informative sections of each in his *Correspondance complète*: "Her verbosity, the fruit as much of her natural disposition as of her combativeness, did not permit her to neglect any detail, making it impossible to reproduce in their entirety all of these documents" (*CC*, 42:7343).

Leigh's lack of appreciation for de La Tour's public defenses of Rousseau is significant for two reasons. First, he does provide the full text of all of her autograph missives to Rousseau, letters much longer than her published diatribes, and altogether more repetitive. While in the following chapter I will consider the editorial theory behind this decision on Leigh's part, in the present context I am more interested in the specific passages that Leigh decided to cut from the public letters. Leigh suppressed those passages in which each fictitious woman letter writer positions herself with regard to de La Tour's other pseudonyms, and with regard to Rousseau himself. These are the most important parts of these letters for my purposes, for I view them as embedded clues pointing to de La Tour's desire for eventual fame.

In Leigh's defense, the playful self-positioning of her various alter egos is meaningless in the letters as published in the *Année littéraire* and the *Vertu vengée*. These cryptic references were placed in these letters for the appreciation of a future reading public, one informed of de La Tour's identity as Rousseau's real-life "Julie." De La Tour's second pseudonymous letter, for example, cleverly points to her real relationship to Rousseau. De La Motte declares that while she herself has only had limited personal contact with "Jean-Jacques," she is surrounded by people who knew him well. In particular, she is able to claim a rich acquaintance with his private letters: "I have read 184 of his private letters, all in his hand, and addressed to different persons, in the cruelest circumstances in which he found himself; every single one of these letters exhibits the seal of its author's soul; breathes his sensibility, candor, selflessness, goodness, indulgence; every one conforms in every point with the excellent moral principles that he establishes in his works, about which he never varied, and above all, with which his own conduct never clashed."[38] While her purpose may have been to pique the interest of any prospective editor of Rousseau's works, "de La Motte's" description of these 184 letters is hardly faithful to the spirit of the actual correspondence between Rousseau and de La Tour. Rousseau did not prove faithful to the ethos of his works in writing to her; to the contrary, his letters demonstrate his (relative) moral perfidy in "abandoning" a devoted admirer. As such, the actual letters are of far greater potential interest to the public than the saintly missives described by de La Motte; but as de La Motte, de La Tour must persist in her role as champion of her "faultless" idol.

When she finally admits in the *Vertu vengée* of 1782 to having used a variety of false names, "Mme de ***" opens herself up to the charge of having been herself less than faithful to the truth. She addresses her use of pseudonyms in her introduction, explaining that editors are loath to publish unsigned letters these days, which makes it hard for someone such as herself, "who wants neither to remain silent, nor to become the topic of conversation," to make her views known. The following contradictory passage implies that the French public is simultaneously anxious to know de La Tour's true identity and quite unlikely to have realized, pseudonyms or no, that her various letters were by the same person: "I had been advised to sign a name to my first letter that would not cause me to lose the advantages of being *incognito*: this little ruse was not in the least to my liking: however, I had to do it, and as is always true the first step was the hardest, and finding that I needed to write again, I believed that I should, the better to deceive the curious, sign my letters with different names, and say in them things that would make the reader believe them to be by different persons; not flattering myself that I had a style distinctive enough to make that precaution necessary" (14).

How much more interesting would be the news that the one woman responsible for all of these letters was also Rousseau's private correspondent and Julie come-to-life, a circumstance alluded to in a manner so discreet as to be incomprehensible, unless one is already aware of the existence and character of de La Tour's private correspondence with Rousseau. The allusion is contained in an introduction to the "Réflexions sur ce qui s'est passé au sujet de la rupture de J. J. Rousseau & de M. Hume," included in the *Vertu vengée* for the first time (52–90). De La Tour had, it will be remembered, intended to publish this letter with the private correspondence in 1770. The mysterious Mme de *** informs the reader that although written in January 1767, the piece has never before been seen, then adds a note: "No; but in 1772 Jean-Jacques read it and honored it with his approval. A circumstance I believe I should not pass over in silence; because, for me, and all those who knew the character of this man of truth, it answers the question so often debated: *Was* La Nouvelle Héloïse *a true story or a novel?*" (2–3).

What can de La Tour mean by this "enigmatic remark," as May terms it? The exact nature of the "circumstance" referred to as deciding the question of the origin of Rousseau's novel is difficult to determine. Are we to understand that Rousseau's approval of the letter decides the matter? Or the mere fact of Rousseau's having read the letter? What importance does Rousseau's status as the "man of truth" par excellence have to bear on the question? And what "others," who so well knew Rousseau, are being called to bear witness alongside "Mme de ***"? The principal purpose of this note seems to be precisely to establish an enigma in the mind of the reader of the *Vertu vengée*. Just as the supposed curiosity of her imaginary reader obliged de La Tour to adopt various pseudonyms in her defenses of Rousseau in the *Année littéraire*, the reader of this collection of letters is assumed to be quite attentive to the notes of the *Vertu vengée*, and quite interested in the identity of the mysterious "Mme de ***." Having revealed for the first time in her introduction to this work that one passionate woman was behind this flurry of missives, de La Tour plants a seed of doubt as to her identity as a real, however elusive, Julie.

The pseudonymous letters that follow this introduction, some now published for the third time, address a number of topics related to de La Tour's "private" relationship with Rousseau, including his views on the woman question. De La Motte's letter contains a defense of Rousseau's views on women, as had the anonymous "Lettre à l'auteur de *la justification de M. Rousseau*" of 1766, also reprinted in the *Vertu vengée* (33–51). Adopting the voice of one of Rousseau's detractors, de La Motte declares Rousseau to be "a dangerous sophist, who used his eloquence only to impose upon a sex whose sensitivity *opens its soul to all sorts of seductions.*" Addressing Fréron, she continues: "Lend an attentive ear, monsieur, and an open mind, to the important truth I am about to reveal to you. All the gratitude women feel for *Jean-Jacques* (for what man would be fool enough to feel gratitude toward him?) has no real foundation: the revolution in our morals and our habits that seems to have taken place since 1762, relative to the very young, is but a pure illusion" (144). The letter from Mme de St. G*** dated January 14, 1779, refused by Fréron, contains a similar reference to Rousseau's influence on women. Carefully humbling herself before the achievements of de La Tour's other pseudonyms, Mme de St. G*** tells Fréron that although her limited income does not permit her to subscribe to the *Année littéraire*, "persuaded as I am, monsieur, that Mesdames *du Riez-Genest* and *de La Motte* owe their success as much to your approbation and to the subject they treated as to their talent, I am emboldened to follow in their tracks" (123). On the topic of Rousseau's reputation for misogyny, Mme de St. G*** declares herself "penetrated as are they with gratitude for the services he rendered to my sex, by emphasizing those qualities particular to it; and by recalling us to our true destiny; finally, by inspiring women to love their duties" (123).[39]

Mme de St. G***'s letter ends with a postscript, in which she contributes her few words against the most famous posthumous attack on Rousseau's reputation, Diderot's *Essai sur la vie et les oeuvres de Sénèque* (Essay on the Life and Works of Seneca, 1778). The *Essai* contains a note that, while it does not directly name Rousseau, obviously refers to the second part of the *Confessions* (as yet unpublished, but widely known): "If, by a not-unparalleled eccentricity, there should ever appear a work in which good men are mercilessly torn apart by a lying villain who, in order to give the appearance of truth to his unjust and cruel accusations, paints himself with odious colors"; if such a dreadful publication should appear, Diderot advises us to throw it away. He argues that the revelation of one's sins is no guarantee of truth; it is rather a probable indication of other, hidden crimes, perhaps of "a life hidden for more than fifty years under the thickest mask of hypocrisy."[40] Diderot was roundly criticized for this attack on Rousseau; Baczko's "Burn Diderot" takes its title from the fact that the *Essai* was offered up in an auto-da-fé before Rousseau's tomb on the Ile de Peupliers, on which were inscribed the words: "Here lies the man of nature and truth."

The most significant aspect of de St. G***'s letter for my purposes is her discussion of the recent, unauthorized publication of private letters by Rousseau. As mentioned earlier, de La Tour's stated purpose in writing this letter was to make adjustments to a notice from the *Journal de Paris* concerning the publication of a *Supplément aux Oeuvres de J. J. Rousseau*. Volume 10 of this supplement reproduced letters written when Rousseau was young, and the notice in question had criticized the inclusion of such private missives in a work published only one year after Rousseau's death. Quoting each contested sentence, Mme de St. G*** first agrees that such a correspondence indeed cannot be considered "a work," but then notes: "*These letters were never intended to be published*: that is true, and that constitutes to my eyes their principal merit. With the exception of some trivial expressions, eminently pardonable in such an intimate exchange, what can one find to criticize? As for me; monsieur, I find that these letters do all the more honor to *Jean-Jacques* in that they were not written to do him honor" (129).[41] Glossing over the moral point that Rousseau's privacy is being violated, de La Tour argues that the letters' indisputable status as private documents unintended for the public eye makes them eminently publishable.

As one might expect of a woman who possessed an enormous cache of private letters by Rousseau that she wished to see published, de La Tour is arguing that the ideal manner in which to "avenge" Rousseau would indeed be to violate his epistolary privacy. According to her argument, the most compelling justificatory documents are by definition private letters, written, it is assumed, by an individual exposing his essential self. As I will explore in the next chapter, de La Tour's advocacy of the publication of private letters was highly unusual for her time, and indicates the strength of her desire to see her exchange with Rousseau published. She was willing to wait—until after her death, if necessary—but she was determined to see her role as Julie made public. The idiosyncrasy of her argument is highlighted by contrast with a statement from La Harpe, in which he declares that the publication of Rousseau's letters is the equivalent of grave robbery: "It is a strange folly to publish in this way, as soon as a famous man is dead, everything that should have died with him. . . . It is to violate tombs, so to speak, as well as the respect due to dead souls; but the publishers, who want to make money however it can be had, do not look too closely at the manner."[42]

The *Vertu vengée* of 1782 was de La Tour's last publication as the anonymous *amie de Jean-Jacques*. Next to nothing is known of how she spent the remaining years of her life. While her death in 1789 shielded her from the turmoil of the French Revolution, the private correspondence she had so carefully cultivated with Rousseau, and so carefully edited for publication, would be quite negatively affected by the cultural upheaval of the Revolutionary years, as we shall see in the next chapter.

3

The Sanctity of the Reader's Response: Eighteenth-Century Critical Assessments of the Missive Letter

Reread your letter: it exhibits an order that unveils you with each sentence. . . . That is the problem with novels; the author whips himself into a heat, and the reader stays cold. *Héloïse* is the only exception; and despite the talent of the author, this observation has always made me think that the basic story was true.
—Letter from Merteuil to Valmont; Laclos, *Liaisons dangereuses*

WHEN MARIE-ANNE DE LA TOUR DIED ON SEPTEMBER 7, 1789, SHE LEFT A number of curious objects to Alexandre Du Peyrou: "I give and bequeath to Monsieur Du Peyrou, inhabitant of Neuchâtel, Switzerland, and a friend of Madame de Montrond, the glass cage containing my three little Senegalese birds; the portrait of my dog, Mouse; and a large case that contains, I insist, only my correspondence with him, with J.-J. Rousseau, and other letters relative to those. I am sure that Monsieur Du Peyrou will receive with feeling this modest testimony to the friendship that attaches me to him" (*CC*, 9:app. 249). De La Tour could rest easy that Du Peyrou would value her lengthy and often explosive exchange with Rousseau as more than a modest gift in the same league with the portrait of Mouse. As Rousseau's editor, one-time friend, and always fervent admirer, Du Peyrou was perfectly placed to see to the publication of these letters. He was also, of course, de La Tour's publisher, having included her pseudonymous *Vertu vengée* in his 1782 edition of Rousseau's works. That de La Tour expected Du Peyrou to capitalize on her status as Rousseau's posthumous defender when publishing the correspondence she had willed to him is made clear when she adds yet one more curious bequest: "I give to this commendable friend the freedom to name the author of the *Vertu vengée par l'amitié,* found in the supplement to the Works of J.-J. Rousseau, Geneva Edition.''

Contrary to de La Tour's obvious expectations, Du Peyrou did not publish the exchange himself. The inauspicious date of de La Tour's death—two months after the taking of the Bastille—may explain this lapse better than any lack of appreciation of the letters' publication value, for at Du Peyrou's own death in 1794 he left careful instructions concerning de La Tour's manuscript with another Neuchâtel publisher, Louis Fauche-Borel.[1] Du Peyrou enjoined Fauche-Borel to publish the Rousseau–de La Tour letters and suggested as editor "either Mme de Charrière, Pastor Chaillot, or Pastor Meuron, in a word, someone well educated.''[2] What happened to the manuscript at this point is unclear; it was, in any case, nine years until a two-volume work, entitled *Correspondance originale et inédite de J.-J. Rousseau avec Mme Latour de Franqueville et M. Du Peyrou* (Original Unpublished Correspondence of J.-J. Rousseau with Mme Latour de Franqueville and M. Du Peyrou), appeared in 1803.

Unfortunately for de La Tour, the lengthy delay caused by Du Peyrou's failure to publish the correspondence during his lifetime did not serve her project well. Had these letters appeared just after her death in 1789, or better yet, shortly after Rousseau's death in 1778, this correspondence would certainly have been a publishing event of some magnitude. The effect might have been all the greater had de La Tour gone through with her original threat to publish the letters in 1770, when Rousseau was alive and his reputation at something of a controversial peak, following the Hume affair. The opportunity to peer into Rousseau's private thoughts, expressed to a real-life Julie whom he then "abandoned," would have intrigued readers and attracted commentators eager to weigh in on the subject of Rousseau's character. When the exchange finally appeared in 1803, some twenty-five years had passed since Rousseau's death, and a series of political and literary revolutions had quite definitively shifted the reading public's attention to other matters.

I begin examining the reception history of this ill-fated correspondence over the two centuries since its publication by considering the value of the missive letter in France when de La Tour undertook her project of establishing a publishable correspondence with Rousseau, that is, in the 1760s and 1770s. I emphasize that while the essays produced on this topic during this period differ in many respects, they share a set of contradictory assumptions that is fundamental to understanding de La Tour's project and how it has been misread since its publication. At the time de La Tour was writing, it was given, first, that true private letters were never to be published under any circumstances; and second, that once published, their aesthetic value was superior to that of any other genre. Truth-value conquers all in these assessments, for it is the unadulterated exposure of one's true thoughts and feelings that inspires both the moral objections to the publication of private letters and the aesthetic celebration of such publications.

The centrality of truth-value to such theoretical considerations makes it all the more strange that the issue of the authenticity of any particular set of private letters was most often resolved with a wave of the critical wand. The general rule was simply that if the reader *perceived* a letter to be authentic, it was so. This heuristic approach was subject to ludic (and revealing) pressures in the prefaces to epistolary novels of the period, as I explore in considering the prefatory material to Rousseau's *Nouvelle Héloïse* and Diderot's *La Religieuse*, but readerly infallibility was nevertheless evoked with high seriousness in discussions of the true missive letter, as in the preface to the 1803 edition of the Rousseau–de La Tour correspondence.

As the nineteenth century progressed, the centrality of a work's emotional effect on the average reader as a criterion for judging its worth was increasingly abandoned in favor of "literariness" or "literary value," a judgment best left to the experts. This shift reaches its apogee with Flaubert, whose legendary concern with indirectness in his novel's discourse and with authorial self-effacement places his writing at the opposite end of the spectrum from eighteenth-century epistolary fiction. While this general shift has been studied in the context of the history of the novel, its effect on the reception of true missive letters has been neglected, perhaps for the very reason that the elevation of literariness as a criterion of judgment resulted in the relegation of the missive letter to critical oblivion.[3] As the emphasis on the creative genius of the author increasingly eclipsed the importance of the emotional effect of truth-value on the reader, the missive letter experienced a dramatic drop in status. By the late twentieth century, as I will examine in my next chapter, the notion that a letter exhibiting no signs of literariness in the Flaubertian sense of that term might be publishable on its own merits becomes laughable.

My only witness as to de La Tour's status in the nineteenth century is fortunately an important player in the literary critical scene I am examining. Charles Augustin de Sainte-Beuve's 1850 essay on de La

Tour represents the perfect middle point, both chronologically and theoretically, between eighteenth-century and twentieth-century views of her chosen genre, the "true" missive letter. In perfectly liminal fashion, Sainte-Beuve both elevates and denigrates the place of missive letters in the literary universe. On the one hand, he insists on the considerable value of de La Tour's letters and accords them considerable attention qua letters; on the other, he reveals the decreasing value assigned to this genre in that he explicitly uses her letters as the means to an extraepistolary end. What most interests him is gaining a better understanding of the character, and thus the works and influence, of Jean-Jacques Rousseau. Just as interest in the emphasis on the man and his milieu would later be expunged from literary critical concerns, the value of the missive letter in-and-of-itself had been considerably effaced by the time Sainte-Beuve turned his attention to de La Tour and her correspondence.

When de La Tour began her self-fashioning as Rousseau's real-life Julie, the genre she chose was to the contrary considered highly significant and worthy of theoretical analysis. The complex generic richness and high status attributed to the epistolary genre in the eighteenth century is evident in the many, many articles grouped in volume nine of the *Encyclopédie* under the collective heading *Lettre, Epître, Missive* (1765). One of the major reasons for the existence of so many subgroups under this heading is the great care taken by the authors of the various articles to distinguish the truly private letter (*la lettre missive*, never intended by the writer to be viewed by a third party) from the only apparently private letter (*la lettre familière*, having the form of a private letter but intended for public viewing).[4] That the latter category is now all but extinct contributes greatly to our current misapprehension of the link between publishability and letters in the eighteenth century. The *lettre familière* was, indeed, central to the Enlightenment project, as Dena Goodman argues in *The Republic of Letters*. For Goodman, the key to the essential move from elite salon conversation to general propagandistic publication was "the letter, the dominant form of writing in the eighteenth century. The philosophes increasingly and creatively used letters to bridge the gap between the private circles in which they gathered and the public arena that they sought to shape and conquer. . . . The epistolary genre became the dominant medium for creating an active and interactive reading public."[5]

The intensity of the publication of letters between famous men,

of pamphlets, literary "correspondences," and other Enlightenment and counter-Enlightenment epistolary vehicles, explains the
care taken in the *Encyclopédie* to distinguish the true missive letter
from those of most interest to Goodman (clearly *lettres familières*).
The most important distinction made between the two types of letters is the correspondent's moral obligation to keep the true missive
letter out of the public eye. In the absence of laws prohibiting the
publication of an individual's letters without permission (such legal
restrictions did not appear in France until after the Revolution), the
Encyclopédie calls upon the addressee of a missive letter to defend the
privacy of its writer quite rigorously: "One must not abuse this type
of *letter* by making public that which was written confidentially; it is
especially odious to hand such a letter over to a third party who
might make use of it; that is an abuse of confidence."[6] We are
thus to understand the epithet "private" when applied to missive
letters at the time as indicating far more than merely "addressed to
one individual." In the *Encyclopédie,* "private" serves to distinguish
lettre missive from *lettre familière* by denying access to the former to
third-party readers, and by extension, to the reading public. The opprobrium attached to handing over missive letters cannot be over-
emphasized here, as it is of central importance to any consideration
of de La Tour's delay in publishing her exchange with Rousseau.
Indeed, the moral censure against publishing missive letters at this
time was so strong that it extended even to one's own letters, as Ruth
Perry observes of 1730s England: "It was considered indecent to
have one's letter published—so much so that Pope went to a great
deal of trouble to hush up his part in the first printing of his letters.
He was, in fact, the first literary figure whose private letters were
published during his own lifetime and at his own instigation. To protect his respectability, and because he knew how much the public
valued private letters, he tried to make it appear that they had been
innocently composed without the expectation of public fame, and
that they had been stolen from him."[7]

The exaggeratedly strong moral stance against showing private
letters to third parties was, as this quotation also reveals, in part the
result of the heightened publication value of such documents in the
eighteenth century. The very form in which the prohibition against
publishing private letters normally appeared served to reinforce
their publication value, for if the purity of the letter writer's belief
that only his intended recipient will see his letter is so strongly as-
serted, it follows that any third-party reader who comes into posses-

sion of such a document can peruse it with the profound assurance that the writer revealed himself quite entirely while writing his letter. The ravished missive becomes all the more valuable in that we believe its writer to have anticipated no such exposure. As Perry dramatically sums up the situation: "Booksellers often advertised the fact that a set of letters had not been intended for publication because privacy, like virginity, invites violation."[8]

Pope's readers were, paradoxically, able to rest secure in their moral uprightness while reading the published volume of his (pseudostolen) letters. Whatever the moral opprobrium attached to handing over one's correspondent's letters for publication, reading letters handed over by others and generally distributed to the public is not generally condemned. By some strange sleight of hand, publication nullifies the moral issues surrounding missive letters. This strange lack of condemnation is born, I believe, of the contradiction at the heart of eighteenth-century treatments of the missive letter. This most admirable form of written expression, in which the writer reveals the unadorned truth with no eye on fame or reputation, is to be locked away from the reading public for the most indisputably ethical of reasons. At the same time, the immoral publisher of such documents can be said, in a sense, to perform a public service. He allows the public access to private letters at no cost to the reader's soul. In turn, the reader justifies this unethical act of publication by benefiting from exposure to Truth. The epistolary theorist also benefits from the reader's access to private letters, for the positive reaction of such third-party readers is the central heuristic device employed by theorists of the missive letter when establishing both the importance of the genre and the authenticity of any particular letter or exchange of letters.

This method of determining authenticity is omnipresent in theoretical treatments of the missive letter. Consider, for example, the most important *Encyclopédie* article on the topic, at least for my purposes, written by the chevalier de Jaucourt. The central tenet of his entry on "Scientific and Literary Letters" is that the standard by which all letters are to be judged is the correspondence of Cicero. While Jaucourt laments the "small" number of extant letters by Cicero (one thousand), he waxes lyrical over the glories that the remaining letters hold for the reader. One important source of the greatness of these letters is the quality of the man who wrote them: "No writing gives as much pleasure as the *letters* of great men; they touch the reader's heart by unveiling that of the writer."[9] Eminent scholars, scientific geniuses, men of state, all produce powerful letters, each in his own way; but just as Cicero alone combined the talents of all such men, only he produced epistolary masterpieces in all subgenres of the letter form. Such extraordinary genius is, however, not enough on its own to ensure the masterpiece status of a correspondence should one essential element be missing: "What makes Cicero's *letters* so precious is that he never intended them to be made public, and that he never kept copies. We thus find in them the unadorned man, with neither disguises nor affectations." Cicero's assumption of privacy when writing his letters is a sine qua non of their superior status; the correspondence provides us, in other words, the occasion to be illicit third-party witnesses to a private act of communication.

When Jaucourt goes on to compare Cicero to his ancient contemporaries, this emphasis on the authentically missive quality of his letters becomes yet clearer. Jaucourt declares other classical letter writers admirable in their way; Pliny's letters are witty and tasteful, for example, but of far less value than Cicero's. This lack does not necessarily point to a deficiency of mind; the inferior quality of Pliny's letters is rather the result of his assumption that his letters would be read by third parties. Pliny is said to have censured himself out of fear of persecution; rather than entering freely into any topic and openly expressing himself, he held back, anticipating a reader other than his intended correspondent. Cicero, in comparison, is declared to have combined naturalness of style with the liberty of expression of a man "talking to himself." For Jaucourt, Cicero's letters thus offer a unique historical window into the last years of "free Rome," for although his correspondents included the most powerful men of his time, he wrote with no trace of obsequiousness. That he also believed the topics he addressed to be unsuitable for the majority of his contemporaries further ensures the truly private nature of these letters. Jaucourt cites this point of view with approbation, quoting a passage from a letter Cicero wrote to a friend who had shown one of these delightful missives to a third party: "You are not unaware that there are good things in our society that, made public, are only mad or ridiculous."

Jaucourt's insistence that Cicero's letters are nearly stream-of-consciousness documents of his thoughts clashes somewhat with the subgenre in question, for the article is supposed to be devoted to "scientific and literary" letters. But despite the reference to this correspondence as a window on a lost world, what is of most importance to Jaucourt in his promotion of Cicero is the authentification of his letters as truly missive. Jaucourt's ultimate goal in this essay is to assert that these prime examples of an exemplary genre were passed through no filter whatsoever. Even the addressees of Cicero's letters are subtly effaced, until the reader becomes an eavesdropper upon that most truly intimate of moments, a man "talking to himself."

In a different *Encyclopédie* article that addresses eighteenth-century letter writers (*Lettres des Modernes, genre epistol.*), we learn that present-day epistolary practitioners share Pliny's flaw of anticipating eavesdroppers. To their great shame, eighteenth-century missive letter writers are said to avoid the great topics not out of fear of the authorities, but rather because they are overly concerned with social niceties. The desire to flatter and please, we are told, has led to banality. While the natural style of modern missive letters is praised—a constant in such discussions, based on a contrast with the rigid rules imposed on seventeenth-century letter writers—it remains true that "[modern letters] contain only insignificant events, minor news, and illustrate the language of an era and a century in which false politeness has spread lies everywhere."[10] Such a letter could obviously never fulfill Jaucourt's criterion of "touching a reader's heart by unveiling that of the writer," be he scholar, scientist, man of state, or even the rare combination of all of the above.

The condemnation of contemporary letter writers in the *Encyclopédie* neglects to mention the presence in eighteenth-century France of such rare, Cicero-like exceptions as Voltaire, not to mention that champion of Truth, Jean-Jacques Rousseau, whose every published work rails against the politeness of the French and the inability of modern men to speak truthfully to each other on any subject. Could not the letters of such men equal those of Cicero, both in content and missive authenticity?

"No" is the resounding answer given in one of the most complex and important eighteenth-century treatments of the private letter, Michel de Servan's "Réflexions sur la publication des lettres de Rousseau, et des lettres en général" (Reflections on the Publication of Rousseau's Letters, and of Letters in General). This short essay was published, significantly, as part of a larger work entitled *Réflexions sur les* Confessions *de J.-J. Rousseau* (1783).[11] The inclusion of a piece on missive letters in a work concerned primarily with Rousseau's recently published autobiography is revealing not only of Servan's specific purpose in writing this work but also of general eighteenth-century assumptions about the missive letter. From an eighteenth-century point of view, letters and autobiography are closely linked by their shared capacity to betray to the public that which should remain private.[12] A lawyer, Servan is intent on establishing both the legal and the greater ethical considerations that he believes apply when one individual chooses to expose another's private acts or thoughts. While he cites the posthumous publication of Rousseau's correspondence as an example of the trend to publish everything, Servan's principal purpose in writing this work as a whole is to join the chorus of those condemning Rousseau himself for disclosing the sins of his close confidants along with his own in the *Confessions.*

For Servan, Rousseau's autobiography epitomizes the perversity of those who would seek to capitalize on the public's taste for the "abuse of personalities."[13] No good ever comes from such attacks, Servan tells us, whether justified or not. We are reminded to "never forget that the first law of society is to do no harm, and that the second is to be useful" (12). In an argument that has not lost its pertinence in our own time, Servan also contends that some revelations concerning public figures are better left unmade in the name of the human right to privacy, and out of respect for an all-too-human frailty. Rousseau, obviously, has failed to uphold this law of civil society in Servan's eyes. Overall, his opinion of Rousseau as expressed in this work is quite harsh. He acknowledges Rousseau's genius, but laments that it was so poorly employed. As a young man, we are told, Servan had been devoted to Rousseau, but was swiftly disillusioned by the opportunity to live next door to the object of his admiration. Based on this experience, Servan pronounces Rousseau something of a paranoid nut, whose success caused him to overestimate his own worth. Servan goes so far as to propose that Rousseau staged the stoning incident at Môtiers, and refers to the Hume-Rousseau affair as "the famous quarrel between Hume and Rousseau, that is to say, between judgment and imagination" (156). Those who have remained devoted to the memory of Rousseau, Servan acknowledges, will not take kindly to his essay (one can imagine de La Tour writing a letter that would reinforce this view), but their blindness to the truth is merely a symptom of their Rousseau-like fanaticism: "I will say nothing that does not appear outrageous to these impassioned minds" (10).

Despite his efforts to discredit Rousseau, it is safe to say that Servan would never countenance using private letters to back up any public attack on Rousseau the man, as was done in the Hume affair.

We know this to be true, in that Servan explains in his "Réflexions sur la publication des lettres de Rousseau" that his experience in the courts of law has led him to a dramatic conclusion concerning letters: "It is a capital maxim that a written work, of whatever type, cannot be imputed as a *fault* or a *crime* unless the author himself has given it over freely. Until then it is nothing; in the words of M. de Voltaire, it is only black on a white background" (111–12).[14] Rousseau wrote the *Confessions* intending it for publication; he can thus be taken to task for his public abuses of others in this work. As for Rousseau's letters, in Servan's opinion the posthumous publication of an author's private correspondence is an unethical misappropriation by unscrupulous editors. Private letters offer the most odious opportunity for abuse of the right to privacy in that they appear to their writers to be as ephemeral as an intimate conversation with a friend. Most letter writers do not understand that a letter's physicality makes it a contribution to the written record, and that any momentary lapse in a letter can lead to public humiliation, especially in an age with a maniacal inclination "to print everything, even the least scraps of letters. . . . We have witnessed the most irreproachable old age dishonored with one blow by the revelation of a mistake made in extreme youth" (115).

The famous are most at risk, of course, of seeing their letters published, and of these the most vulnerable are famous authors who have recently died. Servan declares that a veritable plague is raging among publishers in this domain: "Publishing letters is the fashion today, it is an epidemic, there are few authors whose letters are not published" (84). In pressing his point, Servan employs a striking analogy between the dead writer's soul bereft of its "envelope" and a prostituted woman: "This immortal soul has barely left its earthly envelope when it is spied upon, collected, printed, advertised, and exposed forever on sale at 50 *sous* a volume as an object of commerce and public talk" (100–101). He asks publishers to limit themselves to "purified" editions of authors' works, meaning no doubt that publications such as Du Peyrou's *Collection des oeuvres de J.-J. Rousseau*, which had appeared the year before, should not contain every "scrap" written by the author (not to mention documents such as de La Tour's *Vertu vengée*). In the name of the public good, Servan advocates the strictest of editorial policies with regard to private letters, for the knowledge that one has no control over the posthumous publication of one's writings might lead men of genius to stifle themselves, à la Pliny.

Such traffic in the prostitution of great men's souls requires buyers as well, and in arguing for the cessation of this commerce Servan makes an usual appeal to readers, as well as to publishers. The public is attracted to such overly complete editions of authors' collected writings for the worst of reasons, Servan declares. Admitting what Jaucourt and most other treatments of published private letters avoid mentioning—the salacious attraction of private letters by the famous—Servan declares that the appeal of such documents to lesser men lies in their desire to catch well-known literary figures with their pants down, or rather, as he puts it, *en négligé.* "Sometimes also a man of taste stares fascinated at the style of a superior writer like a voluptuary stares at the *négligé* of a beautiful woman, and ordinarily both are fooled. An author does not lay aside his mind any more than a woman does her face: the letter is the product of reflection, just as the *négligé* has its toilette. This sense of preparation, by the way, is the problem with Rousseau's letters; but take away the title, and this fault is no longer a fault" (84–85). Referring to the reader of private letters as "a man of taste" attenuates the fault involved in being attracted to such letters; perhaps Servan considered that rather than merely attempting to shame readers, it would be far more effective to argue, as he goes on to do, that letters by famous men are not true missives, and thus of no value. He uses Rousseau as an example, explaining that his criticism of Rousseau's letters for being too public in tone and style is a product of the false "title" he is obliged to attach to these documents: "missive letters." Given that there is no true abandon in the private letters of famous writers any more, the lack of spontaneity in Rousseau's letters can be viewed as a fault only if we anticipate its presence.

Like myself, that is, Servan argues that Rousseau would have been highly conscious of the possibility of the future publication of his letters, and would have written with care, especially when his correspondent was unknown to him. Contradicting his own powerful image of the prostituted authorial soul, Servan is thus establishing that the risk of exposure to Rousseau when his private correspondence is published is minimal. He also argues, to put the matter in Jaucourt's terms, that all modern geniuses are reduced to Pliny's unfortunate self-censorship. We conclude that there are indeed, as the *Encyclopédie* declares, no modern letter writers equal to Cicero, but in Servan's eyes the fault lies with the modern publishers, not with the letter writers themselves.

Servan does propose a potential victim should Rousseau's correspondence be published: his obscure correspondent, whose position in life had not taught him the harsh truth of his inevitable exposure. Servan considers the most serious publishing crime to occur not when a famous man's letters are published (he has just declared such letters to be *familières*, not *missives*), but rather when an obscure individual (always male, for Servan) who has written privately to a famous man witnesses with horror the publication of his letters. When Servan transfers his heuristic attentions to the letters of this innocent, unknown correspondent, his conclusions again differ considerably from what we assume he will say. We imagine that the obscure man in question, unlike the worldly-wise famous writer, will in his letters naively share embarrassing personal truths or political opinions with the public. This assumption that an unknown nonauthor is yet more likely than a famous man to pour out his thoughts uninhibitedly and honestly is at the heart of de La Tour's self-fashioning as "Julie," and her readers have over the centuries obliged her by making that very assumption; but in a manner once again contrary to most eighteenth-century treatments of missive letters, Servan declares instead that the danger for the obscure correspondent lies not in the potential revelation of his true private thoughts, but rather in the public's gaining a false image of what he believes. Entering imaginatively into the mind of an unknown individual writing a letter to a famous man, Servan tells us that this letter writer will modify his epistolary style in an effort to please his exalted correspondent. He is performing, or believes himself to be performing, for a difficult and discerning public of one. Like an actor on a stage, he plays a role, but unlike the actor, he is unaware of the possibility of a public audience: "A man who is very reserved in public on matters of religion might, for example, in writing to M. de Voltaire, allow himself pleasantries quite foreign to his character. Publish the letters to Voltaire alongside the responses; and this man will be severely misjudged" (91).

If we accept the fundamental inauthenticity of letters to and from famous men, the power of Servan's metaphor of the letter writer as a woman exposed "against her will" to the eyes of a lascivious public is considerably attenuated. The famous author, at first an innocent soul prostituted in the streets by pimping publishers, is later said to be too cautious ever to be caught naked before potential "voluptuaries." He remains always artfully dressed, posed in his boudoir in anticipation of the presence of voyeurs. The famous man's unknown correspondent is also far from naked, as he is dressed in the garish outfit of his hyperbolic rhetoric. Adorned in borrowed clothes for the exceptional seduction of one, famous client, he will be mistaken for a prostitute only by the uninformed *profanum vulgus*. It is nevertheless in the raw power of such images that Servan's attack on letter readers becomes most effective. Cast as the client of the pimping publisher, the reader is allowed no pleasure from his sins, that is, no authentic glimpse into the private lives of others. Servan would have the public recognize a convoluted truth: that the boudoir environment in which such epistolary exchanges take place is by definition not a fully authentic domain of intimate self-expression.

In spite of Servan's title ("Réflexions sur la publication des lettres de Rousseau"), when he comes to discuss the "deceased famous man" to whom his imagined letter writer addresses his missives, the example he uses is that of Voltaire. This choice is telling, for Servan neglects to mention that he was himself one of Voltaire's "obscure" correspondents, and thus in a prime position to judge of his pseudo-imaginary letter writer's difficulties. Voltaire had died, like Rousseau, in 1778, and Servan may well have been anticipating a *Collection des oeuvres* that would include every last scrap of writing to or from Voltaire, in which his own letters would be exposed to the public. The motivation behind the somewhat contrarian nature of Servan's views on the missive letter comes clearly into focus when one has this bit of information, as does the purpose behind the strongly legal bent his reflections on the publication of "letters in general" take. The main crux of his argument about written documents unintended for the public eye, it bears repeating, is that they cannot be included as criminal evidence unless the author freely gives them over. It is no coincidence that to back up his point of view, the authority Servan cites is Voltaire himself, who would have such documents become literally unreadable ("only black on a white background").

When turning his attention to epistolary ownership, Servan presents his theory as a shock to his readers: "What! they will say, do not Rousseau's letters belong to Rousseau?" No, he tells us; letters belong not to the sender alone but to both sender and receiver equally: "They are common property, and neither of the two may dispose of them without the positive permission of the other" (86). The term "positive" rules out posthumous publication, for it is impossible to obtain the explicit consent of a dead man. Servan's exclamatory rhetoric about the unusual decision to which he has come concerning ownership of missive letters is rather overdone, given that it echoes the general views of his day. That one was not to dispose of such letters without the permission of the writer was accepted as a basic moral proposition. A more pertinent question might be why anyone would bother to publish or read such letters, given that Servan has just dismissed them out of hand as crafted, and thus worthless. The real challenge Servan presents to the view of private letters in the *Encyclopédie* and elsewhere concerns not ownership, but rather what third-party readers should assume when given access to the private letters they are most likely to read, those of the famous. Servan tells readers that in perusing such published correspondences they are not in fact privy to unguarded thoughts. They might as well put the volumes aside; as missive letters, these documents are worthless, because the writer was not "speaking to himself."

This "fact" does not dilute, of course, Servan's intense moral outrage at those who publish such letters, nor does it affect the intensity of his metaphorical references to the exposed, prostituted letter writers, famous or not. One might argue that he is trying every tactic to discourage the publication of letters in order to protect himself— whatever the harm to the integrity of his essay. It is also true, however, that the very idiosyncrasies of Servan's essay ultimately reinforce my views on the peculiarities of eighteenth-century epistolary aesthetics. Its contradictory two-part structure is quite significant. First, Servan would have his reader accept that letters by famous men and their correspondents should be treated as—are in fact?—true private documents, and thus subject to the common moral strictures against publication. For his own peculiar legal reasons, he then goes against the common view to insist that such documents, when published, are inauthentic. According to this intriguing, complex argument, only in the unlikely case that a missive letter writer specifically allows the publication of his private letters and gives them his imprimatur could a reader enjoy the resulting "spectacle" with the assurance of authenticity.

Servan's metaphors apply far better, interestingly enough, to de La Tour's letters than to his own, to Voltaire's, or even to Rousseau's. Her missives, acknowledged by herself in the letters themselves to be unquestionably authentic, present the reader with a novelistic fantasy of unrequited love, in which a real, beautiful woman, *en négligé* in her boudoir (perhaps literally), writes to the man she adores. Here lies the potential appeal of the Rousseau–de La Tour correspondence for the eighteenth-century reader, as she herself envisioned it. As Servan's essay brings out, however, her awareness of the publishability of her correspondence with a famous man was in direct conflict with the very real dilemma she faced in attempting to get these letters published and publicized. In the face of hortatory essays similar to Servan's, de La Tour had to take care to avoid exposing herself to the accusation that she was engaged in the self-serving epistolary prostitution of both herself and Rousseau. She had many tricks at hand, of course, not least of which was her willingness to wait for posthumous fame as Rousseau's "Julie." What better proof that her letters were truly private and herself impeccably virtuous than to make them a "gift of friendship" to a publisher at her death, rather than explicitly handing them over for publication.

By 1803, when the exchange finally appeared, Rousseau was of course long dead, and the missive letter on its way out of fashion. The autobiography, as we see already in Servan's essay, was destined to replace the letter as the locus of authorial exposure par excellence.[15] It was perhaps the awareness that de La Tour's time had passed that led the editors Giguet and Michaud to preface the *Correspondance originale et inédite de J.-J. Rousseau avec Mme Latour de Franqueville* with a fairly lengthy defense of the letters' importance. In this prefatory material, the gray areas of authenticity and privacy evoked by Servan are scrupulously ignored. The editors assure us unqualifiedly that we are holding the authentic item: true missive letters, written with no thought of an eventual third-party reader. Giguet and Michaud also understandably avoid the questions raised by both Servan and the *Encyclopédie* concerning the morality of publishing private letters without the correspondents' permission. They instead devote their editorial preface to telling the reader why this collection of strictly private missives between an unknown woman and a famous man offers a unique reading experience to be savored by the exceptionally sensitive reader.

In other words, the preface to this first edition of the de La Tour–Rousseau correspondence is above all promotional. The basic characteristics of the definition of the private letter in the eighteenth century are present, and yet, as in Servan's essay, they are given a creative twist to fit the argument at hand. Giguet and Michaud are not content merely to present this exchange of letters as significant and worthy of publication; they instead enter the realm of hyperbole so often present in eighteenth-century discussions of the missive letter, stating that nothing like this exchange of letters has ever before been seen. Like Jaucourt pleading for the superiority of Cicero's missives, Giguet and Michaud declare that the letters they are presenting to the public are more authentically "real" than all other similar missives, and thus of far greater value. They dismiss all previous published correspondences by Rousseau as comprising letters expressly written for publication, more or less *familières*, rather than *missives*. Giving no evidence for this claim, they then go on to declare that all previous volumes of Rousseau's letters are inferior for a second reason: they contain only isolated missives, rather than a continuous series of letters. The de La Tour–Rousseau correspondence, in contrast, is declared to be authentically private and to exhibit a clear progression of sentiment "that everyone may comprehend."[16]

The editors anticipate that the reader may be tempted by this insistence on the length of the exchange to conclude that these letters have much to teach us about the most momentous fifteen years of Rousseau's life. Such a reader should be ashamed, we are told, for being so insensitive as to consider perusing these letters merely for what they have to reveal about a famous man. The editors are not however denouncing the immorality of such voyeurism, as did Servan. Reading in this way constitutes for them an aesthetic, not a moral, crime. By reading for insight into Rousseau's life, one makes the mistake of confusing this missive correspondence with—a novel. Read as a novel (for the events of Rousseau's life, that is), these letters offer only entertainment value; one follows a plot, and delights in the changes of fortune of the participants. Such superficial "literary" qualities are, however, the least of the pleasures this exchange has to offer a reader: "So much for curiosity; for those who read only novels, and who are capable of reading these letters in the same spirit in which they read *La Nouvelle Héloïse*. But this correspondence offers a more real interest" (10).

This "more real" *intérêt* (significance, importance) will be appreciated only by those readers who recognize that these letters are more impeccably "real" than any previously published letters by Rousseau. An interesting chiasmus results. Those interested in the facts of Rousseau's life will read this exchange superficially, in the manner of novel readers; those interested in a moving emotional experience (the benefit generally accorded the novel) will accept and appreciate the letters' factuality. According to this logic, breathtakingly contrary to our current standards, the fictional masterpiece *La Nouvelle Héloïse* could only ever rank second to the real letters exchanged by de La Tour and Rousseau. The emotion that the reader, vampirelike, is to imbibe from his or her experience of Rousseau's "letters by two lovers living in the foothills of the Alps" is impure, and thus only superficially satisfying. The novel, by definition, and in spite of the chronological contradiction, is only an inferior "imitation" of the sustaining reading experience provided by this exchange of letters between an unknown woman and the famous Jean-Jacques Rousseau.

Or perhaps one should say: by this unknown woman's letters alone, for the editors go on to establish yet another unexpected hierarchy, this time between the two correspondents. In the context of this preface's assumptions, Rousseau's only claim to fame is that he is the author of a (merely) fictional masterpiece. He fails dismally in a more important arena: remaining faithful to the ethos of that novel in real life. The value of this exchange, we are told, has little to do with the presence of a famous man's missives. For the editors, what this correspondence offers the reader is the opportunity to peek into the very soul of a hypersensitive woman who naively uncovers her deepest self to one man with no thought of public display—a man who then mercilessly turns on her. It is de La Tour's resemblance to the long-suffering Portuguese nun, Marianne, that seems to offer the most to the reader, according to this analysis, for it is only when we are privy to this sensitive soul's sufferings that our reading experience becomes truly inestimable. In a Rousseau-like ultimatum to their readers, the editors declare: "Enlightened observers . . . will find in [this exchange] the heart and the soul in its entirety of a woman who writes according to what she is feeling, and who writes without knowing that she will one day be read by the public. The reader will see fully exposed the character of a man who expresses himself first with the openness of friendship, and who later, without reason, regrets having opened his heart" (10).

In declaring her letters unequivocally private, de La Tour's editors are deterred neither by the private-versus-public debate within the letters themselves, nor by de La Tour's editing job of 1770 (unmentioned in the preface, although the editors were working from this version of the exchange). Nor do they refer to de La Tour's *Vertu vengée,* for according to the terms of their preface, she is not to be considered in any way a public figure. They do include a poem by de La Tour, not a previously published piece, but rather a transcription of verses supposedly written by her "on the walls of the farm of the Ile de Saint-Pierre." Once again, as with the poem appended to Mme du Riez-Genest's letter, de La Tour seems to have succeeded in imposing her verses on Rousseau only in death. This particular poem takes a curious sort of revenge by resurrecting the accusation that Rousseau brought many of his problems onto himself:

> Famous hideaway, inhabited by Jean-Jacques,
> You remind me of his genius,
> His solitude, his pride,
> His misfortunes and his madness.
> Always, alas! persecuted,
> Either by himself, or by the envious,
> Let us contemplate by the flame of philosophy
> A great man and humanity.

De La Tour's poem ultimately celebrates not Rousseau but rather her own devotion to him, in spite of his "madness." The editors, eager to present Rousseau's inexplicable rejection of de La Tour as evidence of his unstable character, approve: "These lines seem to us to paint faithfully the character and the life of Rousseau" (15).

Whether or not, like Servan's work, the primary purpose of this editorial preface is to attack Rousseau's character, the editors' analysis of the missive letter genre remains pertinent to my own.[17] The intense emotion communicated to the reader would be, it is important to emphasize, quite meaningless were these letters not authentic. If fictional, this exchange would be by definition inferior. Placing so much emphasis on the private nature of these letters might seem to call for some justification, but the tricky question of how one can be sure of the provenance of the exchange is taken up only at the end of the sixteen-page editorial preface: "We do not believe that anyone could doubt the authenticity of this correspondence; the proof in such a case is in the work itself; and, if we needed to have recourse to outside evidence, from that very moment the evidence would become worthless" (15).

One could not hope to find more baldly stated the reliance on reader perception that lies at the heart of eighteenth-century epistolary theory. It is not so much the case that if inauthentic, the strong emotion inspired by these letters would be meaningless; rather, if inauthentic, then by definition these letters would inspire no strong emotion. The apparently simplistic and circular, yet in fact aesthetically complex argument implicit in the use of this heuristic device is never fully developed in the eighteenth-century treatments of the true missive letter that I have examined. The most complete treatments of the question of how reader response relates to authenticity are instead to be found, ironically enough, in the prefatory material to many of the century's epistolary novels. If presenting "true" things as true could be left to self-evident proof, presenting that which is "false" as true evidently required some editorial sleight of hand. In turning now to the prefaces of two exemplary French epistolary novels of the eighteenth century, my goal is to tease out what such convoluted and often pseudoserious treatments of the question of value and the real missive letter have to tell us about de La Tour's self-fashioning as a real-life epistolary heroine. Her performance as an *épistolière* was of course quite thoroughly embedded in novelistic discourse, however devotedly her editors may have worked to separate her letters from fiction; in seeking to understand further what was at stake in her exchange with Rousseau, I now examine the theory of the missive letter embedded in actual novels from the same period.

The notion that the letters of an obscure female correspondent could be ranked above *La Nouvelle Héloïse* in readerly impact is made much less shocking by our knowledge that the novel long occupied a shifting, not to say shady, position in the eighteenth-century aesthetic hierarchy. As has been explored at length by scholars of the period, the novel was the genre most often accused of possessing the potential to lead readers astray by seducing them into accepting as "true" that which by definition corresponded to no lived reality. The "dilemma" faced by novel writers, and so famously explored by Georges May, was something of a game, of course, for just as the truth-value attached to missive letters did not lead to a mania for publishing such documents (unless they were written by famous men), the novel suffered no loss in readership due to theoretical concerns about its dubious ontological status.[18] Novel writers were, nonetheless, obliged to "defend" their literary productions as real, however tongue-in-cheek that defense often became (Persian visitors who heedlessly leave their letters lying about; chests of letters discovered in the attics of country estates . . .).[19]

More revealing, for my purposes, is the heuristic device authors often employed to "prove" the authenticity of these letters: their readers' conviction that the letters were real. Many creative methods were available to coerce the readers' response; among the most common was the moral opprobrium cast upon those so insensitive as to doubt the letters' origins. That the average reader was more than aware of the fictional nature of the letters does not seem to have affected the strength of such statements, given at times with no accompanying wink of the authorial eye. Consider the foreword to Françoise de Graffigny's *Lettres d'une Péruvienne* (1747), in which we are told that if we do not believe in the authenticity of these missives, it is because we are hopelessly racist: "Because the light of so much learning has already been shed on these peoples' character, it would seem that one should not fear seeing original letters treated as fiction when they serve only to develop further what we already know of the Indians' lively and natural spirit. But does prejudice have eyes? Nothing ensures against its judgment, and we would certainly not have submitted this work to it were its dominion without bounds" (4).

Or take, for example, the introductory material to the best-selling epistolary novel of the eighteenth century: *Julie, ou La Nouvelle Héloïse*. The manner in which Rousseau carefully negotiates the status of his lovers' letters is of particular interest to my study, and not only because his novel was the fictional template for the correspondence I am examining. We find in the prefatory material to this eighteenth-century best seller one of the most fully developed considerations of reader response to fictional letters, and thus letters in general, from this period. There were compelling reasons why Rousseau so deeply delved into the question of reader response, writing not one but two prefaces to his only novel. He faced a particularly exquisite dilemma in presenting a work of fiction to the public, for he had just denounced fiction as dangerous in his *Lettre à d'Alembert*. How indeed could anyone justify such an apparently hypocritical act? By hiding behind the shibboleth that guided judgments of the missive letter: the reader's perception of authenticity. Rousseau's manipulation of his implied readers in these prefaces seems at first breathtakingly contradictory, and yet it is, in the end, perfectly in keeping with his overall philosophy of Truth in the fallen, corrupt world of shifting Platonic appearances.

The first and more important of Rousseau's two prefaces to *La Nouvelle Héloïse*, the "Préface dialoguée," consists of a conversation between two men, "R." and "N.," as to the authenticity of the "letters by two lovers living in the foothills of the Alps." R. is, of course, a rather thinly disguised "Rousseau, editor of the letters"; N. functions as a stand-in for the novel's readers, all assumed to be avidly curious to learn the true origins of the missives. N. reads Rousseau's novel looking for evidence that these letters are fakes; should he find any such evidence, he tells R., the letters would lose any value in his eyes. Should R. reveal to him that they are real, however, he will reread them with edification for the rest of his life. R. declares to N. that the question is his to decide as a reader. In so doing, R(ousseau) makes quite explicit the unstated premise of the prefaces to most eighteenth-century epistolary novels that were said to consist of authentic letters. The reader's conviction that these "letters by two lovers" are real may well be false; the reader may well know that the letters are fiction; but both author and reader are willing to pretend otherwise, for to do so is a necessary step on the road to readerly edification.

Necessary, because as N. has already told us, he will not read this collection of letters for its moral value unless he believes the missives to be authentic. N. is in one sense a simplified, ideal eighteenth-century reader, in that he is willing to agree that the letters are real, if told that they are by R.; yet he is at the same time a sophisticated reader, "a man of taste." In his quest for falsity of tone, for example, N. puts himself in the place of an author looking to fool the public: "Who would not have begun by saying to himself: I must distinguish the characters carefully; I must vary their styles precisely? Without fail, he would have carried out this project better than Nature . . . This Julie, such as she is, must be an enchanting creature; everything that comes into contact with her must resemble her; all must become Julie around her; all of her friends must have but one tone" (*OC*, 2:28). An "inventor," N. declares, would never dare to produce a work that exhibited such lack of stylistic variety, such sameness of tone; for "that which becomes simple again by force of finesse would not be acceptable to him. But that is the seal of truth; that is where an attentive ear seeks and finds nature once again." The monotonous sameness of the letters that make up this novel are thus, for N., qualified proof that no author was involved—even though his own reference to that which becomes simple "again," by "force of finesse," clearly points to the work of a writer. What N. has discovered with the help of R.'s Socratic attentions is a deeper truth than he sought. The attentive reader of this novel finds not "authenticity" in the standard sense of that adjective as it applies to letters, but rather something greater: nature regained, set with the seal of truth.

The sophisticated metareaders of N.'s pronouncements are to understand that the letters contained in *La Nouvelle Héloïse* are too badly written to have been the product of a *bel esprit*. We seize the truth that Rousseau is the "worst" of craftsmen, a writer constitutionally incapable of rhetorical flourishes; and understand that for this reason, he is the *best* of epistolary novelists. Although R. never explicitly declares that the letters are fake, it was out of an understandable concern that this preface would prematurely reveal the fictional origins of his novel that Rousseau asked for its removal from the first edition.[20] The replacement preface is closer to the generic norm, as when Rousseau condemns as manifestly immoral any reader capable of questioning the work's authenticity. As mentioned in chapter 1, such a reader is relegated to one of several distasteful categories: *les gens de goût,* for whom following the latest style is all; the prudes, who will be alarmed by the letters' content; and finally, the morally bankrupt, be they libertines or philosophes. Yet when Rousseau goes on in this preface to declare these "authentic" missive letters to be a suitable antidote to the moral plague loose in France at the time, he simultaneously hints, even in this revised version, at their fictional essence: "Plays are necessary to the inhabitants of great cities, and novels to corrupt peoples. I have seen the mores of my time, and I have published these letters. If only I had lived in a century when I might have thrown them into the fire!" (*OC*, 2:5).

The contradictions in the "Préface dialoguée" are thus present, albeit much less obviously, in the preface to the original edition. In both prefaces, Rousseau-the-editor hints more or less strongly that the work is a fiction; yet even in the more transparent "Préface dialoguée," R(ousseau) persists, with seeming seriousness, in presenting these letters as a potential cure for the spiritual ailment ravaging France. As Paul de Man has remarked, this clash of epistemes is altogether curious: "The discrepancy between the *persona* of Rousseau as the critical moralist of rhetorical suspicion and that of the man of practical wisdom is puzzling."[21] And yet, in my view, the "Préface dialoguée" needs no deconstructionist forces brought to bear upon it, for Rousseau's ludic games with the status of his letter-novel do not, by eighteenth-century standards, clash with his simultaneous claims as to the curative value of these letters. Rousseau's unusual dialogic preface, by means of the very "clashing epistemes" diagnosed by de Man, reveals to contemporary readers that the anachronism of prefaces to eighteenth-century epistolary novels lies not in some bizarre belief by eighteenth-century readers in the legitimacy of what are obviously fictional letters, but rather in the high generic value assigned to true missive letters at the time. R.'s obstinate refusal to admit what the reader surely must know—what he allows the reader to see, that these letters are fictional—is thus, ultimately, an implicit homage to the "real" missive letter, described in the *Lettre à d'Alembert* as possessing "that celestial fire that warms and inflames the soul, that genius that consumes and devours."[22]

Rousseau was the most likely of all eighteenth-century epistolary novelists to bow down before that which was perceived as True, that is, inspired by authentic inner sentiment, and to castigate the false, characterized by a concern for artistry. In addition to the prefaces to his novel, he worked in the *Confessions* to place *La Nouvelle Héloïse* in as ambiguous a relationship to art as possible. In describing the origins of this work, Rousseau claims that the first letters he wrote were born of a reverie so profound as to be experienced as "real" by the author. Rousseau had withdrawn, disgusted, from Paris and all it represented to "wander in the woods," in search of a more natural life. He had left the corrupt modern world, in a sense, for a Truer reality. As I have discussed in chapter 1, when he began "writing" what would become his novel, he claims to have done so with no authorial intent. He tells us that he wrote spontaneously, almost unconsciously; even in putting together these letters at a later stage, he insists, he had not the slightest intention of publishing them.

Could there possibly exist readers capable of receiving these missives in the spirit in which they were written—that is, without N.'s doubting explorations of their status? Not in the European capital of sin, it goes without saying; as R. tells us, in his "Préface dialoguée," "a novel, if it is well made, at least if it is useful, should be booed, hated, attacked by fashionable people as a flat, extravagant, ridiculous book; and thus, monsieur, the madness of the world is wisdom" (*OC*, 2:22). It is only when he is disdained by "men of taste" that an author can be sure he will be well received by provincial readers. And not just any provincial readers; Rousseau rejects the provincial *beaux esprits* in favor of "true country people." Rousseau pauses to conjure up these Ideal readers: "I like to imagine two spouses reading this collection together, finding in it renewed courage to withstand their shared tasks, and perhaps new ideas to make that work useful" (*OC*, II:23). Such hardworking innocents are incapable of the type of suspicion evinced by readers such as N., whose desire to "know" threatens to ruin the purity of their reading experience. Sophistical prefaces are necessary for readers such as N., surely not for these fireside readers (who with any luck possess a first edition, and thus have no access to the "Préface dialoguée").

The only readers more naive than these hypothetical "true country people" would be those willing to accept the existence of such simple rural folk. Like N., such ideal readers are clearly a necessary device, a part of Rousseau's argument in favor of the usefulness of what is, after all, a novel, as he does not hesitate to admit in the *Confessions*. It is only in reading this autobiography that we understand fully the complexity of Rousseau's prefaces to *La Nouvelle Héloïse*. By declaring his ideal woman's impossibly idealized fictional world suitable only to the tastes of impossibly idealized "true country people," Rousseau places himself, as an author, above reproach. His inner imaginary world is "truer" than the corrupt world in which he is forced to function as an author, a man, and a "man of letters." He has by no means violated his adherence to absolute truth, nor contradicted his attacks on fiction; he has written the Ideal exchange of letters, and shared it with any worthy readers able to receive it as True. Had he lived in "a century when [he] might have thrown them into the fire," the letters would never have been written; he would have been living the fictional life he presents in his letters, with a real Julie.

Julie's perfection, while exhibiting the unidimensionality of allegory, again proves, by its very unnaturalness, the unmistakable authenticity of these letters. Would not an "author" have sought, as part of his ruse, to create a more believable heroine—a heroine for her time? This line of argument allows Julie to be all the more believable to the extent that she remains all the more allegorical in her perfection. Pluridimensional symbolic representation would have been automatically suspect, for it would have made her perfection all too human. As de Man emphasizes, Julie is a Platonic Ideal that, were it to be realized on earth, would make all representation unnecessary (and would preclude as well the existence of real, complex women—but that is another topic).

De La Tour, that would-be real Julie, would of course have been a quite careful reader of Rousseau's prefaces to *La Nouvelle Héloïse*, but she conveniently overlooks the impossibility of the existence of a "real" Julie. Like de La Tour's letters, her resemblance to this paragon of virtue is to be manifestly true, and thus needs neither explanation nor proof. Rousseau, as always, is to the contrary willing to drop his idealism when he begins to find it burdensome, even in his preface. When N. points out that Julie's contagious ability to improve the morals of those around her contradicts Rousseau's previous observations as to female duplicity, R. wisely refuses to comment. "N: 'I am charmed to see you reconciled with women: I was upset that you forbid them to preach to us.' R: 'You press me, I must be silent: I am neither mad nor wise enough to be right. Let the critics chew on this bone.'" Providing the appropriate critical apparatus, or attractive bone, Rousseau then provides a reference for those readers insufficiently familiar with this aspect of his work: "See the *Lettre à M. d'Alembert sur le Théâtre*, p. 81, first edition" (*OC*, 2:25).

Rousseau's fundamental insistence on the truth-value of his letters, even when he fully admits that they are fictional, as in the account of the novel's origins in the *Confessions*, is ultimately as idiosyncratic as de La Tour's claim to embody Julie. To place Rousseau's relationship to fictional letters in context, I now briefly turn my attention to a different, equally complex prefatorial treatment of the real versus the fictional letter, the "Préface-Postface" to Diderot's *La Religieuse*.[23] This unusual piece exhibits the same convoluted homage to the power of the real missive letter present in the "Préface dialoguée," yet it admits, finally, of the superiority of fiction. Attributed to Frédéric-Melchior Grimm, and first published in his *Correspondance littéraire* (1770), the "Préface-Postface" relates the story of the "mystification" of the marquis de Croismare, the supposedly true episode that led to Diderot's novel. According to this narrative, *La Religieuse* began as a plot to lure the amiable Croismare back to Paris from his country retreat, where he was enjoying his sons and his garden, as well as succumbing to an unfortunate spell of religious fervor (he later recovered). By sending him pleading letters from a "desperate young woman," a nun who had escaped the convent and sought a position and a place to hide, Diderot hoped to appeal to his friend's soft heart and oblige him to return to the city to help the young girl. In addition to the admittedly fake letters of the young nun, composed by Diderot, we are given Croismare's actual, unwitting responses, in which he offers the nun a position in his household. Diderot then must kill her off, as there is no actual nun to send; the letter in which a "Mme Madin" describes the young girl's suffering is particularly bathetic. This exchange is intermixed with Grimm's commentary on the progress of the ruse, and on the gaiety of the band of philosophical friends in on the trick. We are assured of the authenticity of Croismare's letters, an assurance born of Diderot's suspicion that his friends were waging a counterconspiracy aimed at his own epistolary gullibility: "All of [Croismare's] letters are real and were written in good faith, a fact of which we had the most difficult time convincing M. Diderot, who believed himself mocked by the marquis and his friends."[24]

This statement makes it all the more striking that, when the question of the nature and value of missive letters is raised in this strange appendix, we are treated to an analysis not of Croismare's letters but rather of the imaginary nun's fake missives. We learn that when Diderot first showed his fellow conspirators his letters, the fake nun's pleas for help were declared too artfully written to be accepted as authentic by their recipient. Based on this reaction, Diderot reworked his missives into lesser examples of epistolary art that were, however, far more convincingly real. Turning to the readers of the *Correspondance littéraire*, Grimm then asks a *Question aux gens de lettres*: "Which are the good letters? Those that might have been admired? or those that would certainly have produced the illusion?" (the illusion, that is, of authenticity).

The select *gens de lettres* who received the *Correspondance littéraire* were more than capable of recognizing that this question was rhetorical. Diderot's epistolary tour de force obviously consisted of eliminating all traces of artful writing from the fake nun's letters, in order to produce letters that appeared to be those of a "real" nun. Like Rousseau, that is, Diderot succeeded in producing the type of writing declared impossible by N.: artless art of the highest order. Grimm seals the answer to his question by declaring of Diderot's initial and revised forays into epistolary deception that "if one had picked up the first in the street, one would have said: 'That is beautiful, very beautiful . . .' and if one had picked up the second, one would have said: 'That is quite true. . . .' "[25]

Once again, we are being treated to an implicit bow of respect to the true missive letter. Or is this only apparently the case? De La Tour's 1803 editors, and de La Tour herself, were counting on a corollary to Grimm's and Rousseau's prefaces. If the best fiction is composed of letters perceived to have been written exclusively for private consumption, then surely letters that were indeed written with only one, private recipient in mind must be considered superior to the epistolary novels that dominated the century's literary landscape. De Man's diagnosis seems borne out here: the prefaces to epistolary novels only *seem* to nod towards the power of the real missive letter, while undermining its claim to truth-value with clever rhetorical games.

I would argue, however, that our own preoccupation with authorial consciousness may be causing us to overemphasize the relative importance of the origins of such letters to the theorizing present in such prefaces as Rousseau's and Diderot's. Consider for example Grimm's imagined scenario of a passerby casually picking up a revealing letter. The need for this naive (even if only circumstantially naive) reader illustrates that the question at the heart of prefaces to epistolary novels is less an ideal of epistolary production than an ideal of reader response.[26] This response, in its most satisfactory and complete realization, takes place in two steps. We are indeed required to be convinced of the "truth" of the emotion present in what we are perusing, in order to be touched fully by the unveiling of another person's heart. But only a subsequent demystification allows us to appreciate this readerly experience, or to be more precise, allows us to appreciate the artfulness of the author who provided us with that primordial contact with another human being. Step one can be folded into step two when one's readers are adequately sophisticated, for, leaving aside Rousseau's nonexistent ideal peasant couple, it is far less important that fictional letters be accepted as "quite true" (*bien vraies*) than that they be unequivocally accepted as "quite true-seeming" (*bien vraisemblables*) by an informed audience of men of letters. So it is that Diderot is able to rely on a group of readers in on the ruse (his friends) for assurance that his second attempt at writing convincing letters by a young nun will successfully fool Croismare.

The necessity for epistolary illusion was born of an aesthetics that posited the superiority of truth over fiction, and then spun off in various sophisticated directions from that basic premise. All of which points to the reason why the facts behind the letters of that other famous epistolary nun, Mariane of Guilleragues's *Lettres portugaises,* were left in peace during the eighteenth century. No one journeyed to Portugal to decipher the records of "Mariane's" convent until the nineteenth century (at which point they were led astray; but that is another story). In eighteenth-century France, the claim that the Portuguese nun's letters were authentic, at its most disputed, was merely an interesting theoretical conundrum. Nor was any concerted effort made to demonstrate the existence or nonexistence of a "real" Julie, either by Rousseau's admirers or by his detractors. Considered in this light, Giguet's and Michaud's insistence that de La Tour's letters are of greater value than *La Nouvelle Héloïse* because the latter is fake quite misses the point about her status, in a manner consistent with the editors' propagandistic motives. As is clear in the "Préface dialoguée" to *La Nouvelle Héloïse* and the "Préface-Postface" to *La Religieuse,* only an expert writer could have produced letters from a "real" female fan worthy of comparison to Rousseau's novel. However much the editors' preface to the 1803 edition of the Rousseau–de La Tour exchange may have appealed to the "undisputed" superiority of the real over the fictional, eighteenth-century readers were not ultimately interested in the provenance of the epistolary production with which they were so often presented. Like the novel reader of any age, they wanted to be entertained, to be astonished, to enjoy a well-written work. As is so often the case with aesthetic treatises, the heightened value assigned the missive letter in the eighteenth century had little influence on the practice of the average eighteenth-century publisher or reader. When readers turned their attention to correspondences that they (really) believed to be real, they most often sought the sort of titillation Servan denounces—and that Giguet and Michaud implicitly promise by denigrating Rousseau's character as revealed in his letters to de La Tour. To paraphrase Servan, readers sought, to a great extent, the opportunity to catch a famous man with his guard down, inadvertently exposing his seamier side.

By 1850, at least in the work of one nineteenth-century theorist, Charles Augustin de Sainte-Beuve, this last factor in the publication of authors' correspondences is more explicitly acknowledged, albeit in high-toned critical terms. Sainte-Beuve begins his essay "Madame de La Tour-Franqueville et Jean-Jacques Rousseau" by echoing the 1803 editors' appreciation that the correspondence "is regular, that it forms a complete whole, that it was not meant for the public."[27] What is of most interest to him, however, is that these letters present the opportunity to glimpse "Jean-Jacques *au naturel,*" a phrase that might well have horrified Servan. Despite this declaration, Sainte-Beuve concentrates the bulk of his essay not on Rousseau but rather on de La Tour, in her role as his much-maligned female admirer. As his rhetoric quickly reveals, for Sainte-Beuve, Rousseau *au naturel* is not an entirely appealing sight; de La Tour *en négligé* is something else altogether.

The theoretical justification for this attention to de La Tour lies in Sainte-Beuve's literary-critical hypothesis that an author can be known by the qualities of his female fans.[28] De La Tour is important in that Sainte-Beuve is interested in, "dare I say, *Rousseau's women,* in the person of one of the most distinguished among them and certainly the most devoted" (63). This essay is one of a series in which Sainte-Beuve explores his hypothesis, indeed the first in that series, for in Sainte-Beuve's judgment de La Tour inaugurated (I would argue intentionally invented) the type of relationship with an author that he is studying. The "pale and touching" Mme de Beaumont may have worshipped Chateaubriand, we are told, "but it is Rousseau who starts this great revolution in France, and who brings women decidedly over to the side of literature . . . the enthusiasm of this sex for him was unprecedented." While including among Rousseau's female admirers such famous women writers as Mme de Staël and Mme Roland ("will they not soon figure in the forefront of the group I am calling Jean-Jacques's women?"), Sainte-Beuve declares of the obscure de La Tour: "She was the first, and she merits a special place in the fame of the man to whom she consecrated herself" (64–65).

In order to fit Sainte-Beuve's formula, women fans must be limpid mirrors that naively and thus accurately reflect the souls of the men they admire.[29] His account of the Rousseau–de La Tour correspondence thus shares with the preface to the 1803 edition a hagiographic image of de La Tour's devotion to Rousseau and an emphasis on the unimpeachably private quality of her letters. In emphasizing, again like Giguet and Michaud, how badly this devotee was treated by her idol, Sainte-Beuve dismisses Rousseau's early suspicion that de La Tour intended to publish their letters as "a bizarre eccentricity," symptomatic of a burgeoning mental breakdown. He accepts the validity of de La Tour's self-identification as Julie, and chastises Rousseau for his inability to embrace this concretization of his fictional ideal. Glossing over the sexualized game playing of the opening letters of the correspondence, he echoes Bernardoni's first letter by declaring de La Tour to be "Julie before her mistake" (66). In the final analysis, this Julie deserving of the name, who even published a *Letter* in defense of her unworthy hero ("it is the honor and the right of women to act blindly in such cases" [81]), is virtue personified for Sainte-Beuve.

Where Sainte-Beuve parts company with de La Tour's 1803 editors is in his assumptions as to the relative value of letters and literary works. The importance of these letters for Sainte-Beuve lies not in the reading experience they provide, but rather in their potential contribution to the peculiar variety of literary history he is practicing: the pursuit of psychological revelations about male authors through the examination of the character of their *admiratrices*. Among the more interesting pieces of evidence Sainte-Beuve presents in this essay is the manner in which de La Tour's faults mirror those of her hero. The most egregious of these flaws is her habit of proclaiming for herself the very virtues Sainte-Beuve would ascribe to her, a failing she is said to share with "all the women of the school of Rousseau." He is most offended by de La Tour's evidence as to the unique quality of her heart: "The testimony that she renders herself is just, and she certainly had a noble heart. But when one truly loves, with a passionate heart and not with a passionate head, does one think of elevating one's heart about *the common class* in order to distinguish it? Women who truly love, the Portuguese nun for example, did she think of that?" (72). In a fascinating replay of *La Religieuse*, Sainte-Beuve is fooled by the stylistic mastery of a male writer, Guilleragues, into accepting the letters of a fake nun as real. He was hardly alone in doing so; the *Lettres portugaises* would be accepted as "real" for another century. What interests me about Sainte-Beuve's evocation of the Portuguese nun is rather that de La Tour's actual letters, however carefully constructed, can only pale in comparison; the limits of her chosen genre—in particular the need to negotiate with a difficult, changeable correspondent—are nowhere as apparent as when her letters are set beside those of Rousseau's Julie, or Diderot's nun, or Guilleragues's Mariane.

Despite his reference to "women who truly love" (*les vraies amantes*), Sainte-Beuve stresses that he is not questioning the sincerity of de La Tour's devotion to Rousseau. For Sainte-Beuve, women letter writers are symptomatic of their time; their letters spontaneously reflect, rather than construct or influence, the style of the male literary greats of their era (yet another interesting take on the relationship between literature and letters). Just as the letters of the Portuguese nun supposedly mirror the exquisite taste of her period's culture, de La Tour's letters are said to have "absorbed" the stylistic flaws that mar Rousseau's writing: "[Her faults] are only the result of a lack of taste and delicacy, characteristic of the period and especially of the type exemplified by Rousseau" (68). By "lack of taste and delicacy," Sainte-Beuve refers, among other details, to the alacrity with which de La Tour and Bernardoni enter into a discussion of Rousseau's urinary problems. The question of coarseness of taste leads into a stylistic critique, as each of the three correspondents is taken to task for an imperfect subjunctive, an offense against the casual ideal of epistolary style. Bernardoni sins with *ignorassions*, Rousseau with *attribuassiez*, and de La Tour with "that horrific word, *consultassiez*" (68). Sainte-Beuve cries out for solace: "O the casual pens of Aïssé, Caylus, and Coulanges, where are you?" (69).[30]

There is an important seventeenth-century name absent from Sainte-Beuve's list of "casual pens" (*plumes négligentes*). The reason for this apparent neglect of Mme de Sévigné may be that her letters go so far beyond the "mere" casual elegance of her seventeenth-century peers, in Sainte-Beuve's estimation. In a different essay devoted exclusively to Sévigné, Sainte-Beuve describes the marquise as having produced writing worthy of the great creative geniuses of the French language: "She sows color with abandon, comparisons, images, wit, and feeling escape her from all sides. She thus placed herself, without wanting or suspecting it, in the first rank of writers of our language."[31] In insisting on the unintentional quality of Sévigné's literary production, Sainte-Beuve of course evokes the familiar myth of epistolary spontaneity, as well as the cliché of feminine epistolary genius. His method of valuing this genius, however, demonstrates a significant move away from eighteenth-century concerns. Just as he values de La Tour's letters primarily for the glimpses they offer into the psyche of a famous male writer, Sainte-Beuve declares the value of Sévigné's letters to be that they rise to the level of true works of literature.

Despite his unusual (by our standards) attention to letters, Sainte-Beuve ultimately judges these two women by criteria shared by his twentieth-century successors. Sévigné's letters go beyond, or rise above, their generic meanness, by virtue of their "literarity"; de La Tour's are, ultimately, and despite his attention to her as an *épistolière*, reduced to the status of data to be mined for information about Rousseau. It is above all in his urge to recuperate a genre on the brink of losing its cachet that Sainte-Beuve prefigures current critical attitudes toward the missive genre, as opposed to the eighteenth-century emphasis on the letter as valuable in and of itself. As mentioned in the introduction, de La Tour's letters might not always have suffered in comparison to Sévigné's, judged by a certain eighteenth-century perspective on literature and letters. Consider the following negative reading of Sévigné from 1785, the (epistolary) fictional context of which makes it all the more appropriate to this study. The detractor of Sévigné's letters is a pseudoeditor engaged in presenting some fictional letters to the public as real: Mlle Fontette de Sommery, author of *Lettres de Madame la comtesse de L*** à Monsieur le comte de R****. The letters are supposed to have been written between 1674 and 1680, at a time, that is, when the style of letters was "diametrically opposed to the easiness and naiveté of conversation," according to the *Encyclopédie*.[32]

Not so the missive letters of the comtesse de L***. As an ideal eighteenth-century fictional creation, she embodies the epistolary values of her author's time. In the (of course fake) "Editor's Notice,"

Sommery describes her heroine's letters as possessing "neither the lightness, nor the variety, nor the turns of phrase of those of Madame de Sévigné; but it is easy to perceive that Madame de Sévigné was writing for posterity and that Madame de L***, to the contrary, wrote unpretentiously, and surely never imagined that her letters would be saved."[33] As with N.'s analysis of *La Nouvelle Héloïse*, "turns of phrase" implies awareness of publication value. Like Julie's letters, like those of Diderot's fake nun, the letters of the comtesse de L*** are declared authentic precisely for what they are said to lack: the literary traits admired by Sainte-Beuve in Sévigné's letters.

In his study of Sommery's novel, Bernard Bray points out that the pseudoeditor's iconoclastic and "disrespectful" interpretation of Sévigné's motives is in the service of the novel's development.[34] He notes that Sommery undertakes a gentler devaluation of the divine marquise in her *Doutes sur différentes opinions reçues dans la société* (Doubts on Various Received Opinions in Society, 1782). In the portion of this work entitled "On Epistolary Style," Sommery begins by upholding an almost Platonic ideal of letter writing as "natural." Bray comments:

> The author offers much praise of this style, insisting above all on the diversity of uses and tones it is capable of carrying: it "is with no doubt the universal style," she writes, before allowing herself a brief comparative study of the epistolary classics. Mme de Sévigné's letters provide the model: they fulfill "most" of the desired conditions, and are "generally and . . . justly admired." It is by comparison to these letters that those of Mme de Maintenon, de Grignan, and de Coulanges will be judged, the last having "with many fewer points of merit than the former . . . that of being more agreeable, because more frank, simple, and full of feeling."[35]

In promoting Mme de Coulanges over Sévigné, Sommery appeals to the same qualities mentioned in Sainte-Beuve's analysis of these two famous women letter writers: the "casual pen" of the one, the stylistic mastery of the other. Sommery's and Sainte-Beuve's conclusions as to the value of the letters by these two *épistolières* are, of course, polar opposites. Mlle de Sommery rejects Sévigné's exaggerated effects, those very stylistic "excesses" that are recast by Sainte-Beuve as extraordinary "colors, comparisons, and images"—as literature, in a word.

Like Rousseau declaiming that he knows the *Lettres portugaises* to have been written by a man, Sommery's bold declaration that Sévigné wrote with publication in mind goes against the "received opinion" of her culture, in more ways than one.[36] Loudly proclaiming one way or the other as to the authenticity of letters was not in the style of the day. This reticence is present in the last text I will consider here, the 1786 *Mercure de France* review of the *Lettres de Madame la comtesse de L**** by Gabriel-Henri Gaillard. As a man, or rather a reader, true to his time, Gaillard plays with the implications of a letter writer's authorial consciousness, rather than feeling compelled to decide one way or the other. He is also not in the least bothered by allowing real and fictional letters to coexist in an ambiguous way. Gaillard first takes up and discusses Sommery's unequivocal judgment that Mme de Sévigné wrote for posterity: "This point may be contested but can also be defended. There is a great air of abandon in most of Mme de Sévigné's letters; but abandon can be imitated and used like everything else."[37]

We are in a sense back in Servan's boudoir, with Sévigné perhaps arranging her *négligé* in an effort to reflect the proper air of abandonment. Perhaps—because Gaillard is uncomfortable judging a woman's consciousness of making a fashion statement, when that woman lived some one hundred years ago. How are we to judge what is "natural" and what is "affected" in the writing of previous periods, he asks? Gaillard points out that the impeccably dressed young ladies of the days of Louis XIV would appear odd to their fashionable counterparts of 1786, just as their language would exhibit "marks of foreignness." Tastes in epistolary style change as quickly as tastes in clothing; Voiture, denigrated by 1786, was in his time "the oracle of good company and the Hero of Literature according to Boileau himself" (160). Sévigné's enduring popularity in this most conversational and thus ephemeral of genres testifies with certainty to only one thing, for Gaillard, her incontestable charm: "It is not a mediocre sign of the charm of Mme de Sévigné's letters that they have resisted the mobility of the genre" (161).

Having declared himself unable due to anachronism to answer the question of Sévigné's authorial consciousness, Gaillard displays a similar lack of decisiveness with regard to Sommery's novel. After considering the authenticity of these (supposedly seventeenth-century) letters, Gaillard declares it a question "we cannot and do not want to resolve" (162). The addition of "do not" is quite revealing; all that Gaillard will venture is that, authentic or fictional (*vraies ou supposées*), seventeenth- or eighteenth-century in origin, the letters of the comtesse de L*** "possess many great signs of truthfulness" (159). With his studied lack of conclusiveness, Gaillard keeps intact the paradox of eighteenth-century epistolary aesthetics; like Rousseau (or rather R.) reviewing his own letters, Gaillard will not, cannot, *does not want* to declare himself as to the authenticity of these letters. He will say, as did Grimm, that should these letters be inauthentic, they would possess all the more merit: "We cannot say whether they are authentic; we would hope that they are not, for they then would possess all the more value" (177). Like Grimm, Gaillard is pointing toward the notion that literary creation must, due to the artistry involved, be valued more highly than the "unskilled" letters of a seventeenth-century woman with little learning; but he does not, will not, make a definitive judgment as to authenticity.

In the following chapter, I explore de La Tour's fate when the verdict that literary creations are more valuable than nonliterary documents quite thoroughly triumphs over the coyness in Gaillard's review concerning authenticity and epistolary fiction. Deprived of the near-magical quality attributed to the missive letter in the eighteenth century, deprived as well of any redeeming literary qualities à la Sévigné, letters such as de La Tour's are now routinely considered the dross of the universe of the written word—admitted into consideration, unlike laundry or grocery lists, yet below such other "nonliterary" genres as the private journal. De La Tour does wring some praise from her twentieth-century critics, albeit for only one aspect of her letters: her unceasing devotion to Rousseau. This supposedly maniacal attachment to her favorite author has attracted the admiration of all of her readers, regardless of period; as literariness and Rousseau's reputation became increasingly established, however, the explanation of de La Tour's devotion has changed. By the late twentieth century, in contrast to Sainte-Beuve's analysis, she is admired not for her oh-so-feminine virtue in having stuck with a difficult or "mean" correspondent, but rather because she chose to admire an author of incontestable literary genius. Twentieth-century critics are quite immune to Sainte-Beuve's fascination with this woman's personality and admiration for her "virtue," just as Sainte-Beuve seems immune to the independent aesthetic value of her private missives. The standard opinion of de La Tour in the context of the current literary hierarchy is perhaps best summed up by Raymond Trousson's assessment of her in his biographical study of Rousseau: "She was a sentimental and disappointed woman who had married badly, at times acted a bit silly, and sustained a touching amorous friendship for the great man, without every letting herself be rebuffed by his harshness."[38]

4

Authenticity Devalued:
Contemporary Epistolary Theory

HENRY JAMES'S SHORT STORY "THE REAL THING" (1893) TEACHES THE
reader, along with the painter-narrator, that authentic artistic representation is best accomplished without reference to the real. When
an impoverished genteel couple comes to the painter's studio seeking to earn money by modeling, he at first mistakes them for custom-
ers in search of a portrait. Following the awkward exchange cited
above, he agrees to take on Major and Mrs. Monarch as models, for
their clearly visible social status seems to qualify them for certain
types, such as generals and queens. To the painter's surprise, his efforts to capture the couple's impeccably "real" social qualifications
in his book illustrations fall hopelessly flat. He soon returns to the
lower-class professional models he had previously used, pondering
the relationship between reality and representation all the while.

When James later turned to the question of the value of missive
letters, the relationship between the "real" and artistic value was
again in the forefront: "The best letters seem to me the most delightful of all written things and those that are not the best the most
negligible. If a correspondence, in other words, has not the real
charm, I wouldn't have it published even privately; if it has, on the
other hand, I would give it all the glory of the greatest literature."[1]
For James, the letter writer's lack of awareness of future publication
means that letters are written without artistic intent and are thus
likely to be the most negligible of written things; but, should a corre-

134

spondence by some happy miracle embody epistolary perfection, it is by virtue of the very unlikeness of this success worthy of elevation to the status of great—indeed of the *greatest*—literature. Publishing privately—showing one's letters to friends?—aside, it is clear that James retains an antique awe before the exceptional letter as spontaneous masterpiece, even as he feels compelled to "elevate" such a letter out of its lowly generic status by endowing it with literarity.

In this chapter, I consider the fate of the Rousseau–de La Tour correspondence as such vestiges of generic respect for the private letter disappear quite completely in the course of the twentieth century. Awe is quite entirely absent from current discussions of the genre; with few exceptions, correspondences are now considered publishable exclusively for the information they provide about famous authors or public figures. The production and the quality of collected correspondences has by no means decreased, but the scholarly effort and skill that editors currently exhibit in publishing an author's correspondence do not lessen the implied relationship between the writer's private letters and his or her literary works. The former are to be used as data for the study of the latter; it is the public, literary masterpieces alone that deserve praise and serious attention, not the private missives.

So it is that R. A. Leigh's *Correspondance complète de Jean-Jacques Rousseau* (fifty volumes, 1965–98), despite its status as a masterpiece of the genre of authors' correspondences, has the overall effect of demoting letters to and from Rousseau to the status of supporting data for critical analyses of his literary and philosophical works. The effect of this fall in value is quite striking in the case of the Rousseau–de La Tour letters. R. A. Leigh's assimilation of this exchange into the voluminous, chronologically ordered *Correspondance complète* separates the letters from each other, scattering them across many volumes. In the process, Leigh quite unintentionally destroys de La Tour's carefully constructed "work." More importantly, the genre to which this collection belongs separates the two parties of the exchange into "author" and "fan." Rather than preserving de La Tour's status as one of two correspondents, Leigh quite thoroughly strips her of any value unrelated to Rousseau's fame as a literary figure.

After considering Leigh's *Correspondance complète*, I explore how the status of de La Tour's letters changes once again when they are assigned increased heuristic value with the rise of reader-response criticism. De La Tour's long, expressive missives constitute a unique data source for Claude Labrosse's study of the reception of *La Nou-velle Héloïse*, but the resulting analysis, I argue, too easily assumes the transparency of de La Tour's letters, in the service of using them as raw data. I consider as well the first separate publication of the Rousseau–de La Tour exchange in 1998 by Georges May, an event that would seem to undermine my contention that these letters were devalued when subjected to the standards of twentieth-century epistolary aesthetics. However, in his editorial preface to *Jean-Jacques Rousseau/Madame de La Tour: Correspondance*, May's primary goal is to convince his readers, imagined as well-educated nonacademics, of the "unlikely" benefits of such an exchange. The readers May imagines for his edition of these letters clearly share the contemporary devalued view of private missives I am outlining here, and the manner in which May argues against this devaluation is also highly revealing of contemporary attitudes toward missive letters.

Until May's 1998 edition of the Rousseau–de La Tour exchange appeared, anyone interested in these letters had to skip from volume to volume of Leigh's *Correspondance complète de Jean-Jacques Rousseau*. The effort would have been rewarded by the thoroughness with which Leigh chronicled this exchange. In the heading to each of de La Tour's letters, we find her full legal name at that particular point in her life, followed by her maiden name ("Marie-Anne Alissan de La Tour, née Merlet de Foussomme," or "Marie-Anne de Franque-ville, née Merlet de Foussomme"). There are cross-references in the index to each volume of the correspondence, to aid the hapless researcher in finding all of the letters listed under de La Tour's evolving names. Leigh was equally concerned with precision and exhaustivity in reproducing de La Tour's letters; we are given the complete text of the autograph version, when extant, and the editorial notes give variants from the 1770 edited copy of the exchange made by de La Tour.

Leigh's presentation of de La Tour's letters is thus in keeping with the three principles guiding present-day editors of authors' correspondences, namely, exhaustivity, respect of chronological order, and faithfulness to the autograph.[2] The editorial criterion most pertinent to Leigh's treatment of de La Tour's letters is exhaustivity, for one has the definite impression that, had he not been obliged to take quite literally the *complète* of his title, these exceedingly minor missives would not have been included, at least not in full. Leigh may endow de La Tour's letters with all the considerable scholarly apparatus accorded to the letters of Rousseau himself, but if one looks more closely at his notes to de La Tour's missives, it becomes quickly apparent that Leigh considers them "the most negligible of written things." For him, de La Tour is no abandoned heroine in the Portuguese mode; she is merely an extremely bad letter writer and an excruciatingly annoying woman.

Consider the editorial note to the following stagy mid-letter pause in de La Tour's letter to Rousseau of September 20, 1764: "If you pleased me as the author of Julie, as author of *Emile* you must have enchanted me; and then, independently of your talents, and your new goodness toward me, what a crush of interesting things! The state of your health; that of your fortune; your departure, its circumstances; in a word, all the disgraces you paint so strikingly in your *Lettre à M. de Beaumont* . . . . They bring me a letter, it is from you, I recognize your writing . . . O my friend! my complaints cease." Leigh is hardly required, by editorial standards, to comment on the verisimilitude of the interruption scenario de La Tour describes in her letter. One senses that he is simply too annoyed to let the moment pass without comment, however "self-evident" the device may be: "This letter contains a rather tired literary artifice, perhaps in imitation of *La NH*. It is self-evident that Mme [de] La Tour was not interrupted at the moment that she was writing this text. It is evident that it was recopied, at one sitting, from a draft. And those thirteen suspension points that mark the interruption . . . That is a quite artificial spontaneity" (*CC*, n. to 21:3517).

While not moved to argue with Leigh's assessment of the lack of subtle artistry in de La Tour's letter, I would point out that imitation of *La Nouvelle Héloïse* is precisely the point. Her correspondent was meant to notice this similarity, to recognize her as the incarnation of Julie, and to feel himself a Saint-Preux come to life, as he had when receiving her portrait (letter of Oct. 16, 1763). De La Tour's allusions to *La Nouvelle Héloïse* aim to make these letters more publishable, more of interest to both Rousseau himself and to an eventual public. For Leigh, such "imitation" is damnable. Judged by the standards of a collected correspondence of a famous writer, it is artificial and thus reveals nothing of value; judged by creative, literary standards, it lacks originality.

Whether Leigh's attacks on de La Tour are excessively critical or not, the content of these notes is perfectly in keeping with his view that such documents are solely valuable as repositories of biographical, historical, or at the limit, psychological data linked to Rousseau.

Leigh is not concerned with readerly impressions and writerly sensibility; indeed, such sentimental indulgences seem to leave him impatient to get on with the serious work of his edition. Giguet and Michaud would never have called into question the intensity of de La Tour's "suffering"; nor would Sainte-Beuve have done so, despite his criticism of her style. Leigh does not hesitate. When she writes: "You know that your silence is painful to me, monsieur. . . . Furthermore, you have taught me to suffer; and I thank you: what knowledge could be of more frequent use to me," Leigh bitingly comments: "Really, Mme de La Tour was exaggerating. Well before meeting JJ, her conjugal life was a long calvary, especially for *a sensitive creature* like herself" (*CC*, 12:2027; my emphasis). Far from celebrating the occasion for intimate knowledge of the feelings of a paragon of womanly feeling, Leigh mocks de La Tour's rhetoric and insists on biographical verisimilitude.

One might justify Leigh's interventions by arguing that one of the greatest failings for the editor of an author's collected correspondence would be to misrepresent the letters he is preparing for the public. As Pierre Riberette comments: "A part of the task of the editor of correspondences, not to say the essential part of that task, can be summed up in two words: search and investigation. Seek out the raw document first; then inquire around and about it, in order to make it admit to everything it may be concealing."[3] This process of investigation includes, for Riberette, ferreting out the true nature of the relationship between the letter writers: "There is still one more area in which the discernment of the editor is put to the test: the nature of the relationship between the author and his correspondent. . . . The annotator's role is to clarify the nature of the relationship, at least implicitly, and from time to time to point out, under the conventionality of the language, a friendship about to form, a nascent romantic attachment, or else a passion about to die out."[4]

Leigh is thus well within his editorial rights, according to Riberette, in revealing that he views this particular correspondent of Rousseau as a parasite who attached herself to a famous author on tenuous emotional grounds. Nevertheless, I would argue that Leigh's attention to the style of de La Tour's letters goes too far to fit Riberette's notion of "clarification." Leigh at times seems merely annoyed at de La Tour, and these moments of annoyance often correspond, significantly, to the portions of her letters that I am citing as evidence of de La Tour's hidden intention to establish and maintain a publishable "private" correspondence with Rousseau. Her all-too-obvious allusions to *La Nouvelle Héloïse*, designed to flatter her correspondent and establish her credentials as a real-life Julie, are a case in point. Consider as well Leigh's note to a letter written early in the correspondence (Jan. 1763), in which he calls our attention to a passage de La Tour has quoted from a previous letter from Rousseau: "One remarks the precision, the pedantry even of her manner of quoting: the words that are not found in Rousseau's text are not underlined" (*CC*, n. to 15:2431). Similarly, in a note to a much later letter (Apr. 1771), Leigh writes: "Mme Alissan de La Tour's manuscript letters are meticulously corrected. One sees, in ms. I, a rather amusing example. She had first written 'à,' then crossed out the accent! Correction taken to this point is extremely rare in the eighteenth century" (*CC*, n. to 38:6857). We might ask: Rare in what circumstances? In personal letters? At the hands of the editor of a correspondence intended for publication? What I read as editorial meticulousness is characterized in Leigh's notes as a ridiculous obsession with detail inappropriate to a private letter, and thus illustrative of a perverse character. Rousseau also reacted to the overcorrectness of the letters, but he suspected the subterfuge of a "M. Julie," rather than a bizarre obsession with orthography. Like myself, Rousseau detected authorial desire when faced with such unusual care lavished on a private missive.

The force of Leigh's moralistic condemnation of de La Tour is most evident in his reaction to a plaintive missive written after she learned that Rousseau had been in Paris for some time without informing her of his presence. The very length of Leigh's note, given a generic model of concision, indicates the depth of his editorial feeling: "Nothing demonstrates better than this letter the annoying nature of this admirer of JJ. Instead of saying to herself that this poor refugee, exhausted by his continual displacements and even more by his moral suffering, did not know which way to turn and did not have the energy to inform everyone personally of his arrival in Paris, she invents complicated and specious reasons to explain his 'silence,' in order to have the pleasure of victoriously refuting them. Why did she not simply go and greet him?" (*CC*, n. to 28:4919). For Leigh, de La Tour is the very epitome of the *profanum vulgus* at whose hands the persecuted Jean-Jacques suffered. To a letter written much later, Leigh again appends a note expressing his annoyance with de la Tour and sympathy for Rousseau: "It was in part to avoid finding himself in such situations that JJ increasingly took refuge in the society of several less indiscreet intimate friends" (*CC*, n.

to 39:7019). Leigh sees Rousseau's rejection of de La Tour not as evidence of mental unbalance and meanness of sprit, as had his predecessors Giguet, Michaud, and Sainte-Beuve, but rather as an eminently reasonable response to quite unreasonable demands. Leigh makes only one truly positive remark about de La Tour. To her penultimate letter, which ends "I will always be what I am for you" (June 28, 1776), Leigh adds: "These are not vain words. After JJ's death, Mme de [La Tour-] Franqueville defended his memory in a series of polemical writings aimed at his detractors" (*CC*, n. to 40:7089).

The protective concern for Rousseau that Leigh admires in de La Tour's public letters as the *Amie de Jean-Jacques* is omnipresent in his own editorial asides. His criticisms of de La Tour may stem in great part from an admirable editorial devotion to the author whose epistolary life he is chronicling. As did Sainte-Beuve, Leigh misreads the intensity of de La Tour's published defenses of Rousseau as exclusively symptomatic of her passionate admiration and devotion to this great writer. The difference between the two assessments is important to note: Sainte-Beuve praises only the private letters; Leigh admires only the public missives. For Sainte-Beuve, de La Tour's private missives record the virtue of a woman who truly loved Rousseau, while her public missives are an unfortunate defense of an unworthy man ("it is the honor and the right of women to act blindly in such cases").[5] For Leigh, the private letters are pestering and badly written; the emotion they contain is often feigned. De La Tour's public letters, however, attack the detractors of a man who is clearly, for Leigh, worthy of such an act of devotion.

In moving from Sainte-Beuve to R. A. Leigh, by way of Henry James, we leave behind quite decidedly the assumption that both women and private letters are to be kept free from exposure in the public sphere (I am, again, referring to the obsessions of theoretical commentaries, rather than actual practice; just as letters were frequently shown to third-party readers in eighteenth-century France, it is hardly accepted today that one might publish the letters of others without permission). Just as commentators no longer feel called upon to praise the retiring virtue of women writers, public debates over the morality of publishing private letters, by men or women, have now all but disappeared, along with the letter's centrality to legal, social, literary, and other pursuits. Rather than focusing on the ethical question of publication, or the theoretical question of intention, efforts to define the private letter now generally begin with a base definition centered on the physical origins of the document. As Mireille Bossis formulated and answered this central question in 1986: "What is a letter in its simplest form? It is a message written by one individual to another individual who is far away . . . a substitute for direct speech, which distance has made impossible."[6]

The Rousseau–de La Tour letters exhibit all the formal markers of a private exchange, including postal marks and ruptured seals. In addition, the signatures "Rousseau" and "de La Tour" are those of two individuals whose historical existence is verifiable. Limiting the Rousseau–de La Tour letters to the strictly pragmatic function of overcoming distance raises immediate problems, however, for de La Tour chose the letter form not because insurmountable physical distance separated her from the author she wished to contact—she lived in Paris, Rousseau just outside of the city in Montmorency—but because a visit in person would have been too forward for any woman of her social status to undertake without an appropriate companion to introduce her. Such a visit would have been all the more unseemly on the part of a woman who was attempting to pass herself off as a second Julie. It is also more than likely that Rousseau would have refused to see de La Tour, even if she had been accompanied by a suitable male friend known to Rousseau himself. When a close acquaintance, Alexandre Deleyre, brought a woman friend to visit Rousseau without first asking permission, Rousseau became quite angry at the intrusion of a stranger into his life and house.[7] The barrier to face-to-face contact was thus not essentially geographical but rather social, and de La Tour's choice of the letter form indicates recourse to the written word for reasons other than strictly utilitarian. The stylized social function of such a letter is but a step away from the hypothetical ur-letter appealed to in the definition above, but the implied change in the rhetoric of self-presentation is fundamental.

Having established a basic definition of the missive letter, current discussions of epistolarity tend to move on to the question of when, if ever, this eminently pragmatic form of communication can or should be elevated to the status of literature. Yet while the question of literariness is central to current discussions of the genre, this quality is, interestingly enough, not equated with stylistic value at the present time. Instead, the decision as to whether or not a correspondence is "literary" depends on values such as scholarly usefulness or the historical interest of the correspondence. (Yet another reason for publishing has remained essentially unchanged since the eighteenth century: public interest in the intimate lives of famous persons; but this rather base consideration is absent from critical discussions of the genre, as it was generally absent in the eighteenth century, Servan excepted.)

In one of the most interesting treatments of the topic of literarity and letters, "On the Renewal of the Study of Literary Correspondences: The Example of Flaubert" (1991), Claudine Gothot-Mersch addresses the question of the literary value of letters by identifying two distinctly different potential uses of authors' correspondences. She argues that while authors' letters can serve simply as documentary evidence, aiding the scholar in studying the writer and his works, such letters can also rise above their epistolary status to become themselves the objects of textual analysis. Quite unlike James, however, Gothot-Mersch is not fetishizing the letter as an object worthy in itself of such concentrated attention. Either use of authors' letters that she identifies—as documentary evidence or as objects of textual analysis—relies on the unspoken assumption that letters provide insight into an author's nonepistolary oeuvre. It is also important to note that a correspondence does not, for Gothot-Mersch, constitute a "work" worthy as a whole of analysis, for it lacks an organizing principle (*projet d'ensemble*). In turning her attention to the textual analysis of authors' correspondences, she is interested instead only in those few select passages worthy of elevation to the status of literature—only those passages in which Flaubert "makes literature" (*fait de la littérature*). While for James, writing in 1899, an entire letter might miraculously achieve literary status, for Gothot-Mersch only certain passages of letters by an otherwise established author may be rescued from epistolary obscurity and "recuperated" as literature. Even then, such passages are not actually to be appreciated in and of themselves; for Gothot-Mersch, their value lies in their status as a "laboratory of the work." They are to serve as a sort of palimpsest for critics interested in the origins of a literary masterpiece.

Vincent Kaufmann's *L'Equivoque épistolaire* (1990) is a book-length example of the use of recuperated passages. Kaufmann is interested in the psychological value of this literature-making technique; after examining the correspondences of such authors as Proust, Kafka, and Flaubert, he concludes: "For some writers, epistolary practice is, independent of its eventual aesthetic value, an obligatory passage, a privileged means to gain access to a work." Kaufmann connects the renewal of interest in private letters to the rebirth of the traditional author, declaring that the letter may be "the literary yeti," the famous missing link between "the man and his work."[8]

Several capital distinctions aside, Kaufmann calls to mind Sainte-Beuve, who in justifying the morality of publishing the letters of the young Manon Phlipon (later Mme Roland), remarks: "It must however be said, that publishing her letters in their entirety was not a complete betrayal of the young girl who wrote them; in more than one passage it is clear that she is thinking of the use to which one might put them. One catches a glimpse of the author."[9] Sainte-Beuve points to Manon's self-conscious reference to the letters of Mme de Sévigné, and to her great concern that her convent friend Sophie Cannet preserve the letters she receives. But Kaufmann cannot, as does Sainte-Beuve, assume that the publication of private letters has a distinct value in and of itself—thus the "ambiguous" nature of the epistolary genre. Kaufmann delineates the relationship between the two spheres, the "real" and the literary, by metaphorically splitting the writer's life into two countries divided by a border. On the one side is time devoted to living; on the other, time devoted to writing. Letters become, in this geographical trope, liminal objects: nonliterary, although written, documents. An author's correspondence, by this analysis, represents a unique phenomenon of "transfusion" or "osmosis" between these two separate spheres. In the case of a famous writer, rather than labeling some letters "literature" and others "trivial," Kaufmann would leave authors' letters in "a sort of featureless terrain," an enigmatic zone in which "life at times passes into the work, and vice versa."[10]

Kaufmann's treatment of the letters exchanged between Flaubert and Louise Colet is particularly relevant to my study, for he views Colet as a would-be transgressor of borders. Colet was allowed into Flaubert's physical life as a lover, and into the no-man's-land of his letters as a correspondent, but she was cut off from the protected zone of his true literary production. Kaufmann views Flaubert's correspondence with Colet as a necessary technical aid in the composition of his novel; in his letters to his lover, whom he was deliberately keeping at a physical distance, Flaubert allowed himself to wander in "the empty epistolary landscape" as an aid to ridding himself of the "art of personality." Kaufmann notes that for Flaubert, letters were the emblem par excellence of the intrusion of authorial voice into writing, a voice epitomized by eighteenth-century authors such as Voltaire, capable, in Flaubert's opinion, of writing beautiful letters, but little else of value.

Kaufmann supports his argument concerning *Madame Bovary* and Louise Colet by pointing out that, once the novel was well under way, Flaubert broke off the relationship. Sainte-Beuve similarly notes that Mlle Cannet was dropped as an epistolary confidante when Manon Phlipon fully entered the public world through her marriage to Jean-Marie Roland. The role of the correspondent of the working author, in other words, is often far from rewarding. Judged by the standards of Gothot-Mersch and Kaufmann, it can be quite entirely devoid of value, if an author's authorial concerns do not bleed adequately into his letters. Judged by this criterion, Rousseau's refusal to answer de La Tour's many questions concerning his work and his habits damned her to a far less interesting role than that of Colet. As a result, Leigh's presentation of de La Tour mirrors not Kaufmann's study of Colet, but rather Gothot-Mersch's condescending smile when she briefly considers Flaubert's correspondence with his niece, Caroline Commanville. These letters include neither literary experimentation nor useful biographical information, and Commanville's decision to publish them in a separate edition is for Gothot-Mersch rather laughable. She does allow, however, that Flaubert's niece may have been motivated by something other than the mere desire to see her name in print: "We smile to see Caroline Commanville publish separately the letters that she received from her uncle; but the case is not unique, and may be the result of reasons other than vanity."[11] These "other reasons" are not developed; perhaps pride in her uncle? In any case, I would argue that the reference to "vanity" might be better expressed as "the desire to see her own name in print."Like Caroline Commanville's letters to her uncle, de La Tour's letters to Rousseau represent what might be called a zero-degree literariness of the sort that Gothot-Mersch outlines in her study. While it is true that de La Tour's letters provide some biographical information about an individual whose status as a literary figure is indisputable, they do not focus on the ongoing creation of his literary and philosophical works. The publication of such letters now requires prefatory justification, even when composed by the writer himself, as we see in the case of Guilleragues's *Correspondance* of 1976. The editors, Frédéric Deloffre and Jacques Rougeot, had already elevated Guilleragues to the status of author by their hotly contested claim that he was the man behind the *Lettres portugaises*.[12] In the interest of cultivating Guilleragues studies, they went on to publish his letters, for as they point out in their foreword to the correspondence, these documents had previously been scattered through various "public depositories the details of which will be given for each letter." Unfortunately for the future of Guilleragues studies, Deloffre and Rougeot are compelled to excuse the official and rather pedestrian nature of the extant letters. They nevertheless justify their publication by arguing that even in these unlikely documents, the reader discovers support for Guilleragues's disputed status as an author: "All these letters share a common character, an admirable style: appropriate, sustained, harmonious. However, the main interest of this correspondence lies in providing a moral portrait that, as much in the humorous asides as in the sad sensibility, corresponds well to what one might expect from the author of the *Lettres portugaises*."[13]

One interesting lacuna in Gothot-Mersch's and most other theoretical studies of authors' correspondences is that of a truly rara avis, from which Caroline Commanville's and de La Tour's exchanges with famous men could not be more distant: a correspondence elevated to the status of literature for internal considerations alone. Such a work qualifies as literary not in parts but as a whole. Some correspondences come close, without quite qualifying, such as the exchange between Flaubert and George Sand. Both participants are well established as literary greats, and they frequently discuss their creative projects in their letters. Yet even Sand's and Flaubert's letters pale in comparison to those at the top of the scale of epistolary literariness: those of the ever-exemplary Mme de Sévigné. The connection of Sévigné's letters to literature is not peripheral but central. Her letters are elevated out of their normal generic lowliness to the stature of literary texts exclusively by virtue of style, and it is her letters alone that bestow upon her the title "author."

As I explored in my introduction, this exceptional status has made Sévigné's authorial consciousness the subject of an unusual debate, unusual, that is, by our contemporary standards. Where other correspondences are concerned, the relation to literature is assumed to be absent, and the question of authorial consciousness thus moot. It follows implicitly that for letters in general, the idea that the writer might have been consciously striving to write in an elevated style (the only style associated with "authorial consciousness" in our own time) is generally deemed an absurdity.

The total absence of authorial consciousness in letter writers not already established as authors is assumed in Marie-Claire Grassi's study *The Art of the Letter at the Time of* La Nouvelle Héloïse *and Romanticism* (1994). Grassi's approach is quite unusual in that she turns her attention to the style of letters by "nonauthors," a term of my own invention that conveniently sums up the type of letter writer on whom Grassi focuses. In order to purify her corpus of potential contamination by a letter writer who might occasionally "make literature," Grassi excludes from her field of reference the missive letters of established writers such as Voltaire, Rousseau, Flaubert, Proust, and Sartre (her list). The tight rapport between "the writer, the work, and the correspondence" that Gothot-Mersch and Kaufmann have studied is declared by Grassi to constitute a barrier to the study of "a general epistolary comportment."

Michel de Servan makes use of a similar assumption in his "Réflexions sur la publication des lettres de Rousseau" of 1783, although, significantly, the question of the literariness of letters by authors versus nonauthors was not at issue for Servan. His concern is rather with the letter writer's consciousness of potential third-party readers, as well as with whether or not these readers can assume that any particular letter reflects the true thoughts and beliefs of its writer, famous or obscure. Grassi's concerns could hardly be more different in spirit from Servan's; consciousness of future publication or of potential third-party readers is simply not an issue for her, even when established authors are writing letters. Instead, much like Gothot-Mersch and Kaufmann, Grassi assumes an inevitable stylistic bleeding between the public prose of an author and his private letters. For Grassi, a private letter by an author is always a potential laboratory for developing future written production worthy of publication. Grassi's reasons for excluding such letters from her study of epistolary practice in the eighteenth century are complex, but she ultimately bases her decision on matters of style, not authorial consciousness.

Considered from the point of view of Grassi's theoretical precepts, Rousseau's globalizing artistic consciousness excludes his letters to de La Tour, or to any correspondent, from clear classification as one of the two "great types of letters" she establishes: real and fictional. As in Kaufmann's analysis, Rousseau's letters would for Grassi exist in a no-man's-land between the real and the fictional. Understood in this way, letters by Rousseau written before his famous novel was published might well be useful for a study of *La Nouvelle Héloïse*, for the study of fictional letters is in Grassi's frame of reference a matter of tracing a trajectory that moves from the real to the incontestably literary. Such a process constitutes a "retracing of the itinerary of the transposition that leads from reality to fiction."[14] Grassi does not pursue such concerns, in contrast to Gothot-Mersch and Kaufmann, for again, her chosen field of study is those letters she deems incontestably "real," the missives of those "unknown to history." Letters by these "unknowns" meet two criteria, the second guaranteed by the first: obscurity, and lack of literariness.

The originality of Grassi's study lies in considering the rhetoric of a genre that I have quite purposely neglected in the course of my consideration of de La Tour. It is, however, the genre to which de La Tour's letters have been assigned since their first publication: authentically real letters by obscure persons written with no thought of publication in mind. Such letters offer in Grassi's opinion a uniquely pure data source: "The real letter remains without doubt a privileged locus for seizing, unmediated, a thousand intimate expressions at the heart of a privatization of social space."[15] In studying such letters, Grassi concentrates on thematic organization, rhetorical structure, level of language, level of intimacy, etiquette, and other revelatory aspects of letters the assumed stylistic "purity" of which guarantees the quality of their testimony concerning the privatization of social space in the eighteenth century.

None of the commentators just discussed (Bossis, Gothot-Mersch, Kaufmann, Grassi) consider the possibility that the letter writers they are studying might have imagined the future publication of their missives—even letter writers as famous as Flaubert. One of my purposes in this study, as mentioned in the introduction, is to address this lacuna in current considerations of eighteenth-century missive letters. Rousseau's awareness of the publication potential of his letters, as I have explored, makes him highly conscious of those moments in his letters when he "makes literature," in Gothot-Mersch's terms. He often seems to be playing the role of the "famous author writing private letters," particularly when he first writes to de La Tour as Julie: "Excuse me this moment of enthusiasm. You are beyond praise; praise profanes true merit, and I promise that you will never receive it from me" (Nov. 24, 1761). He clearly has posterity in mind when he imagines that de La Tour will one day be known to the public as his faithful *Amie,* after she defends him during the Hume affair. At such moments, it seems as if Rousseau is imagining the publication of his exchange with de La Tour as part of a greater posthumous self-defense. Nevertheless, Rousseau never wavers in one aspect of his responses to de La Tour: he refuses to discuss his literary works with her, choosing not to respond, for example, to her question as to why Julie tells Saint-Preux that were she free to choose, she would still marry Wolmar (letter of May 6, 1764). He responds positively to her letters only when she limits herself to the subject of her admiration and love for him.

Flaubert and Sand, certainly conscious of the possibility that their letters might one day be published, were willing to use the vehicle of their correspondence to discuss their creative work; Rousseau, significantly, was not willing to do so with de La Tour. He at times made the prohibition against discussing his works quite explicit. In 1762, after reading *Emile,* de La Tour remarks that she will need to move beyond the blinding effect of Rousseau's prose before she can judge the work's content: "I will reread it until, the charm of the style having lost some of its power over my mind, I am able to declare that it is truly the things themselves that attract me. You write so well that there is no illusion that you are incapable of creating" (Sept. 16, 1762). Rousseau forcefully stanches any such future commentary as to the content of his work: "As for my book, you will judge it as you wish, you know that I have always separated the author from the man." She is quite free, however, to express her feelings for Rousseau "the man," as he makes clear soon after: "Whoever is not passionate about me is unworthy of me" (Sept. 26, 1762).[16]

Rousseau might have seized the occasion of his exchange with de La Tour to engage in the justification of his often-disparaged works, but he did not. Just as Rousseau is exquisitely aware of the publication value of his private letters, he exhibits a typically eighteenth-century sensitivity to the division between missive letters and works written expressly for publication. These two considerations might, again, appear contradictory to our sensibilities, yet as discussed in chapter 3, they in fact went hand in hand in the eighteenth century. As a "man," Rousseau writes letters; as an "author," he writes for the public. Rousseau insists on this separation early on in the exchange, when he establishes his theory of private epistolary commerce. When writing letters, he will write only when he wants to do so, and will take the tone of the moment rather than worrying about his correspondent's feelings: "I am not polite, madame; I feel in my heart sufficient reason to allow myself not to be." He then tells de La Tour that he forces himself to write politely and with care only when addressing the public. An author's character is to be judged by his words; a man's words are to be judged by his character:

Furthermore, I write with great difficulty when I want to cultivate my style: I am fed up with the profession of author, the restraint that it imposes is one of the reasons that make me renounce it. By trouble and care I can finally find the appropriate turn of phrase and the right word; but I wish to put neither trouble nor care into my letters, I seek in letters a respite from being incessantly in the public eye, and when I write with pleasure, I want to write at my ease. If I write neither what or how one should, what does it matter? Do I not know that my friends will always understand me, that they will interpret my words by my character, not my character by my words? (Nov. 10, 1761)

In addition to refusing to "make literature" in his letters to de La Tour, Rousseau resists her efforts to entice him into Sévigné-like discussions of the goings-on in Paris. In a letter of 1764, for example, she drops a clever reference to the posthumous reputation of the *amie* of another famous man, Louis XV: "It has been so horrible this last month, that Mme de Pompadour must have quit this life with less regret. She demonstrated in her last moments that her soul was a mixture of force and weakness: a combination that will never surprise me in a woman. I am not surprised, furthermore, to see her as generally regretted as she had been generally despised or hated" (May 6, 1764). Such gossip evokes no response from Rousseau, nor is de La Tour successful in eliciting from him the type of detailed commentary on his day-to-day life and habits that would later ensure the publication value of Balzac's letters to Mme Hanska (the lesser of the two potentially "literary" attributes of private letters, according to Gothot-Mersch). In a statement that clearly invites Rousseau to do what it asks him not to do, de La Tour declares at one point that she will stop insisting in her letters that Rousseau enter into a discussion of his health, his pleasures, his way of life—"although I desire passionately to see you enter into some details" (Mar. 10, 1764). That she sought to increase the interest of their exchange by enticing Rousseau into discussions of his work, or of the day's great events, illustrates that the lessons of Mme de Sévigné's eighteenth-century fame were not lost on de La Tour. Unfortunately, her correspondent was uncooperative; his only lasting interest in maintaining the correspondence was to hear her proclaim her passionate response to himself, as a man.

When the advent of reader-response criticism brought a new set of theoretical givens to bear on letters in general, and on de La Tour's letters in particular, this focus on Rousseau paid great dividends. In *Lire au XVIIIe siècle: La Nouvelle Héloïse et ses lecteurs* (1982), Claude Labrosse treats de La Tour's letters as important documents, indeed as the most important documents, available on his subject. In order to use her letters as he wishes to do so, however, Labrosse must view de La Tour as a writer completely devoid of craft and quite unconscious of the publication value of her letters. Labrosse's reader-response approach is based on the assumption that de La Tour's letters provide unfiltered data for a study of a fictional masterpiece. His introduction points out that the assumed transparency of the act of reading has long allowed it to escape analysis; I will argue that Labrosse makes a similar, mistaken assumption concerning the assumed transparency of de La Tour's letters to Rousseau—an assumption shared, moreover, by all of her commentators.

Labrosse argues convincingly that the importance of Rousseau's novel to literary history, along with the many intense reactions it evoked among his contemporaries, makes this work "an original and exceptional case of reading . . . an ideal testing ground for an exploration of novel reading."[17] In exploring this fertile ground, Labrosse considers an impressive array of documents, including prints of key scenes in the novel, Rousseau's own commentaries, and published attacks on the work. His major focus, however, is the detailed analysis of readers' letters, which allows him to develop a complex theory of the eighteenth-century reading experience. Labrosse imagines a general eighteenth-century reader who "enters into" a fictional universe in a manner far more profound than Proust's celebrated description of loss of self and sense of place in the moment of reading. Labrosse's process involves three steps. Reading, the first step, is followed by a postreading reverie based on images born of the reading experience. The third step is the instantiation of the desire to enter into the reading experience; in other words, the reader is moved to draw or to write. As Labrosse indicates by referring to the product of this act as *parole*, this process is not creative in any true sense. The reader's specific "utterance" is generated by a general linguistic system: the work that he or she has just read.

Labrosse gives us an example of a normal experience of this eighteenth-century process by citing a letter from 1778 by Manon Phlipon, the future Mme Roland, who is a recurrent figure in my own study, both for her extensive and well-known correspondence, and for her fascination with Rousseau. In a letter written, once again, to her childhood friend Sophie Cannet, Manon describes a delicious reverie into which she had fallen, *La Nouvelle Héloïse* in hand, tears flowing. She had been reading a passage in the novel about music, and had suddenly heard strains of actual music rising up from the street. As the music and thus the effect dissipated, she writes: "I wanted to take up my reading again, my father arrived, we ate dinner" (107; her letter is, I assume, the *parole* generated by this experience).

The return from soaring reverie to the table, from the ethereal to the *terre-à-terre*, is in Labrosse's view blocked in a person such as de La Tour, or "Marie-Anne," as he generally refers to her. She instead falls victim to a malady to which only such exceptionally susceptible readers as herself are vulnerable: "Trapped by the fantasy that inhabits and hypnotizes her by means of fiction, her words remain alienated and embody previous texts" (105). This unusually intense response merits Rousseau's most devoted reader an entire subchapter to herself, entitled "Essai d'analyse d'un comportement imaginaire" (Attempt at the Analysis of an Imaginary Comportment). De La Tour is unable, in Labrosses's analysis, to grasp the true nature of literature/language. He proposes that readers such as de La Tour are not content with a sign composed merely of signifier and signified, not content, that is, to allow their immersion in the world of the novel to remain in the two-dimensional realm of the imaginary. Such readers need a referent, a visible manifestation of their experience. De La Tour needs to believe that she embodies Julie, and that Rousseau is her Saint-Preux: "By pushing J.J. to identify with Saint-Preux, by establishing a confusion between the letter novel and the correspondence she is engaged in, Marie-Anne falls, drifting with neither end nor object, toward the unreal and the impossible. . . . Fiction can dissolve and absorb the image of men and women and inspire in them a destructive anguish" (117).

Diagnosing the source of this aberrant reaction to fiction, Labrosse declares that de La Tour's letters testify to a near-psychotic need to escape her own living situation. More specifically, he attributes de La Tour's refusal to abandon her imaginary comportment as Julie to her intolerably bad marriage. Labrosse is far from alone in diagnosing de La Tour as a frustrated, failed wife who sought escape through a relationship with a famous man. Raymond Trousson, despite his apparent pity for "Marianne," as he refers to her, describes her relationship to Rousseau in a similar fashion: "Rousseau participates halfheartedly, refuses to accept the conflation of the epistolary novel and a correspondence, while Marianne attempts to take on a chimerical identity for him. . . . This disappointed and frustrated woman dreamed of living a dream."[18] As quoted above, R. A. Leigh mockingly refers to de La Tour's marital problems ("Her conjugal

life was a long calvary, especially for *a sensitive creature* like herself"
[*CC*, 12:2027]).

These interpretations are all the more striking in that we possess
very few details as to exactly how "intolerable" or "frustrating" de
La Tour's married life may have been. It is known that Jean-Baptiste
de La Tour lost a lucrative position due to his irresponsibility; that
at the time of her first letter to Rousseau, de La Tour had been living
apart from her husband for several years; and that she abandoned
his name in 1774.[19] To move from these few facts to the hypothesis
that the crumbling of her marriage unhinged her mind is quite a
leap. Like Trousson and Leigh, Labrosse assumes an insight into de
La Tour's psyche that goes far beyond my own attempts to establish
evidence of her authorial consciousness. Labrosse stands out among
his fellow commentators, however, in declaring that de La Tour's
letters represent a psychotic version of the inevitable step three in
the process he has described as common to all eighteenth-century
readers.

De La Tour's extraordinary fifteen-year persistence in claiming
the right to identify with Julie would indeed qualify, according to
this model, as evidence of mental instability; but the complexity of
the missive letter's status at this period in history precludes, in my
opinion, Labrosse's psychogenic conclusion. There is, first of all, a
recipient to be kept in mind; de La Tour was not simply writing in a
private journal. The need to negotiate with and appease Rousseau at
every turn hardly fits the drifting image of de La Tour that Labrosse
creates. Nor does the presence of a third party, for Bernardoni was
an active participant in the early letters of the exchange, those of
most interest to Labrosse. In addition, the compositional care taken
in producing these letters, as remarked by Leigh, eliminates the type
of automatic writing generated by a psychotic reverie that Labrosse
is proposing.

The seriousness with which Labrosse studies de La Tour is beyond
doubt more flattering than Leigh's dismissal of her as an annoyingly
persistent woman who wrote bad letters, yet in the end Labrosse is
interested in de La Tour's exchange with Rousseau only as an exem-
plarily pitiable case history from the annals of reader response. He
qualitatively separates her from the other readers he analyzes, accepting her rhetoric at face value. He must do so, in order to remain
faithful to his own interpretative assumptions, for at the heart of Labrosse's study is the extraction of the letter-writing individual from
the process of writing a letter. Readerly practice is merely praxis, the

automatic result of an unconsciously internalized system of response. Readers' letters are, in other words, culturally determined artifacts, and thus readable as a pure database: "Making a text speak is the act of the subjects, agents, and actors who put it into words or discourse. These subjects are not individual names or periodical titles. Behind each of these names and constituting it are mechanisms, machines, institutions" (21). This method of reading letters from novel readers to authors in the eighteenth century may produce rich insights, as is the case in Labrosse's study overall, but it ignores the extent to which the eighteenth-century epistolary novel lent itself to conscious game playing and simulation on the part of both authors and readers (Samuel Richardson being the obvious point of comparison).[20]

Labrosse gives an engaging psychological analysis of Rousseau's possible motivations for continuing a correspondence he insisted many times was of no interest to him, although again the analysis is marked by a romantic transfiguration of de La Tour: "She reactivates and attempts to carry out the myth of Pygmalion. Like a siren out of fictional seas, she attempts to lure J.J., who hesitates on the shore, at times skeptical, at times fascinated by this singular colloquy with his own chimera, or double" (117). It is the "or" that stands out in this last image, for me, in that it indicates that de La Tour is not simply a chimera, the heroine of a novel imagined into "life" by Rousseau. She plays an active, creative role in making herself into Julie, "doubling" his role as author. Like her other commentators, Labrosse takes de La Tour's rhetoric of feminine inadequacy far too literally, for it is de La Tour who reactivates the myth of Pygmalion, who doubles Rousseau's role in creating Julie. She cannot do so explicitly; de La Tour knew that by Rousseau's rules of real-life epistolary order, a woman was allowed to play Galatea, and only Galatea. She could be an object, but not a subject; she could not make any overt reference to her letters as the creation of a creator, however proud she might be of her success.

Labrosse misses the creative aspect of de La Tour's letters because he views them as merely the *parole* of a linguistic system. If her letter writing cannot constitute a unique "work" in its own right, de La Tour's self-presentation as a Julie come-to-life must be diagnosed as the search for an impossible ontological transformation: "The experience that might lead a young woman to claim a literary existence for herself is beyond imagining" (116). Perhaps unsurprisingly, Labrosse ultimately comes to speak of his "Marie-Anne" as a fictional character: "We see here the need and the process expressed in fiction by certain fundamental characters such as Don Quixote and Emma Bovary" (116). Along with her male and female fictional counterparts, de La Tour would seem to have read one novel too many—in her case, of course, *La Nouvelle Héloïse.*

Emma Bovary is nevertheless highly pertinent to de La Tour's case. In "For a Restricted Thematics: Writing, Speech, and Difference in *Madame Bovary,*" Naomi Schor reads Flaubert's masterpiece as the story of the self-fictionalization as a woman of a male author coming (abortively) to writing. For Schor, Flaubert's famous "Mme Bovary, c'est moi" reflects that his novel constitutes a portrait of Emma as writer. Schor emphasizes Emma's desire to become the heroine of the books she reads, a painful yearning that mirrors Labrosse's description of de La Tour. Schor connects this unfulfillable wish to the moment when Emma acquires the tools of a writer—that is, a *letter-writer's* tools, bought by Emma as she begins her affair with Rodolphe: "Imbued with eighteenth-century literature, Emma cannot conceive of a literary production other than a novel by letters, and the taking of a lover is the necessary condition for this form of writing. Once she becomes Rodolphe's mistress, Emma begins her epistolary novel."[21]

What is missing in Flaubert's masterpiece to support a vision of Emma as novelist is any burning desire on her part for fame *as a writer.* Whatever her relationship to Flaubert's self-conception as an author, I would argue that, as a character, Emma does not want to write a novel, she wants to *be* a character in a novel—an eighteenth-century epistolary novel. It is the mistaken assumption of an identical naive mimetic desire in de La Tour that makes her such a pathetic creature, in Labrosse's interpretation. Emma is a fictional character whose words are circumscribed by the linguistic entity in which she "lives." She quite fully and restrictedly inhabits certain literary clichés of her time. De La Tour, to the contrary, was a flesh-and-blood woman who wrote *through* similar clichés by assuming the signature of a fictional character. She manipulated literary stereotypes to attain eventual publication.

The reception history of de La Tour's letters since their first publication in 1803 demonstrates the vicissitudes attendant upon a real woman's efforts to attain the status of author by manipulating a fictional paradigm. The latest evidence that de La Tour succeeded in creating an enduring, publishable "work" despite such obstacles is an edited volume of her letters with Rousseau published by one of the great names in eighteenth-century studies, the late Georges May. I have been citing this edition all along, and my tour of the reception history of de La Tour's letters over the last two hundred years ends with a short consideration of May's preface to his *Jean-Jacques Rousseau/Madame de La Tour: Correspondance* (1998). It is significant that, unlike Leigh and the editors of Guilleragues's letters, May does not adhere scrupulously to the editorial dogma prescribed for authors' correspondences. He follows Leigh's text of the letters based on the original autographs, but only to a point. While Leigh transcribes the original handwritten documents in all their grammatical and orthographic irregularity, May chooses to modernize the letters. This modernization illustrates that his volume belongs to a quite different theoretical paradigm of published letters, for he is not reproducing these letters exclusively for specialists. The readers implied in his preface are members of a more general, however highly educated, public.

Also in sharp contrast to Leigh, the de La Tour one recreates from May's notes to her letters is an intelligent eighteenth-century woman capable of appreciating a well-written novel. Rather than ascribing to her a near-psychotic obsession with Rousseau, as do Leigh and Labrosse, May diagnoses a more admirable, and fairly common, need to console the author of a work she admires: "What causes the slippage from admiration of the work to adulation of the author is the impression or certitude that he has described himself in his work, that he is the victim of a passionate love, a love in reality either unhappy or unfulfilled, a belief that would not fail to awaken in some of his readers the need to console, or even to compensate."[22] For May, de La Tour quickly distinguishes herself from Rousseau's many other admirers by her *délicatesse*, a quality for which Rousseau himself admired her letters, it will be remembered: "[Marianne] quickly distinguishes herself by the sincerity of her emotions, as well as by the delicacy of her manner, the quality of her style, and what was called at the time the beauty of her soul" (9). May proposes that without the strong-handed action of her friend, de La Tour would have contented herself with merely worshiping from afar. He then asks, and answers, the key question: "What would we have lost? The answer will vary with the reader" (11).

May's list of possible reader responses to his question begins, predictably, with the value of the information to be gleaned from the fifty or so letters Rousseau contributed to this exchange. Rousseau's reasonableness in dealing with de La Tour's oversize devotion belies, for May, his popular reputation as a nasty, somewhat insane man. At the same time, May imagines that many readers, both male and female, will admire de La Tour for her refusal to allow Rousseau to discourage her in her quest to live out the existence of an ideal, caring female fan: "[Readers] will also enjoy getting to know a woman who is visibly wounded, but who never displays her pain; subtle and gifted; cultivated and modest; courageous when she takes up her pen again to defend Jean-Jacques, and at the same time discreet and reserved; in love, and chaste" (12). Rousseau's Galatea is indeed an allegorical rendition of the perfect female reader, by this analysis. She effaces herself and devotes her life to promoting a great writer.[23]

The desire this exchange inspires in the reader to ascertain the true nature of the relationship that existed between these two correspondents is its most attractive quality, for May: "One of the delicate pleasures one may experience in reading these letters consists of seeking in them, as if undertaking a police investigation, the evidence on which to build one's own interpretation and reconstitution of the facts" (14–15). In contrast to previous critical responses to this correspondence, the "facts" to which May refers concern exclusively the intensity and the details of the platonic love affair between the two correspondents, not the existence of the love itself. In May's opinion, "there is no doubt . . . that the two correspondents fell in love with each other in the end" (14). Echoing on a minor note the views of the original 1803 editors, May ends his survey of imagined reader responses with the highest level on which he values these letters: "But, beyond what we learn of her or of him from these letters, it is as a chronicle of an unhappy platonic love relationship that these letters will hold the attention of those readers interested in affairs of the heart" (12).

Only at the very end of his introduction does May address the more specialized question of the genre to which one might assign this correspondence. He raises, that is, the question of de La Tour's authorial consciousness. May's response to the notion that de La Tour wrote with publication in mind is revealing in its hesitation and in its appeal to de La Tour's confused state as she prepared her letters for publication.[24] In May's view, de La Tour's 1770 editorial project "seems to indicate on the part of Mme de La Tour the feeling that their adventure naturally lends itself to a transposition from reality into novel, demonstrating to what point reality and fiction remain inextricably blended in her mind. Is this not why she kept copies of her own letters, which might reveal that the idea of publishing them was not new to her?" (25).

Precisely what May means by de La Tour's sense that her (sentimental) adventure with Rousseau would easily lend itself to a transposition from reality to novel is unclear, and this lack of clarity is inextricably bound up in twentieth-century assumptions as to the difference between literary production and the missive letter. As these terms are used in May's preface, "reality" corresponds with private letters, "novel" with the same letters edited for a public. Even if de La Tour intended to publish the exchange, as her editing job of 1770 indicates, this intent does not at all imply, for May, authorial consciousness during the composition of the original letters written to Rousseau. These letters remain "pure" in their missiveness; then, when edited, quite thoroughly lose their missive quality, and become literature ("a transposition from reality into novel"). May is, in other words, quite careful not to let de La Tour's possible literary project interfere with the transparent "authenticity" behind the story told by this fifteen-year exchange, for these letters are of most importance to him in that they chronicle a platonic affair, the tragic aspects of which will hold the attention of readers curious about such things.

May's unwillingness to question in any real sense the legitimacy of the emotion behind de La Tour's letters to Rousseau may be the reason why he concludes his preface on an interpretive note quite thoroughly devoid of didacticism. After declaring that the "textual status" of this exchange will remain undecided, May invites the reader to drop this question as ultimately constricting: "Readers of this volume are thus invited to choose according to their tastes in the name of a liberty that is clearly accorded to them by the very writers of the letters that compose it" (26). The contradictions that arise from any attempt to place this exchange in a particular generic category are left open by May in an appeal to readerly liberty, a freedom supposedly authorized by Rousseau and de La Tour, the writers (May uses the term *signataires*) of these letters.

In defense of more interpretive restrictiveness, I would add that this exchange loses none of its interest if we accept that de La Tour was a woman who sought to insert herself into the literary publishing milieu of her time. There is evidence, I would argue, that she invites us to view her as a quite consciously creative writer, as when she states at various points in her letters, private and public, that women are capable beings who are in general underestimated as artists. As mentioned in chapter 2, her most striking defense of women's creative abilities comes when she mentions that she is having her portrait painted by a woman, then assures Rousseau that the image will be a faithful reproduction. Equally significant is de La Tour's seizing upon Rousseau's new habit of making *lacets* or braids to pass the time as evidence that he was "no longer as rigid concerning the analogy that one's occupations should have with the faculties attached to one's sex" (Aug. 31, 1762). As I have also explored in chapter 2, sending her poems to Rousseau was as misguided at that point as it would have been at any other, given his quite consistent rejection of women writers; but her alacrity in doing so illustrates how very much she would have liked to have been recognized by him as a creator in her own right.

While I would not insist that other interpretations of de La Tour's letters are categorically wrong, I do believe that my argument as to their generic significance limits our interpretive options. We cannot, as May would have us do, read these letters as we would read an epistolary novel: naively suspending any question as to the unexpressed motives of the "characters" in order to increase our enjoyment of a story. More importantly, we cannot continue to view private letters from women such as de La Tour as so many "Portuguese" expressions of pure emotion. As Labrosse's and Leigh's reactions demonstrate, too little has changed since Sainte-Beuve's day in terms of how readers of this correspondence characterize de La Tour's psychology. Things should change, for attention to authorial consciousness in eighteenth-century letter writers opens our eyes to the exceptional status accorded the "real" letter at the time, as well as requiring us to question our own assumptions concerning the use of such documents for literary criticism.

De La Tour's sex has obviously been a determining factor in the reception history of her letters as I have just presented it. The tender condescension accorded de La Tour by many of her previous commentators demonstrates how very predisposed they were to view her as a sad victim of matrimonial trouble, a semihysteric who sought salvation through a famous man. In the following chapter, I explore the more general implications of my arguments concerning de La Tour for gender studies. I do not argue that de La Tour was a proto-feminist, despite the statements just quoted above as to her views on women and art. Whether or not de La Tour had precocious feminist inclinations is not an aspect of her intellectual makeup to which I believe I have access. Far from overt feminist declarations, de La

Tour's appeals to women's potential seem to me to be aimed at opening a small window through which she herself might enter the public arena, as an *épistolière*. She was in my view more than willing to accept her assigned place in society, and to adopt a secondary role of erecting statues to her hero Rousseau, with one important caveat: she wanted to see her name in print.

5

Postscript: De La Tour, James Boswell, Henriette ***, and Gender Theory

> As they came closer, they perceived in one corner of the canvas
> the end of a naked foot emerging from a chaos of color . . . but
> what a living, delicious foot! They stood petrified with admira-
> tion before this fragment that had escaped an incredible, slow,
> progressive destruction.
>
> —Balzac, "Le Chef-d'oeuvre inconnu" (1845)

HONORÉ DE BALZAC'S ALLEGORY OF ARTISTIC MISPRISION, "THE UN-
known Masterpiece," contains the tale of the mysterious, wealthy
Frenhofer, who has been working on a single painting for ten years.
Reputed to be a masterpiece, the work is hidden from even the readers' eyes until the final pages of the story, when we are finally allowed to view it through the expert gaze of two aspiring artists. The
young men are horrified by the ruined potential they detect in the
work before them. "There is a woman under there!" one exclaims,
but while they receive glimpses of a Galatean figure stepping forward to greet them, they are able to perceive clearly only the end
of one "delicious, living foot," one single area of representational
perfection emerging from a chaos of color.

There exists a certain variety of feminist literary criticism in which
works by women of previous eras become analogous to Frenhofer's
"unknown masterpiece." Read in this light, the literary works of
early modern women are so many verbal palimpsests that offer us a
tantalizing glimpse of what might have been produced had their authors been free from societal oppression. Such a reading seems at
first to embrace gender constructionism, by transferring the woman
writer's agency to that amorphous cultural construct, patriarchy; yet
at the same time, it is the critic's duty to detect any "delicious, living" traces of the writing woman's "real" voice. In the language of

the theoretical debates of the last two decades, this latter task "essentializes" the woman writer's latent voice as authentically feminine, a lost treasure covered over by a foreign, repressive patriarchal discourse. The feminist critic who follows this theoretical paradigm assigns herself the difficult heuristic project of teasing out what is authentic in the constructed "chaos" of women's texts.

In this last chapter of my study, I argue that the reception history of de La Tour's letters is an important cautionary tale for contemporary feminists. We have been acting in great part from the assumption that literary works by early modern women constitute obscure records of what these women "really" wanted. At the same time, we have assumed that letters by those same women are fully divorced from the issues surrounding literary production.[1] Even more so than private journals, women's letters have been assumed to offer us unadulterated access to the "real thing," to authentic women's voices speaking of their problems and desires without fear of exposure. When women writers have—as they often have—expressly stated that they never wished to see their letters, journals, travel journals, even novels, published, or that this or that published work was "taken" from them and published against their will, we have been willing to believe them, as such statements seem to conform to our notions of the workings of patriarchal oppression. More practically, these pronouncements confirm the impeccable authenticity of the "private" nature of these documents.

Scenarios as novelistic as purloined letters and writers who watch in despair as their fiction appears in public should, however, alert us to the possibility of authorial desire in such "nonauthors." These women may well be manipulating a variety of assumptions, gendered and generic, in order to assume the mantle of authorship with none of the corresponding issues that going public necessarily entailed. In this chapter, in addition to comparing de La Tour to other correspondents of Rousseau, male and female, I attempt to untangle the complex web of fiction, authenticity, conservatism, and self-promotion surrounding women and letters as I view these phenomena in eighteenth-century France. De La Tour's inscription of herself in French literary history as the devoted fan of a Great Man may not satisfy the paradigm of the strong woman writer, nor even of the resisting woman reader, but the unusual authorial project that she and others like her undertook is an essential part of the history of the publication of women's writing.

* * *

The importance of women's letters to eighteenth-century European literature is evident in the lengthy list of heroines who gave their names to the canonical epistolary masterpieces of the period, not the least of which is Rousseau's *Julie, ou La Nouvelle Héloïse.* As feminist critics have often pointed out, however, it is eighteenth-century male writers who continue to enjoy the heights of authorial renown with their "women's letters," despite the presence of many female epistolary novelists among the best sellers of the time.[2] The common explanation of such neglect, and a compelling one, is that nineteenth- and twentieth-century critics, at least until the advent of feminist literary criticism, relegated these women writers to oblivion based solely on their sex. There is of course more to this important chapter in canon formation; women writers and those who "promoted" them in the eighteenth-century often did their best to fit these works into the mold to which later critics, Sainte-Beuve foremost among them, would appeal. Most astonishing among such clichés was that a woman could write a lengthy epistolary novel and still be given little credit for her "creative" effort.

Consider Choderlos de Laclos's commentary on Fanny Burney's first work, *Evelina,* in which he marvels at Burney's ability to create a novelistic masterpiece when her only aim was to amuse her sick father: "Without shyness and without pride, no thought of an author's glory mixes with the sweet outpourings of Nature; she is far from suspecting that she has created a book."[3] Where did Laclos get the bizarre (to our eyes) notion that Burney was able to write an entire novel "unwittingly," with not the slightest thought of one day publishing it? From none other than Burney herself, who was hardly unusual among the women writers of her day in collaborating with her readers in the presentation of her fictional work as accidental, "spontaneous," written with no thought of fame—as one would write a letter.

This type of denial of authorship obviously goes far beyond the standard prefatorial denials of a Montesquieu, a Rousseau, or a Diderot. Why did women writers so often deny themselves the status of author, even when they were writing and publishing clearly fictional works? There were many possible motives for participating in this rhetoric of "nonauthorship," even if one was writing a novel. In addition to preserving one's virtuous reputation as a retiring woman, nonauthorship may have been viewed as a proactive shield against the harsh critique of one's work, for it seems underhanded indeed for a critic to attack a bit of writing that a scribbling young woman "never intended" for display to a public audience.[4] Such a work qualifies for the protection Servan would see accorded to private letters, especially if published by a woman's relative "without her consent," as de La Tour claimed of her poems: "It is a capital maxim that a written work, of whatever type, cannot be imputed as a *fault* or a *crime* unless the author himself has given it over freely. Until then it is nothing; in the words of M. de Voltaire, it is only black on a white background."[5]

Examples of eighteenth-century French women who expressed anger that their works were published, and have been accepted at their word, include Marie-Jeanne Roland (1754–93), who is said to have been "furious when friends published her travel journal, *Voyage en Suisse* (Tour through Switzerland), without her permission."[6] Roland went on to make quite a career for herself as a "nonauthor," publishing in her husband's name and even claiming in her *Mémoires particuliers* (Private Memoirs), begun in prison before her execution, that she was writing "merely to pass the time." Her rhetoric in this last of her works underwent a radical change, however, when she realized that she was certain to be executed, and her manuscript more than likely lost. Suddenly, Roland was declaring in writing her passionate desire to have made a name for herself as a writer—as a historian, to be precise.[7]

A more telling example, in the context of a study of de La Tour, is that of Mme de Villedieu, of whom Faith Beasley writes: "One female letter writer . . . would have preferred that her personal correspondence remain outside the public domain. In 1668, Villedieu's editor, Claude Barbin, published her love letters to M. de Villedieu without the author's consent. The short, but very passionate *Lettres et billets galants* resembles the anonymous *Lettres portugaises*, also published by Barbin, which appeared in French in 1669."[8] Resembles these letters, I would note, to quite a suspicious degree. Villedieu (Marie Catherine Desjardins, 1640–83) was already a published author in 1668; is it possible that she wished to extend her fame by becoming an acknowledged *épistolière?* Was the publication of her letters as much a trick played on a willing public as that of Pope's correspondence, or of Guilleragues's *Lettres portugaises?* Was the latter, published in 1669, indeed inspired by Villedieu's success?

While it seems likely that we will never be able to answer such questions, it is imperative that we ask them, I believe, rather than relying on the notion of a woman "ravished against her will" of her (highly publishable) private letters. I would similarly put into doubt the precise generic value of the letters of Julie de Lespinasse (1732–76), protégée to the famous *épistolière* Mme du Deffand. The letters Lespinasse produced during her ill-fated love affair with the comte de Guibert have long been praised as models of the passionate, spontaneous, "authentic" missive in the Portuguese mode. To cite only one of the many encomiums to Lespinasse, Jean Bloch writes: "Lespinasse's letters to the comte de Guibert hold a median position between private correspondence and the fictional soliloquy of the famous seventeenth-century *Lettres portugaises*; Lespinasse's letters can be read as literary masterpiece and emotional outburst at one and the same time."[9]

As I have argued in the last chapter, the notion that some letters, although authentically "real," may be lifted out of their generic lowliness and made "literary" is central to current evaluations of the letter form. Bloch would do with Lespinasse what Roger Duchêne has proposed for Sévigné: qualify her letters as "involuntary (literary) masterpieces." What has never been proposed—although the likelihood for Lespinasse is strong, I would argue—is that this woman writer deliberately created a correspondence that fit the Portuguese model, as a bid for future (and perhaps only posthumous) fame. I am not calling into question—not overtly—Lespinasse's feelings for her lover; but given the era in which she wrote, her association with many famous male writers, and the success of her letters, the question of intention must be posed, and in a very eighteenth-century manner: Was she, to whatever extent, writing, saving, "creating" these letters with publication as a missive masterpiece in mind?

Lespinasse and Roland were of course hardly alone in scrupulously avoiding the status of author. As I note in my introduction, Mme de Graffigny resisted calling herself an author despite having to her credit a best-selling novel (*Lettres d'une Péruvienne*, 1747) and a very successful play (*Cénie*, 1750). Suzanne Necker is yet another example of the denial of authorial desire by an obviously talented and skilled woman writer—a denial made all the more significant in her case by the contrast she offers to the nineteenth-century success of her novelist daughter, Germaine de Staël. Necker vehemently denied any desire to publish her many writings, and was, like Roland and Lespinasse, seemingly content with fame as a *salonnière*. In an important study of Necker's relationship to publicity, Dena Goodman addresses the obvious discrepancy between the time and energy that Necker devoted to her essay and journal writing and her position on publication. Her work did appear in print, although only after her death, published under the title *Mélanges* (1798) by her famous husband. Goodman notes the keen irony of Jacques Necker's prefatorial insistence that his wife shunned publicity, offered as proof that she was a virtuous, modest woman and wife: "The posthumous publication of the work of Suzanne Necker, like that of women before her, thus did not establish her as a writer. The obstacles faced by a woman who wanted to be a writer in early modern France could not be overcome even by publication."[10]

And yet Goodman, despite her obvious (and understandable) annoyance at Jacques Necker's effacement of his wife's skill and effort as a writer, accepts without question Suzanne Necker's own vehement statements that she never envisioned the publication of her writing. This acceptance is indeed crucial to Goodman's conclusion that "an emergent writing self is captured in the *Mélanges,* like a bird in a cage."[11] I would argue that the self we see in the published writing of this woman is indeed her "true" writing self, at least to the extent that she desired to show it to us. I would add that we can read a desire for fame into her journal writings that may have been quite well satisfied by the type of publication her husband prepared for the public. Suzanne Necker may even have colluded in this project; the very intensity of her statements concerning publication calls them into question, just as hyperbole in general signals a rhetorical ploy.

In an equally important article on Julie de Lespinasse, Goodman argues that this eighteenth-century woman's apparent split personality (graceful *salonnière,* hysterical letter writer) reveals a basic disgust for a life spent pleasing others through self-effacement.[12] Lespinasse's letters, in other words, are for Goodman symptomatic of her repressed need to make her own personality felt. My proposal that Lespinasse sought fame through the posthumous publication of her "extraordinarily expressive" private letters would not necessarily be in conflict with Goodman's psychological reading of Lespinasse, but it would allow her more agency in passing on a particular image of herself to posterity: that of a real-life Portuguese nun. Like Suzanne Necker, Lespinasse may well be an instance of the phenomenon I have been exploring throughout this study: an apparently retiring, conservative woman whose writings nevertheless reveal a quite burning desire for a publicity unaccompanied by the tarnish of self-promotion.

The best evidence of this fully conscious, unstated desire on Necker's part is quoted by Goodman herself, as she considers Necker's *éloge* of none other than Mme de Sévigné: "[Necker] saw the recognition of the nonpublishing Sévigné . . . as signaling a significant advance in French culture: until then only great men had been universally honored, but now 'a woman whose virtues were without *éclat*, and whose pen was dedicated solely to friendship, receives the same recompense destined for genius or heroism.'"[13] Imitating Sévigné, or appearing to do so, allowed women to become known as "writers" without risking "authorship." This type of fame strikes contemporary readers, and rightly so, as seriously lacking in éclat; certainly lacking in grandeur, if compared with that of a Voltaire, a Rousseau, or a Diderot. However, such "authorship" may well have been experienced as fully satisfying to women such as Necker, Roland, Lespinasse, and even that relatively minor figure whose case I have been exploring, Marie-Anne de La Tour. The elevated status of missive letters in the eighteenth century goes a long way toward removing the bizarreness of such a project, to our contemporary eyes.

As I have argued in my introduction, we must be particularly sensitive to one aspect of de La Tour 's relative obscurity: her lack of a male champion. Du Châtelet had Voltaire as both lover and promoter, just as d'Epinay had Grimm, not to mention her troubled relationship with Rousseau. Suzanne Necker's work was published by her well-known husband, Roland also became known through the important role her husband played in the Revolution, and Lespinasse's primary claim to fame, despite her letters, is as d'Alembert's lover and Diderot's fictional interlocutor in the latter's *Rêve de d'Alembert*. All these women came into and remained in the public eye, in other words, at least to a great degree, through their association with famous men. It may well have been in an attempt to gain a contact in the literary milieu of her day that de La Tour wrote to Rousseau; she had, in any event, to rely on this quite unreliable interlocutor in order to ensure the publishability of her letters. Without Rousseau's name to grace her title page, these documents were merely the uninteresting output of an unknown woman and failed poet. Her struggles to control her correspondent, as I have demonstrated, had the useful outcome of making quite evident the goal behind her correspondence with him: publication and fame. No one made the path to "nonauthorship" smooth and satisfying to de La Tour; she was on her own. Women such as Graffigny, blessed with the complacent "Panpan" as correspondent, could avoid such revelatory epistolary moments.

I have nevertheless consistently stressed in my study of de La Tour not the obstacles she faced, but rather her active manipulation of her society's and Rousseau's views on women and letters. The oppression experienced by women seeking to publish their writings in a field heavily dominated by men is an important area of research, yet what I am most interested in pointing out about studies such as *Going Public: Women and Publishing in Early Modern France* (1995), in which Goodman's article on Necker appears, is that the dangers of exposure are too often given far greater consideration than the benefits of going public with one's writing. The sheer number of women whose writings appeared "against their will" is one indication, to me, that the benefits far outweighed the supposed cost.

In the introduction to another important collection of essays on the topic of women and publicity, *Writing the Female Voice: Essays on Epistolary Literature* (1989), Elizabeth C. Goldsmith sums up the critical attitude of which I am speaking: "To be virtuous was to be modest, self-effacing, above all not talked about, and most certainly not published. To publish a woman's letters, even if the purpose of publication was to praise female epistolary style, was in some way to violate her personal integrity."[14] I would counter that one way in which to ensure that one remains both (relatively) modest and self-effacing, while simultaneously ensuring that one is talked about, is to arrange to have one's letters published "against one's will." The "certainty" that this publication would have been perceived as a violation by the woman letter writer enhanced the value of the writing in question for the eighteenth-century public, albeit in a manner most unsuitable to a feminist aesthetic. This "certainty" also, once again, enhances the value of such works for contemporary feminist critics. If women letter writers would have indeed been horrified to see their letters published, this vigorous resistance necessarily enhances the authenticity of the information to be gathered from such documents.

I am not denying, I should perhaps now point out, that there exist actual private letters by eighteenth-century French women written with no thought of publication in mind; nor that many women would have been quite legitimately horrified should such letters have suddenly appeared in print. My study of de La Tour is intended instead to raise the possibility that any particular woman letter writer, or journal writer, or novel writer, for that matter, however much she may have held to a rhetoric of nonpublicity, might have been quite pleased to see her writing published "against her will."

Like Burney, Graffigny, Lespinasse, and Necker, de La Tour presents herself as a private creature more or less forced into the limelight; that she and they have done so successfully reflects to my eyes not victimization, but rather an intelligent awareness of social and literary conventions.

The edited collections of articles on the relationship between women and publicity that I have cited above are important moments in the study of eighteenth-century women writers. Most importantly, they seriously address the limits of women's socioeconomic situation with regard to publishing during this period. They consider in detail, that is, the complexities of eighteenth-century women's relationship to authorship. Earlier discussions of women and the letter genre, from the 1970s and 1980s, tended to ignore real letter writers in favor of fictional texts, an approach in keeping with the most theoretically compelling notions of the day, especially the Death of the Author. The inevitable reference in any study of gender and letters at that time was the debate between Peggy Kamuf and Nancy K. Miller over the meaning of the authorship of the *Lettres portugaises* (1669).[15] This seventeenth-century work has made frequent appearances in my study and will now be the subject of one last, focused commentary.

The centuries-long success of Guilleragues's literary ruse in passing off these letters as the incontestably real missives of an abandoned, heartbroken woman was the result, to a great extent, of his readers' desire that private letters reveal that which is most scandalous: a woman's—a nun's!—illicit love affair. Guilleragues depended greatly on the myth of women's perfect suitability to this supposedly natural genre, even though the style of "Mariane's" letters heavily reflects the literary clichés of the day.[16] When these letters were finally demonstrated to be fictional by Deloffre and Rougeot, the author of the *Lettres portugaises* became the object of understandable admiration, both for the literary qualities of his epistolary novel and for the longevity of his ruse.

This admiration did not extend to one influential feminist critic, Nancy K. Miller. In her article " 'I's' in Drag," Miller accused Guilleragues of capitalizing on "the always renewable figure of feminine suffering."[17] Peggy Kamuf, in "Writing Like a Woman," took the calmer, more "sophisticated" pose that we should concern ourselves only with the play of the text itself, and let the matter of authorship lie. In response, Miller wrote "The Text's Heroine," in which she carefully considered what authorship of this work by a man or a woman might mean. She concluded that, whatever her own poststructuralist leanings, this question must matter, for "the textualization—hence glamorization—of female suffering around the male is an important issue for women."[18] But what if this book were only falsely attributed to Guilleragues? What of Mariane the nun, should she have actually existed? For Kamuf, who fully embraces the lessons of poststructuralism, the question is moot; for Miller, however, if Mariane had existed, she would be a victim of and not a "glamorizer" of female suffering. Miller declares that if someone were to prove that a nun had actually written these letters, the work would tell a different story, "since the story of the woman who writes is *always* another story."[19]

In "Authority, Authenticity, and the Publication of Letters by Women," the article she contributed to *Writing the Female Voice,* Goldsmith is ready to tell this story: "Mariane herself, if she existed, would no doubt have wanted her identity to remain unknown and her letters unpublished."[20] But what if we consider a possibility Miller does not propose; what if Mariane the nun had indeed existed, and had quite thoroughly exaggerated, or at least intentionally exploited, her suffering—the better to publicize her letters and to promote her reputation as an *épistolière?* The agency that I would accord my imaginary "Mariane" in her self-glamorization as a long-suffering epistolary heroine raises quite a different series of questions for feminism than those considered by critics such as Miller and Kamuf, questions more appropriate to the present climate in gender studies. Like most contemporary feminist critics, I reject the paradigm according to which women principally inscribed their suffering and their frustration in their writing. I also reject the poststructuralist freedom of leaving aside the issue of sex in order to play with the "gendering" of texts. In so doing I avoid the trap of exploring the letters of a famous literary heroine created by a man, when my object is to discuss women's place in literary history.

I am aware that my vision of de La Tour and others like her as out to maximize their public exposure implies a nonfeminist corollary: that some real women were more than willing to capitalize on the very glamorization of female suffering diagnosed by Miller in Guilleragues's *Lettres portugaises.* But the extent to which de La Tour's publishing project was or was not feminist does not overly concern me; I have noted the moments in her letters to Rousseau when she appears to trumpet the equality of women artists, and I accept that she was possibly making a case for herself as a writer in the process, either to Rousseau alone or to a potential public. She may also have been trying, given her knowledge of his antifeminist politics, to provoke a reaction from her correspondent, that is, to garner more letters. Nevertheless, such moments do not constitute the most crucial aspect of this correspondence for me. I am primarily interested in presenting de La Tour as an actor in her own literary cultural milieu, a woman writer who consciously and cleverly set up her own posthumous reputation. She embedded claims to nonauthorship in her public, pseudonymous letters, proof enough that she knew how to play with such self-presentation. Writing to the *Année littéraire* as "de La Motte," de La Tour declares: "I believed that the role of a *woman friend of Jean-Jacques* did me the most honor, and fit me best, and that I should limit myself to filling it."[21] That her project of gaining fame involved explicitly humbling herself before an author considered by many of his own contemporaries to be shockingly misogynist apparently did not bother de La Tour, nor does it bother me, as a feminist. I am instead fascinated by how this one obscure woman was able to insinuate herself into literary history.

Feminist or not, de La Tour clearly relied on an exquisite awareness of Rousseau's sexual politics when attempting to charm him, or at times even to provoke him, with her letters. The proper rhetoric for approaching Rousseau man-to-man was an equally gendered matter, as is beautifully illustrated in a set of letters written by the young James Boswell. Three years after de La Tour sent her first letter to Rousseau, Boswell was equally successful in exciting his correspondent's interest. By exploring the differences in how these two correspondents, one male, one female, seduced the famous recipient of their letters, I explore as well the extent to which they can be labeled representative of their respective sexes. I am interested, that is, in the extent to which the apparently private letters of these two individuals have been and should be read as "sexed." The notion of authorial intention again plays a dramatic role, as the quite different critical responses to their correspondences demonstrate.

When Boswell wrote his first letter to Rousseau in December 1764, the latter was living in exile in Môtiers (he and de La Tour were engaged at the time in a disputatious exchange about his lack of an immediate response to her portrait). Boswell wrote to Rousseau not from England, but from Môtiers itself, for he was on a tour of Europe designed to bring him into contact with the Great Men of his day; in an irony inspired perhaps only by geographical proximity, his next visit would be to Voltaire, who had recently published the defamatory *Sentiment des citoyens.* Boswell's goal was to gain access to Rousseau's home without the aid of the letter of presentation he carried, as we learn from a missive sent to a friend back in England in which Boswell describes the choice to write his own letter as a deliberate test of his epistolary skills. He composed his "masterpiece" in several drafts, and the evolution of these drafts reveals a progressive insistence on his self-presentation as both an honorably straightforward man and an ardent admirer of Rousseau.

The initial version begins: "I am a former Scotsman who is traveling. I write French badly. My spoken French is even worse. I have come here hoping to see you" (*CC*, 22:3694; I am translating from Boswell's indeed rather poor French). After heavy rewriting the next day, the final version begins in a manner yet more redolent of Boswell's "manly" appreciation of his worth: "I am a gentleman formerly from Scotland. You know my rank. I am twenty-four years old. You know my age. . . . I present myself monsieur as a man of singular merit. As a man with a sensitive heart, a quick and melancholy mind. Ah! if all that I have suffered does not win me singular merit in the eyes of Monsieur Rousseau, why was I made as I am? why did he write as he did?" (*CC*, 22:3694 bis). As carried away as Saint-Preux among Julie's undergarments, Boswell then breaks into exclamations, excusing his excess of epistolary emotion in advance: "Excuse me, monsieur. I feel myself moved. I cannot hold back. O dear St Preux! Enlightened mentor! eloquent and lovable Rousseau! I have the feeling that a quite noble friendship will be born today." Boswell ends his letter on a note that might serve to sum up de La Tour's entire epistolary relationship with Rousseau: "I impatiently await your response."

Boswell triumphs, for Rousseau answers: "I am sick, suffering, unable to receive visitors. However I cannot refuse the visit of Monsieur Boswell, provided that out of respect for my condition, he make it a short one" (*CC*, 22:3695). As Boswell proudly proclaims to his friend (writing now in English): "I wrote him a letter which I was sure would recommend me, for I told him my character, & claimed his regard as what I had a title to. I wrote with manly confidence, & told him I was not afraid to stand the test of his penetration. I must give you some of my expressions" (*CC*, 22:3697). Basking in the glow of attention from the famous French author, Boswell stayed in Môtiers from December 3 to December 15. As he took leave, he reports: "M. Rousseau embraced me. He was quite St. Preux Attendri. He kist me several times, & held me in his arms with elegant cordiality. O! I shall never forget that I have been thus" (*CC*, 22:app. 334).

Obviously, Boswell's reputation for unsurpassed self-publication through association with others was not limited to Samuel Johnson, despite the latter's famous retort: "Sir, you have but two topics, yourself and me. I am sick of both." The question I am asking of Boswell's letters to Rousseau, in the context of this study of de La Tour, is the extent to which one can label his epistolary strategies "male," rather than merely indicative of an idiosyncratic talent for personal promotion that borders on the maniacal. Neither Boswell nor de La Tour, as a letter writer, can be considered "normal"; unlike the vast majority of fans, they did not hesitate to hound the objects of their attention when necessary. They each, indeed, made something of a career of parasitic fandom, Boswell with far greater success, needless to say. Fortunately for my purposes, by a coincidence linked to Rousseau's international fame, they shared a correspondent. Whatever their true opinion about the content of Rousseau's philosophical and fictional writings, they each manipulated Rousseauvian ideals to a specific epistolary end: the receipt of a letter. Neither hesitated to make claims of startling narcissism as to their self-worth in order to justify imposing upon their famous correspondent, but the form of this self-presentation differed dramatically for each in one important area: while de La Tour maintains a humble self-effacing rhetoric that emphasizes her total lack of *esprit* and her aversion for fame, Boswell displays an objective summing-up of his superior qualities, intellect included. It is this difference in the rhetoric of their claims to exceptionality that makes these correspondents of Rousseau representative of their respective sexes.

While this conclusion may seem hardly surprising, I must emphasize again that what is new in my study is the assumption that de La Tour was carefully controlling her self-presentation in her private letters with an eye to gaining secondhand fame. The sex of these two letter writers comes most fully into play not in the production, but rather in the reception of their letters. Readings by subsequent "recipients" of Boswell and de La Tour's letters—the future readers both writers hoped for—reveal a striking difference in the authorial consciousness attributed to each.[22] Consider Rufus Reiberg, who has read Boswell's letters as a "dramatized quest for identity" that includes the possibility of a desire for future publication: "[Boswell's] passion for attracting the notice of the great and the celebrated resulted in a number of epistles designed to elicit brilliant responses which could then be displayed in his cabinet at Auchinleck as evidence of his intimacy with the Great and the Celebrated. And he may well have had plans for publishing such correspondence."[23] De La Tour's readers, as described in previous chapters, have to the contrary uniformly assumed her to be a naive fan who truly—and quite "simply"—loved the object of her epistolary attentions. In the context of Reiberg's attribution of a "dramatized quest for identity" to Boswell, the most striking reader of de La Tour is Labrosse, for whom her letters constitute the search for a "dissolution of identity" in which the thought of display and possible publication play no role whatsoever.

Consider as well subsequent readings of another of Rousseau's correspondents, the anonymous "Henriette ***," whose identity has never been established.[24] Her exchange of letters with Rousseau began several months after Boswell's, but resembles de La Tour's far more closely in that Henriette also emphasizes her humbly self-effacing character and her intense abhorrence of publicity. A yet more important resemblance to de La Tour, for my purposes, is that Henriette also edited her exchange with Rousseau for publication, supplying substantial commentary to flesh out the rather short supply of letters. Henriette also provided her manuscript with an introduction and a lengthy closing essay on the fate of women such as herself (single and without marital prospects). The exchange was published in 1902 by Hippolyte Buffenoir, who chose the title *J.-J. Rousseau et Henriette, jeune Parisienne inconnue, manuscrit inédit du XVIIIᵉ siècle* (J.-J. Rousseau and Henriette, A Young Unknown Parisian, An Unpublished Manuscript from the Eighteenth Century).[25]

In writing to Rousseau, Henriette took as her base text not the allegorical *Nouvelle Héloïse*, but rather the pedagogical description of women's role in society found in "Sophie," book 5 of *Emile*. Surely, she pleads in her first letter, she should be considered an exception to the restrictions Rousseau would see placed on women's intellectual activities, given her situation? She is a woman in her mid thirties, single, possessed of a mediocre fortune, and with no prospects for marriage: "So that what is unseemly in general, might become for me a reasonable thing, and perhaps even necessary. It is this question that I present for your examination" (*CC*, 19:3192). Henriette's desperate need for counsel justifies the rather lengthy autobiographical account that follows, and into which she inserts considerable philosophizing on the nature of intellect and on woman's place in society, all ostensibly to aid Rousseau in prescribing a course of action: "I seek only a calmer and happier state of soul. This natural and legitimate motive gives me more confidence to hope that you will be willing to tell me, monsieur, if I am on the right path, or if I am going astray."

We learn that Henriette was raised to marry well, but that her father's financial problems have left her single. She has tried and rejected the devout life, and has also considered and rejected living among the "peasants." She now sees only one option left to her: a life of quiet study. In devoting herself to the life of the mind, she emphasizes, she is not seeking to make a name for herself. Indeed, her most spectacular failure in solving her dilemma has been to try to live in society as a "woman of letters," or rather, as a "man of letters." Deprived of the status of wife and mother, she tells Rousseau, she at one point sought to supplement her single femaleness by engaging in male activities: "I thus resolved to mold my mind as much as I could according to what I imagined to be that of a worthy man, to take up his occupations, his manner of thinking and his conduct in society, to rid myself of all pathetic womanly behavior, and above all of the air that announces that one is seeking to please."

This transvestism did not succeed, we are told, for Henriette could not rid herself of her "woman's heart." To lose the natural feminine qualities that emanate from this organ would mean death for Henriette, she tells Rousseau, for femininity is the very essence of her being. Her brief portrait of herself proves this statement, as it also, like de La Tour's self-portrait in words, echoes Rousseau's ideal of the perfect woman. Henriette is lively, we learn, yet gentle and complacent; indifferent to glory, of course; possessed of extreme sensibility—of course; proud, yet timid in society. She diagnoses herself as having been previously too concerned with society's prescriptions for her as a woman. While she would like nothing better than to take her place and to do her duty to others, "society having decided that I am nothing, and made me an outcast with no role nor match, why should I obstinately insist on fitting myself to anything?"

Her proposal for her future, on which she hopes Rousseau will set his seal of approval, is thus the product of bitter experience. Yet she does not plan to live entirely alone, as at first seems to be the case; her current goal is to continue to study in the hopes of one day meeting a man capable of a lasting friendship (she dismisses women as incapable of such loyalty). She imagines her ideal man as in need of an intelligent ear for his thoughts, as he would be frequently reduced to silence by the fools among whom he found himself. She will listen, and will place no restraints on their relationship; men, after all, must be free to come and go as it pleases them, to be always well received, and to never fear "constraining reproaches."

Could this one superior man in need of female companionship be the inimitable Rousseau himself, that other societal outcast in whose writings alone Henriette has found the voice of reason combined with that of compassion? This possibility is never explicitly raised. In any case, had he joined Henriette, Rousseau would not have risked involvement with a woman writer, that species he claimed to abhor. Henriette closes on this point, emphasizing that in her desperate quest for advice, she has been driven to the hard "work" of writing this letter ("I have taken up the pen, so foreign to me"). This unaccustomed occupation has, however, been a surprising source of pleasure, in that it has distracted her from her problems, and thus demonstrated once again her need for intellectual engagement.

As was true of his reading of de La Tour's first letter, Rousseau immediately suspects "Henriette" of epistolary duplicity: "I am not fooled, Henriette, as to your letter's goal, nor by your dating your letter from Paris. You are seeking less my advice on what to do than my approbation for the choice that you have already made. Between each of your lines I read in bold letters: *Let us see if you will have the courage to condemn someone who writes and thinks as I do never to write or think again*" (*CC*, XX:3256). Rousseau believed that behind the name "Henriette" hid none other than Suzanne Curchod, the future Mme Necker cited above. At the time he received "Henriette's" letter, Curchod was governess in the home of Rousseau's Swiss friend Pastor Moultou. Having met her, Rousseau seems to suspect Curchod of trying to engage him in a public debate in which he will be obliged to defend his views on women. This first letter to Henriette must thus be read as conditioned by Rousseau's belief that he is writing to Curchod and, through her, to a potential public readership.

As was the case with Bernardoni and de La Tour, however, Rousseau's suspicions do not, strangely enough, suffice to stop him from responding to Henriette/Curchod. He will not "condemn" such a woman as she claims to be, he writes, declaring that there is indeed no possibility for her of returning to appropriately womanly activities. Alas, once a mind has begun to reflect, there is no turning back—an argument he had made for the human species in general in his *Discours sur l'inégalité*. But the letter's author is nevertheless mistaken in her plans, according to Rousseau, for she has misidentified the true source of her sufferings. First of all, falling into poverty does not absolve a person of seeking happiness. Second, she will claim, he supposes, to possess more sensibility than others do, but in his view, the self-diagnosis of oversensitiveness is always merely self-love: "It is in the last analysis pride in comparing oneself to others." He also accuses Henriette of wanting a court of men rather than true friends. She claims to want to listen; he declares that she wants to talk, and to be admired: "You are like a sibyl seeking to pronounce her oracles, your real project is not so much to listen to others as to have your own listeners." We recognize the type he is condemning: the *salonnière*, a role in which Curchod would later excel.

The pleasure Henriette admits to feeling in writing her long description of herself should have demonstrated all of this to her, Rousseau adds, rather bitingly. Rather than studying to ornament her *esprit*, Henriette should study with the goal of nourishing her soul. She is to distract herself from "everything," not just from herself, and in the process she may find not only her true self but also the acceptance of others. In an allusion to the myth of Galatea, Rousseau then declares to "Curchod" that he had previously viewed her as an empty bronze statue, an admirable if meaningless masterpiece. Only now that he knows her to be unhappy does he believes that there is hope for her, for her ability to be self-critical demonstrates that "there is still some real heart to you."

In her second letter, Henriette insists that she has not sought glory in her limited society (*CC*, 21:3493). She insists as well that she continues to need Rousseau's advice. He sends it, in a second letter that is much gentler in tone than the first. He is now convinced (or at least claims to be) that she is indeed an obscure *Parisienne*, not "a different person who was in Neuchâtel exactly when I received your letter" (*CC*, 22:3621; he had not named Suzanne Curchod in his first letter).[26] Despite his many worries, Rousseau agrees to continue writing to Henriette because she interests him so much. He adds, in a hyperbolic moment characteristic of some of his statements to de La Tour: "I know few people who attract and no one who astonishes me more than you." He is nevertheless not sure what to tell her: "You are a painful and humiliating enigma for me. I believed I knew the human heart, and I know nothing of yours." If she truly is not seeking outside approval, and yet is indeed incapable of finding happiness "in herself," he is at a loss. In yet another echo of his letters to de La Tour, Rousseau adds that he will continue to correspond with her if she wishes, but can promise no "exactitude" in his responses, and that he will never forget her.

Henriette responds with another long letter, in which she argues that a soul is meant to have a mate (*CC*, 23:3986). A month later, in March 1765, she sends a fourth letter (*CC*, 24:4209), in which she reveals that she is now in the country and much better reconciled with her lot. Without Rousseau's counsel, however, she knows that her life will be meaningless. Please write, she begs him, and by the way, will he soon be leaving his present home? She has heard rumors. In addition, she has read his latest work and finds it worthy of him. This fourth letter was not included in Henriette's edited manuscript, and thus was not in the Buffenoir edition of her letters. Given that Rousseau had not responded to her third missive, perhaps she cut this one from her work the better to demonstrate that she was not after all an importuning woman who did not know how to let a man go. She did however include a fifth letter, in which she reiterates her situation and again begs Rousseau for advice (*CC*, 28:4908). No response was forthcoming this time, either.

The saga took a turn for the worse in 1770, when Henriette sent Rousseau a note upon learning that he was in Paris. He refused to see her, on the grounds (again familiar to the reader of de La Tour's letters) that she was unknown to him. Only if she furnished adequate evidence of her true identity would she be admitted into his presence (*CC*, 38:6801). In her commentary in the *Jeune Parisienne inconnue*, Henriette interprets this refusal as characteristic of Rousseau's general lack of loyalty, citing the example of the Hume affair, albeit in a "self-effacing" manner: "Given that he was able to break with such a man, how much more natural is it that he would be able to forget Henriette."[27] She also tells us that on reading this last letter from Rousseau, "I felt my heart constrict and my senses go cold. I remained frozen in place."[28] She ceased her efforts to see her correspondent, she tells us, and should end her narrative at this point as well; but she feels a debt toward others in her state, those whom she addresses as "unfortunate young women." It is for such spinsterly victims alone that she will go on to reveal the end of her tale, namely, that she went further even than Rousseau advised, abandoning study, retiring to the country, and devoting herself to helping the poor and the sick. In so doing she has come to know, if not happiness, a true contentment in her virtue.

In his note to Henriette's first letter, and in striking contrast to his reaction to de La Tour, R. A. Leigh expresses his appreciation for this "beautiful and touching" missive (*CC*, n. to 19:3192). He compares Henriette's situation to that of Julie de Lespinasse, and equates their writing talent as well, adding: "In fact, there are passages in the letters of this unknown woman that one might place alongside the best pages of Mme de Charrière." Leigh's most important statement concerning Henriette, for my purposes, is that this woman was only obscurely aware of her "vocation" for writing. He berates Rousseau, who was more than capable of remarking this potential, for not revealing it to her and encouraging her to write. Leigh's praise of Henriette's ability as a writer is strong, yet he is praising not so much the letters that we possess as the potential works of (epistolary) fiction he imagines her having produced, à la Charrière, if Rousseau had encouraged her.

That Henriette's published letters might constitute "writing" worthy of publication outside of a complete correspondence of Rousseau is not considered by Leigh, although he was aware, of course, of Buffenoir's 1902 publication of these letters. The gulf between Buffenoir's and Leigh's assumptions about the value of these missives is another striking testimony as to how precipitously the letter form dropped in value over the course of the twentieth century. Buffenoir's prefatory material reflects the same view of letters present in Henry James's evaluation of the genre quoted in chapter 4, and was made in roughly the same period. Both men express a near-mystical appreciation for the attraction of such documents for the reader; Buffenoir even harkens back to an eighteenth-century reliance on Horace's *utile dulci*, for he begins by dividing the work's potential reading public into two groups. The first is composed of a general readership, for whom these letters offer the opportunity "to know better and feel more strongly the magic attraction of the eighteenth century."[29] It is unclear how this magic quality is related to the effect on such readers of Henriette's pathetic "cries," said to be sure to excite "pity and the most sincere sympathy," but the strange, anachronistic quality Buffenoir attributes to this work is clearly related to its genre: real letters, expressing sincere, heartbreaking emotion.

While this first, larger group of readers enjoys the letters' "magic," a second group stands poised to profit more dramatically from Buffenoir's publication. These readers, destined to fulfill the "useful" of *utile dulci*, are identified as early twentieth-century spinsters who find themselves in the same situation as their eighteenth-century sister. By publishing Henriette's manuscript, Buffenoir declares, he seeks to "save the Henriettes of our day from a funereal isolation" (viii). He would have these "unfortunate women," en masse, do as this "young girl" claims to have done: retire to the country and spend their lives doing good works (Henriette tells Rousseau, it will be remembered, that she is over thirty years old).

The feminist impulse to read an eighteenth-century woman's letters as the record of her struggle with patriarchal oppression seems more than justified when one has just read a commentary such as Buffenoir's. In addition to ridiculing his dismissal of all unmarried women, I feel, as a feminist, a strong desire to "save" Henriette from the fate that Buffenoir would gladly have even his own contemporaries suffer: solitary entombment in the country. I want, that is, to reach back in time and argue with Leigh and against Rousseau that Henriette's desire to show off her intelligence and learning is eminently commendable and should be encouraged. Going beyond Leigh, I feel compelled to postulate the latent existence of my own feminist anger in Henriette's apparently acquiescent letters, and to look for clues in her writing of any suppressed urges to reject Rousseau's misogynist philosophy and to make her own decisions concerning the future cultivation of her mind.

Such is the very reading accorded Henriette by Mary Seidman Trouille in chapter 2 of her *Sexual Politics: Women Writers Read Rousseau* (1997). Trouille's chapter on Henriette is entitled "The Failings of Rousseau's Ideals of Domesticity and Sensibility: The Plight of Henriette." By "plight," Trouille refers to the sad trap in which single women with a penchant for intellectual pursuits found themselves in eighteenth-century French society. In Trouille's opinion, Henriette's decidedly well-written letters give "eloquent expression" to this fate. Trouille also proposes that Buffenoir's claim to publish these letters for the first time may be false: "Given the immense popularity of Rousseau's writings in the decades following his death and the reverence with which they were generally regarded, it seems unlikely that a publisher would have refused a manuscript such as Henriette's that featured several of his unpublished letters."[30]

The insight that there would have been a mass audience for Henriette's letters does not, however, imply for Trouille the possibility of a plan on Henriette's part to engage Rousseau in an exchange over the role of women with an eye to displaying the product later. The status of Henriette's letter book as a piece of published writing does not strike Trouille anymore than it strikes Leigh; neither notices that this woman did indeed become a published writer, albeit of private letters. Like Leigh, Trouille accepts the verbatim truth of Henriette's letters, and blames Rousseau for not encouraging this woman to take up a writing career. Unlike Leigh, however, Trouille laments that Henriette herself did not struggle harder to break out of the conventional mold into which Rousseau forced her. Trouille ultimately analyzes Henriette's failure to pursue a writing career as motivated by a need for Rousseau's male approbation: "Perhaps she sought his approval in order to reassure herself; for, beneath her air of defiance and independence, Henriette seemed to lack the self-confidence and strength of character needed to pursue her unconventional role."[31]

Should we accept Henriette's guidelines for spinsterly happiness at face value, they do indeed, as Trouille argues, indicate a damning incorporation of principles that served to limit the life of a budding woman intellectual. But while Trouille relies on the transparency of Henriette's letters to make her argument that this woman fully accepted Rousseau's view of women, I am far more suspicious of Henriette, as was Rousseau before me. She may well have been misrepresenting the circumstances of her life in her letters, and may just as well have been exaggerating the effect of his responses on her life, the better to sell her manuscript. Perhaps she did go on to pursue a further writing career as "anonymous," or under her real name. At the limit of the possible, she may have been de La Tour, for Henriette's situation as she herself describes it is strikingly similar to de La Tour's: a woman living on her own with a penchant for intellectual activity and something of a talent for writing, forgotten by Rousseau when he went to England, refused permission to see him when he moved back to France in 1770.

Such imaginings aside, my most important quarrel with Trouille comes when she interprets Henriette's decision to publish these letters as "an unconscious rebellion against an overbearing mentor."[32] Like the critics cited above, Trouille assumes that only a powerful, unconscious motive could have caused a woman to publish her private letters in the late eighteenth century. Again, this assumption is highly motivated, for if this psychological barrier to publication does not exist, then we are not assured of the validity of the views and emotions expressed in the letters of early modern women. The authenticity of Henriette's letters is central to Trouille's overall argument. Her proposal that Henriette's decision to publish represents an "unconscious" rebellion against Rousseau's misogyny kills two birds with one stone: it allows Henriette's letters to remain fully in the realm of the private, while simultaneously bestowing upon her writing the cachet of feminist rebellion.

I should no doubt now pause to emphasize that my view of Henriette as a conscious agent in the construction of this correspondence does not take away from the misogyny of preaching to women that they must steer carefully clear of any intellectual participation in the public sphere, nor from the tragedy of wasted women's lives, in any era. My view does, however, implicate Henriette herself in perpetuating these conservative views of woman's proper role in society. Rather than explaining away Henriette's statements as internalized restrictions accompanied by an unconscious rebellion, I am speculating that Henriette may indeed have been as conservative in her views on women as was Rousseau. She was at least, as was de La Tour, perfectly willing to present herself in a conservative mode, if that self-presentation guaranteed the receipt of letters from Rousseau and the eventual publication of her work.

My view of "Henriette ***" is ultimately that her personal beliefs concerning woman's proper place in society cannot be extrapolated with any certainty from these published "private" letters. Like de La Tour, Henriette represents a phenomenon of eighteenth-century publishing values that has been misunderstood in our own day, by critics of all persuasions. Rousseau's rightful paranoia concerning the publication value of his letters led him to the same conclusion as myself about both of these women: that the sentiment in their first letters was neither spontaneously expressed nor innocent of design. While he was (probably) wrong about their identities in both cases, mistaking one for a man and the other for a different woman, Rousseau was in my opinion correct in believing that de La Tour and Henriette sought to engage him in the type of intellectual discussion that would ensure the future publication of their letters. To get around his opposition to such a correspondence, the women appealed to the private nature of their chosen genre, to their innate retiring "feminine" nature, and to their own obscurity, as evidence that they had not the slightest intention of going public with their letters. Both women then did exactly what Rousseau suspected they would do from the first, editing a manuscript for publication and arranging to have themselves presented to the public in an appropriately positive light as "nonauthors," all the while berating Rousseau for heartlessness and insincerity.

These two correspondences reveal women with a clear desire to write and to publish who found a way to do so. Neither protofeminist heroines nor sad victims of patriarchy, de La Tour and Henriette resemble James Boswell in their voracious desire for fame—perhaps reflected fame, perhaps posthumous fame, even an oxymoronic "anonymous fame" in Henriette's case—but fame, nevertheless. Guilleragues seems to have been content with a similar fate, concerning his "authorship" of the *Lettres portugaises.* It is undeniable that heavy strictures were placed upon women in the name of "virtue" in eighteenth-century France. Appealing to these strictures when venturing into the proscribed public forum could only help further one's cause as an author. Quite often, it seems to me, a woman writer's fallacious claims of "nonauthorship" constitute her "authentic" woman's voice, to the extent that such a voice can be heard.

My position raises some compelling theoretical questions. If women did at times willfully misrepresent their writing as private in order to promote themselves as "nonauthors," does this mean that the poststructuralists are right after all in claiming that there are no grounds on which one can claim to pare away a text's rhetorical layers to uncover a core "Truth"? The declaration that these two women sought primarily to please has the bizarre potential of placing me back among those critics against whom I was arguing in the beginning of this chapter, for whom "authenticity" in women's writing is only ever the result of unintended slips. While I have been primarily considering women's letters, the results of such a method of reading are most clearly evident in treatments of women's autobiographies. As a genre, autobiography seems at first to offer insight into the authentic thoughts and feelings of women, more so, at least, than fictional works; but again, critics interested in discovering the living woman beneath the obscuring rhetoric of patriarchy find in autobiographies only a frustratingly tantalizing echo of what they seek. Nancy K. Miller describes her experience of reading women's autobiographies as akin to "shaking hands with one's gloves on," while in an article on Marie-Jeanne Roland's *Mémoires particuliers,* it is only when Roland's intimate sexual revelations are briefly accompanied by an expression of anger at men that Brigitte Szymanek writes: "Roland for the first time revealed a woman's voice."[33] Perhaps the best illustration of this critical phenomenon comes in the conclusion to Sidonie Smith's *Poetics of Women's Autobiography*: "I have found women's autobiographies to be both eccentric and alive, whatever their limitations . . . women's stories frustrate expectations and thoroughly enchant the reader because they are vital, unconventional. From them erupt, however suppressed they might be, rebellion, confusion, ambivalence, the uncertainties of desire."[34]

With gender constructionism fully in place, only careful critical excavation can uncover a final layer to the palimpsest of a woman's autobiography. That this nugget of truth exists for Miller, Smith, and Szymanek, is clear. Each does indeed seem to believe that "there is a woman under there!" as one of the onlookers exclaims of Frenhofer's ruined masterpiece; but as each points, horrified, to this remnant of a writing woman, "a fragment saved from an incredible destruction," they simultaneously condemn the rest of her work to the status of mere conciliatory dross. I view the insights of many such critics, Nancy K. Miller in particular, as of enormous benefit to scholars, insofar as they have brought to our attention the true frustration and anger felt by women who believed their talents to have been consistently overlooked by virtue of their sex. Too often, however, these insights are accompanied by a blanket rejection of most of what women have written for centuries. In the course of their studies, these scholars deny the existence in these works of precisely that which they seek: direct contact with an individual consciousness of a previous era.

How did it come to pass that so many pages have been devoted to lamenting the destruction of potential masterpieces by early women writers? My experience as an Anglophone critic working on French texts from an American feminist perspective has taught me that the answer to the question "Who is to blame?" depends a great deal on geographical circumstance. From the vantage point of one side of the Atlantic, it would appear that the French are to blame with their airy Theory, exported to the United States sometime in the 1960s or 1970s and embraced fully by feminist studies in the early 1980s. Conversely, looking westward from Europe, it is the American feminists themselves who are to blame. In their unexamined rush toward radical equality between the sexes, together with an insufficiently theoretical understanding of Continental philosophy, *les Américaines* have arrived at a point where they are able to read only by imposing their own acrimonious grid over the works they examine.

This description of the present state of affairs is only somewhat exaggerated. Lamenting the presence of the "French disease" in American literary studies is now a bit passé, given that the heyday of poststructuralism came to an end in the early 1990s; across the ocean, however, the critique of American feminism and its potentially nefarious effects is thriving. A well-written attack can reach best-seller status, as was the case in 1995 with Mona Ozouf's *Women's Words: Essay on French Singularity*. Ozouf's book was born of her anger at American feminist critics who had turned their attention to Marie-Jeanne Roland's *Mémoires*, cited above, and considered to be the first modern autobiography by a French woman.[35] Ozouf views the constructionist studies of Roland by American feminists to be an affront to this intelligent and resourceful woman's memory. As her title indicates, *Women's Words* was born of Ozouf's stated desire to let Roland and other French women writers "speak" to us, in their own words, about it what it meant to them to be a woman.

Going to the opposite extreme of the American feminists she is attacking, Ozouf displays no theoretical angst whatsoever in declaring that she hears and understands Roland's views clearly from across the divide of more than two centuries. This serene rejection of interpretation is far from what I have in mind as a model for contemporary humanist gender criticism. Ozouf is quite right in urging us to "listen" to the voices of women born long ago in order to learn how they themselves experienced their lives as women. She is also right in arguing that we should not merely attribute answers that make us uncomfortable to the internalization of patriarchal belief structures. Yet Ozouf is also quite thoroughly wrong in ignoring the source of the occasional bursts of anger and frustration undeniably present in, for example, Roland's *Mémoires*. Women's voices speak to us from the past in a dialogue with the public they so ardently desired to reach; conforming to her readers' assumptions about women may well have been uppermost in Roland's mind as she began to write her autobiography, but the certainty of imminent death, and her apparent belief that her manuscript would be destroyed, seems to have "liberated" her from such constraints. However uncharacteristic her outbursts in the overall context of her work, they are part and parcel of her text. Rejecting the most radical manifestations of constructionist gender theory does not require rejecting the insights of feminism as a whole. There is a middle ground. My own polemic has, in other words, a positive goal: to go beyond the limits of constructionism by applying the "reasonable woman" standard to the conundrum of authorial intention, in order to create an image of a woman writer allowed her own beliefs and situated in her own time.

The rejection of unsuitable rhetoric in the writing of early modern women has, however, a time-honored, entrenched place in feminist literary studies. In "A Room of One's Own," the mother of feminist literary criticism frowns equally upon negotiation and overt anger in early women's writing: "One has only to skim those old forgotten novels and listen to the tone in which they were written to divine that the writer was meeting criticism; she was saying this by way of aggression, or that by way of conciliation."[36] It is a relief for Woolf to turn to works by men from the same period, even the most flawed, for they seem "so direct, so straightforward after the writing of women."[37] Woolf is relying, of course, on an androgynous model of the artist, a model she famously declares available to women only when they gain financial dependence and freedom from "woman's work." The result is a reversal of the critical procedure I have described above. Woolf seeks the "authentic" androgynous artist's lack of passion, dismissing both cultural negotiation and anger as dross; later feminist critics seek the voice of the angry woman, and dismiss both cultural negotiation and androgynous banality as dross.

I would argue, and I am hardly alone in doing so at this juncture, that whatever her views on the "woman question," the *manner* in which a woman writer negotiates, incorporates, and occasionally protests the limitations her culture placed on women's writing is a constitutive aspect of her writing, and constitutes as well, in my opinion, much of its beauty and value. Women writers of the past must be viewed as autonomous individuals whose works reflect a reality quite different from our own, a reality at times quite difficult for us to seize, but nevertheless equally authentic.[38] The reception history of de La Tour, a minor figure and hardly a suitable feminist heroine, proves my point quite nicely. While I find her occasional protofeminist statements to be heartfelt, what her letters most clearly communicate to me is a desire for fame as a writer. She sought that fame actively and eagerly in a manner not designed to attract the positive attention of feminists or nonfeminists, for she was quite willing to construct an image of herself as "merely" a female fan, "merely" a writer of "private" letters, at most, a builder of monuments to a famous man. She was quite willing, that is, in the end, to grab her reflected glory where she could find it.

Appendix: The Rousseau-de La Tour Correspondence, September 28, 1761–January 15, 1762

Bernardoni to Rousseau, September 28, 1761.
Ah! such is the inconstancy of women! While reading *La Nouvelle Héloïse*, I had promised myself never to write again; I said it to everyone, determined never to change my mind.

Projects vanished as soon as they were formed,
here I am writing, and to whom? To Monsieur Rousseau himself. I can preserve my pride only by remaining anonymous: a sad creature who scarcely knows how to assemble the twenty-four letters of the alphabet, daring to enter into the lists, face uncovered, against the most famous pen of past, present, and no doubt future centuries, that would be an insufferable audacity. You will thus not learn, monsieur, who I am: but you will learn that Julie is not in the least dead, and that she lives to love you. This Julie is not myself, you can see that by my style; I am no more than her cousin, or rather her friend, just as was Claire; if I do not possess the merit of the latter, I do at least have the same feelings and zeal. I have told my divine friend that Julie's soul breathes in her, with the exception of her mistake; all who know how to appreciate her agree with me; she disputes this claim out of excessive modesty, and assures us, with that lovely candor that only demonstrates her to be all the more that which she will not admit to being, that she would like, even at the price of Julie's fall, to resemble her in every way; and that she is only sure of not committing this sin, because she is sure of never finding a Saint-Preux (supposing of course that she is not married).

I said that I would tell you; I was challenged to do it; I am telling you, that is the subject of my letter. If this act seems mad to you, so much the better, you will thus not believe me mad, as the good Chaillot argued to the charming Claire. As for the rest, believe me as much as you like; I figure in all this only as one more of your admirers in the world, whose opinion is so far beneath you, that it could only be indifferent to you. To return to my Julie, whose existence you surely never suspected except in your brilliant and fecund imagination. Be however assured that you modeled her after my original, feature by feature, as if she had been known to you. The same sublimity of soul, the same delicacy, the same piety toward her parents, the same tone with her servants, who adore her, the same sensitivity for the unfortunate; as much wit and intelligence, as much grace, as many talents, as much wisdom, as much ease in speaking, and more than all that, the same generous ways with a husband quite different from Wolmar. Believe a woman who praises another, whose superiority she has felt over the ten years that they have been intimately linked. Julie exists, monsieur, do not doubt it; and why would you doubt it? M. Rousseau certainly exists, is the one fact more surprising than the other? This Julie, who has a decided antipathy for new acquaintances, would give anything to make yours. She does not dare flatter herself that it will happen, but she hopes at least that I will show her an answer from you: it is only for this reason that she has permitted me to speak to you of her. If you wish not to disappoint her, address your letter, to whom? Oh! that is a problem, wait; leave the top blank, please; signifying nothing will signify that it is for me, not to the postman who is not in on the game, but to Mme the marquise de Solar, Parc-aux-Cerfs, across from M. de Séjean Versailles, an address that you will have the goodness to put on an envelope containing the letter. It will be faithfully delivered to me; and Mme de Solar will not tell you who I am, she knows me no more than do you, of whom I have the honor of being with all the feeling that you know so well how to inspire, the very humble and very obedient servant.

My husband knows and approves of what I am doing.

Rousseau to Bernardoni, September 29, 1761.
I hope, madame, despite the beginning of your letter, that you are not an author, that you have no intention of becoming one, and that you are not provoking me into a battle of wits, a type of fencing for which I am as averse as incapable. Nevertheless you promised yourself, you say, never to write again in your life; I promised myself the same thing, madame, and surely I will keep that promise; but this engagement is relative only to the public, and does not extend to the exchange of letters, which is a good thing no doubt, for your own letter would, I greatly fear, cost me an infidelity. To the editor of one Julie, you announce the existence of another, one who really

exists and whose Claire you are, I am charmed for your sex and even for my own, for whatever your friend may say, as soon as there exist Julies and Claires, Saint-Preux will not be lacking; warn her of that, I beg you, so that she may be on her guard; and you yourself, should you be, which I do not presume, as mad as your model, do not believe that her example suffices to protect you from folly. Perhaps all that I am telling you will seem quite thoughtless; but it is your fault. What to say to those whom one would like to believe very likable and very virtuous, but whom one does not at all know? Charming friends, if you are such as my heart supposes, may you, for the honor of your sex and the happiness of your life, never find Saint-Preux; but if you are like the rest, may you find only Saint-Preux!

You speak of making my acquaintance; you no doubt do not know that the man to whom you are writing, afflicted with an incurable and cruel illness, fights every day between life and death, and that the very letter that he is writing to you is often interrupted by distractions of a quite different sort. Nevertheless I cannot hide from you that your letter has given me a secret desire to know both of you and that if our exchange ends here it will not leave me without some anxiety. If my curiosity is satisfied, it will be even worse: in spite of age, suffering, reason, experience, a solitary man must not expose himself to the sight of Julies and Claires when he wishes to retain his tranquility.

I have written to you, madame, as you prescribed to me, without seeking to inform myself of that which you did not want me to know. If I were indiscreet it would not be impossible for me to discover who you are; but were you Mme de Solar herself, I will never learn anything about your secret other than what you tell me. If it is your intention that I guess who you are, you will find me quite stupid; but then you probably did not expect to find me clever.

Bernardoni to Rousseau, October 5, 1761.
No, monsieur, I am not at all an author; and have never had, as you so very well put it, the intention of becoming one: I have only the precise amount of wit necessary, to feel all my insignificance in this regard. I well understood that you would quite misunderstand the beginning of my letter; but I only noticed this blunder while perceiving a thousand others. I would have had to redo my entire letter. The more I would have started over, dreamed, reflected, the worse and more unintelligible it would have become. I left it as it was; I will do the same with this one. It is my habit to say whatever springs to

mind, when my limited intelligence provides me with nothing else. Your penetration will supplement what I write. You no longer wish to write for the public: I am upset for the public and for your publisher: as for me, I will console myself by rereading a hundred hundred times what you have written, in which I will always find the charms of novelty. The reasons that I had for remaining *incognito* are more pressing than ever. I have no desire that you *discover* who I am. You must think me quite devoid of intelligence, if you did not believe that I believed you smart enough to be stupid on purpose. I render you in this regard, as in all others, the justice that you deserve; and in order to prove it to you I am going to give you, in complete confidence, a way to remove the possibility of your discovering my identity by chance. Do not show our letters to anyone: there are those who come to you who know the writing of the *inséparables*. Dare to believe at present that I am working in your favor. Not only am I not Mme de Solar, it also the exact truth that she does not know me, and that it is by an intermediary that your letters come to me. I say nothing to you of Julie: she is writing to you; you will judge her. We promised each other to write you separately, without showing each other our letters, until they were ready to go out, and to redo nothing, even if we had said the same things. They will at least have been said quite differently. I leave to her the response to the passage in which you express *your incapacity and your aversion for a battle of wits*: that will be ample matter for comment. I should have also let her respond to all your other points, should have admired her, and stayed quiet. I am writing to M. Rousseau, my letter will be sent alongside that of Julie: all that should make me tremble; but emotion conquers vanity. While I do not have the honor of being known to you, I have that of knowing you: to know you, and to take a lively interest in you, is one and the same thing. I wish thus to join my efforts to those of my friend, in engaging you to refuse none of the help that can be given to reestablish your health. Could you have really thought that we were ignorant of its deplorable state? Are you such that it can be ignored? Not only do we know that you are sick, we also know that you insist on remaining so. *I have lived long enough,* you say. Come to my aid, eloquent Milord. *Cruel one,* you would say, *if you have lived enough for yourself, must you not live more for others, etc.?* Is it only to set conditions for us, monsieur, that you wrote your divine letter? Are you not also made to practice what you preach so well? Are you capable, by your example, of dragging the public into an error from which you seemed to want to save it by your advice?

The public is already inclined to believe that your intention was to have Saint-Preux's argument prevail over that of Milord. In spite of you, I adopt the opinion of the latter; and Julie wishes you to adopt it. Out of love for her, see Brother Côme; an expert in more than one domain, and particularly in that of the illness that torments you, and drives us to despair. You answer will decide whether or not I continue or cease the epistolary exchange that you wish to engage. If you wish to take no care of a life that has become precious to all of Europe, I do no wish to cause myself new regrets. That is my last word.

De La Tour to Rousseau, October 5, 1761.
I am monsieur that admirer of whom a woman quite enlightened with regard to every other subject spoke to you as Julie. I am quite far from perceiving all the resemblances that Claire finds between this admirable woman and myself: you should take my word: I have nothing in common with her, except the often fruitless desire to be useful to the unfortunate: an upright and sensitive soul; and the most tender inclination for Saint-Preux's character. All the other qualities that my friend attributes to me are as of yet only the objects of my emulation: in a word, it is my model that she has sketched in her letter, and not my portrait. You will find in my style neither the lightness nor the gaiety that embellishes that of my dear Claire. I possess infinitely less wit than she: I have only one manner of being, thinking, feeling, speaking; and I do not know how to choose, as she does, among all possible tones, the one that best fits the circumstances. Furthermore, I was born more serious; and I do not have the courage to banter with you. I am even quite close to regretting having authorized the enthusiasm of my ardent friend: I admit to you that I did not believe you would answer: the opinion that I was given of you made me try this test out of pure curiosity; and I did not count on its success. I should however have realized that it is not easy to resist the grace Claire puts into her expressions, and that a man such as you show yourself to be in your works would not want to resist. But . . . but why am I writing to you then, since I do not have the talent to amuse you; and I do not claim to interest you? Why? Because I never said that I would not write again, because Julie wrote, and because Claire writes much better than I do; and because I have many things to tell you.

Nothing, aside from *La Nouvelle Héloïse*, has affected me as much as your letter, monsieur. The honesty, the delicacy, the care, the discretion that reigns in it, enchanted me. But I was deeply moved by what you said about your health. You should not have published *La Nouvelle Héloïse*; or, you should devote all of your care to curing a disease you make incurable by persuading yourself that it is. For you surely do not wish to hurt anyone; and you hurt me more, by afflicting my soul with a share in your pains, than you have served me by rectifying my mind through the communication of your insights.

I am flattered, monsieur, by the willingness you seem to demonstrate to consent to make my acquaintance: but I do not wish to know you (as my Claire has also the honor of writing to you, I speak here only for myself). What good would come of it? I have nothing of any value but my heart: scarcely does it find in this life the occasion to show itself

> *Ben s'ode il ragionar, si vede il volto*
> *Ma dentro il petto, mal giudicar puossi.*
>
> *[It is simple to understand what he says, and to read his face,*
> *But as to what is in his heart, one cannot easily judge.]*

You would thus gain nothing. As for myself, I do not admire coldly enough to expose myself to seeing you. Would that be watching out for myself, as you advise my friend in your last letter? A man who made Saint-Preux speak would be too dangerous for a Julie held in the bonds of marriage. I admit that he would not say the same things: but anything from his mouth must be engaging. I already feel too strongly how disagreeable my situation is, to place before my eyes an object of comparison as despairing as yourself: and then, what woman could hope to appear estimable in the eyes of a man who knew, or who imagined, Julie? No, I do not wish to know you. That is unforgivably contradictory, after having allowed my friend to express to you my desire to see you: you will take me for a madwoman, and you will be right. Believe, however, that if I carried out my original plan, I would be yet more mad.

Of all the advantages that my seductive Claire has over me, I envy her only that of having obtained a letter from you, monsieur: and I beg you to treat me as favorably as her. I fear that this prayer would be indiscreet, if my intention were to impose more than once on a man whose time is as precious as your own. But I passionately desire to possess one of your letters; and I will never again write to you. May the cessation of an exchange that I should never have begun, leave you with no *anxiety*. Is if for you to feel the lack of anything? If Julie really existed, you are certainly Saint-Preux; and in that case, her memory must occupy you entirely. If she is only the masterpiece of your imagination, believe me, keep to your chimera: the Creator never made a work as perfect as your own.

Farewell, monsieur, that which Claire let you glimpse of the conduct of my husband, in order to put my behavior toward him in the best light, makes anonymity obligatory for me: I am unable to name myself, without attacking him: I believe that you know him: I would thus risk taking from him your respect; it is too great a good for me to wish to deprive him of it: thus, you will not learn who I am. It is enough for me that you know that I have for you all the feelings that one may obtain from the idea that what is known of you gives of your soul, your heart, your mind, and your character.

Bernardoni to Rousseau, October 15, 1761.

What! monsieur, you who are so familiar with the science of the heart, you were able to mistake the feelings of my Julie, and myself! This must in truth be the case, as it pleases you to hold out so rigidly against us. It is not possible to suppose that our letters did not reach you: less so that you have any reason to doubt the lively and sincere interest that we take in your health; if it causes us to combat the resolution that you seem to have taken to succumb to your sufferings, rather than employing the one efficacious remedy, is that a reason to snub us? Fie! Nothing is more villainous; one would hardly excuse such behavior in a spoiled child; it approaches ingratitude. Perhaps you will offer as justification that we threatened to break off contact with you if you did not submit to us? You believe quite simply that we have said our last word on the matter, as if women were never permitted to change their minds, when it was to their advantage. I must tell you, I do not recognize Saint-Preux in all this; or if he were like this, your Héloïse loses in this moment a good part of its merit, in my eyes. Not to offend you, but I place much higher my Julie, who begs you, who even orders you to prefer her to your plan to let yourself die. Read, read attentively what she writes to you; weigh each of her reflections, return to its principle; pity yourself, if you dare. Ah! No response! No, I cannot get over it. It is only the alarm that your present state causes me that is able to suspend my just reproaches. I will not leave you alone until you repair promptly the damage you have caused. Truly, we are quite worried about you, monsieur; and we would be greatly obliged if you calmed our fears without delay, by the indicated method of Mme de Solar, Parc-aux-Cerfs at Versailles.

P.-S. Well, blush, fall to your knees, if you are capable of remorse. At the very moment that I was closing my letter, written and ready to leave without the knowledge of my friend, I received one from her that encloses one for you, which she asks me to send you or to throw into the fire, as I please. It would be thievery to choose the latter option: live up to the one I am choosing.

De La Tour to Rousseau, October 16, 1761.

What have I done, monsieur, that you refuse me an answer? Are you angry that the enthusiasm of friendship gave me a name that you have caused to be praiseworthy? A Julie such as myself, does she not merit some regard? The sentimental tone of my first letter, did it revolt you? Do you accept only the homage of wit? Is it Claire's that you favor? Did I appear to you too ambitious in wishing to be treated like her? Did I speak too frankly? Can truth not flatter itself that it will be well received by you, because it offends your modesty? Or rather, are you more ill? Although this last reason would be the most bearable to my vanity, it is the one I fear the most. But need I search anywhere other than in myself for the source of the disobliging distinction in how you treat me? I recognize in it the character of my star, I succeed in nothing.

> *Non comincia mai fortuna per poco,*
> *Quando un mortal si piglià à scherno e à giuoco.*
>
> *[Fortune is not content with half-measures,*
> *When she goes after a mortal out of spite or for play.]*

Goodbye, monsieur, pardon me for allowing myself the satisfaction of sharing with you the pain you are causing me. Perhaps I should not have given myself the pleasure: but she who expects nothing from others, is excused for permitting herself the consolation that she is able to procure for herself.

Rousseau to Bernardoni, October 19, 1761.

The pleasure that I feel, madame, in receiving a second letter from you would be tempered or perhaps increased by your reproaches, if I were able to fathom them; but I try in vain to do so. You speak to me of a letter from your friend; I received no such letter, other than the one that accompanied your own of the 16th, and was of the same date, and this letter, no offense, is not that of a woman, but rather of a man or of an angel, and either option is equally frustrating to me. You seem to complain about my negligence in responding, and the more I merit this reproach with regard to others, the more your own ingratitude increases, for I responded to your letter the day after I received it, and, by an increase in diligence that I would gladly do without, here I am responding to the second the day after as well. The real evil is that while giving yourself a man for a woman friend, you remained a woman; and the joke is all the more cruel in that you only fooled me by half. Two men might play a thousand such tricks on me and I would only laugh: but, I know not why, I am unable to imagine your tête-à-tête with M. Julie collaborating on your letters and all the mockery addressed to the poor dupe, without feelings of anger, and, I fear, something even worse. If to avenge myself I imagine you as horrible, you can easily imagine that does not work: I thus avenge myself by imagining you as charming, so much so that as charming as you are, I could make you jealous of yourself. The only thing that displeases me about this vengeance is the fear that it will turn back on me.

A new madness that I must admit to you. While reading this distressing letter, while examining its every fold in an attempt to find that chimerical Julie whom I could not stop myself from regretting to the point of tears, I happened to discover that the postal stamp had pressed through the envelope to the paper, from which I concluded that the author of this letter had not written it in your room; this discovery immediately disarmed my fury, and I understood that I was excusing you only for the plot to fool me, rather than for the collaborative tête-à-tête. For God's sake, madame, you who can perform miracles, tolerate the indiscretion of my prayer; I ask you on my knees to change this man back into a woman: abuse me, lie to me; but please, make of him, as you are able to do, another Julie, and I will give to you both the hearts of a thousand Saint-Preux in one.

As for the letters that you say were previously written to me, and that you say must have reached me, you must not suppose this to be true, madame; you must be persuaded of this: I did not receive these letters. If I had received them, I might not have responded to them, at least not so quickly, for I am lazy, ill, sad, busy, and have never in my life been a faithful correspondent in the exchanges that interested me the most; but I would never have denied receiving your letter, and I would never have denied my blame for not responding. I judge from the content of your reproaches that the letters concerned my health, and I am touched by the interest that you are taking in my condition. Far from trying to die, it was to continue to live until the last possible moment that I gave up on the ruses of doctors. Twenty years of torments and experiments have been sufficient to teach me the nature of my illness and the insufficiency of their art. My life, although sad and painful, is not a burden to me; it is not without its pleasures as long as those such as yourself deign to take an interest in me: but to fight in vain to prolong it would be to use it up and shorten it. The little that remains to me is still dear enough that I wish to enjoy it in peace. My decision is made, I do not like to argue, and I do not wish to contradict you; but I will not change my mind. Farewell, madame; here will probably end our short correspondence: enjoy the easy triumph of leaving me with the regret of ending it. I am sensitive, easy, and naturally quite loving; I cannot resist caresses; with one letter you have already subjugated me; I admit also that your pretend Julie added much to your empire over me, and that now that I know she does not exist, her idea increases the heartache that remains as I think of the trick you played on me.

Bernardoni to Rousseau, October 24, 1761.
It happened again! Oh! I would strangle M. de Chauvelin and all his helpers if I had hold of them. Yes I would love to break their bones. I have just sent someone to put all of them to the question. If our letters are found again, you will have them; and if they are not found, you will have the copies that Julie and I required of each other. She wants you to have mine; I want, with more reason, that you have hers; and this packet will surely reach you, unless our ambassador dies on the way. And on top of all that you take my female Julie for a male. The more you see of her style, the more you will feel her imposing vigor. I like the little vanity of men, who make man and angel synonymous. I would excuse such behavior in a common man; but I have trouble overlooking it in the great, sublime Rousseau, who knows so well how to say that *the soul has no sex.* No, monsieur, it does not; remember that always! Julie adds to all the graces of her own sex, all the solidity of your own: nature exhausted itself in joining in her the perfections of both, and in sparing her the frivolity of the one, and the ferocity of the other. I cannot show her to

you, as she does not want to be seen: but if you wish to come to Paris, I will show you just her foot, through a cat door, and you will agree that this pretty appendage does not belong to a man. I admit that I myself, who have seen this rare combination every day for some time, I am still so astonished by it that I would not know what to think, if M. Julie had not taken it into her head to come close to dying in childbirth! You are now convinced, I hope, unless in your stubbornness you decide to believe that Vulcan's ax was somehow involved. There are still many Vulcans in the world, but no Jupiter. What delights me is that you take women for men, and men for women: for after all, I had promised myself I would tell you about this one day or the other, given that I do not want to adorn myself with peacock feathers, and now is the time, or never, for this confession. My third letter, that is, the second you received, was written entirely by my husband, except for the postscript. Here is what happened. Seeing Julie truly afflicted by your silence, we decided, he and I, to ask you the reason. That was a problem for me, as I had announced that I had told you I would not write again, unless you promised me to work at preserving your life. He combated my resolve, I resisted, he insisted, I would not give in. Finally my husband (these men are masters) took up the pen, scratched out the letter that you have seen and, a pistol at my throat, forced me to copy it. Note that his pistols are affectionate supplications: the way to resist those! No, I know nothing more despotic than those devilish men who demand nothing. Admire my husband's fine character; he is no less humiliated at being taken for a woman, than Julie is vain for having been taken for a man. Does that not prove a bit that in fact the soul has no sex? This little dog took off with your letter; I do not have it in sight to respond to it as I would like. She has made that her task, you will benefit from that decision, in any case. Farewell, monsieur, I do not dare fight your resolution; but it makes me despair. I will nevertheless sacrifice my own for you, as long as I do not bore you with my chatter. Proud of the least resemblance between Claire and myself, I will not hide from you my pride in having, as does she, an only daughter named Henriette, who calls Julie her second Mother. *Is that not, my sister, to cough and spit like her?*

De La Tour to Rousseau, October 25, 1761.

I do not have a mind for detail; and I am afraid that I will make a mess of the story I have to tell you, monsieur: but this is not the moment to consult my vanity: a matter far dearer to me than vanity obliges me to reveal in full my projects, and my conduct toward you; thus, at the risk of explaining myself badly, and boring you, and causing you to reject me once again in the most mortifying way, I am going to give you a faithful account of what I have done and thought with regard to yourself.

In reaction to your first letter, certainly capable of encouraging my Claire to continue an exchange that seemed so agreeable to you, she wrote you a second letter, in which she begged you to do all that you could to prolong your days; and this letter was in itself a further reason to live. I dared to join a letter to her own: I will not tell you what it contained: the things that I say do not merit repeating. These two letters were brought in the same envelope on Tuesday the sixth of this month to M. Chauvelin's place: I do not know by what unhappy chance, for us, they were prevented from reaching you: but although your little regard for my good faith authorizes me to doubt you, I believe that you never received them. I am sending you these letters; in order to correct or punish you. We kept copies of them; because we promised each other, Claire and I, to give each other doubles of all that we wrote to you; and that is the only agreement between us, with regard to our letters. Not possessing the advantage of living together, we write them separately; with no sharing of ideas; and we give them to each other only at the moment that they are sent off: most often without even seeing each other.

I am a woman, monsieur; and I do not have the ridiculous pretension of raising myself out of my sphere: to be a good and honest woman, in every sense, seems to me to be an honorable task, when it is performed well: I want nothing more; nor anything less; and I do not think that I have strayed, in the little that you have seen of me, from the sweetness, simplicity, and modesty that fits that title. I would be quite offended by your claim to incredulity, if I perceived it as a censure of my behavior; and if it were not clear that it was only an excuse for your silence. You pretend to doubt that I am a woman, in order to dispense in my case with the regard that your sex owes my own (a regard too dearly earned, in any case, to be contested); and it is only to blush less at having tricked me, that you claim that I am tricking you. But allow me to say, monsieur, that your games are too cruel to be considered the distractions of a beautiful soul: one who tries to do good, does not enjoy doing evil; and you have done me harm: yes, you may congratulate yourself. Nothing disagreeable about the metamorphosis you are demanding has escaped my notice. And yet I am not complaining: my heart is not one to become annoyed; and I will not say, my project was that M. Rousseau write to me; I failed; he obstinately refuses to write to me; and whether this be because he fears that I am not likable enough, or because he fears that I am too likable, *either option is equally frustrating to me.*

And so, monsieur, will you do me the honor of responding? Will you resolve yourself to determining in my favor the meaning of all the equivocal statements contained in your last letter to my friend? My esteem for you is so precious to me that I tremble to add by my demands to the faults the accumulation of which would no doubt weaken it: thus I will not press you more. Farewell, monsieur, the loss of the two letters of which I am attaching copies to this one have inspired me to send a messenger: he is under orders to stay over in Montmorency if you are unable to respond immediately. For you will at least answer Claire? You will not betray a preference that, if I were not so sure of your tact, would make me believe that you had discovered who we are? Farewell, I say again; and with cause. I have expressly forbidden the messenger who is carrying this enormous package to tell you who I am: I beg you not to test his faithfulness. Eh! what good would it do you, what good would it have done you, to know who I am? You would have hurt me more directly; I would not have felt it more.

De La Tour to Bernardoni, October 26, 1761.

The zeal of D . . . , who wanted to go to Montmorency on foot, is the reason, my Claire, that our dispatches have not left; for it is too nasty to put a dog outside. But I will win, he will go by horse; and tomorrow morning. I am sending you our oracle's letter, and my sad response. He will laugh well at your epistle, if he laughs as much as I did. It is original, *miraculously* well written, and will contrast marvelously with the mournful tone of my own. You will please come to dine with me on Tuesday; in that way, you will likely arrive at the same time as our courier. Bring me the two letters that I gave you; your husband will have had the time to copy them by then. I do like your warning not to steal anything from you. Lack does not make me a thief, mademoiselle; and your treasure is in its entirety in the envelope that contains my *widow's mite.* So no bad jokes about how I depend on the wealth of others.

Rousseau to de La Tour and Bernardoni, October 26, 1761.

To the *inséparables,* men or women,

I must admit to you, messieurs or mesdames, I am as mad as you have wished me to be. My exchange with you is becoming more exciting to me than is appropriate to my age, my estate, and my principles. In spite of all that, my badly healed suspicions will not permit me to continue without misgiving. That is why I am not writing to Julie by name, because if she is as you claim, which I desire, or rather which I should fear, it is less offensive if I do not write to her than if I write to her in a manner other than is appropriate. If she is a woman, she is more than an angel; if she is a man, this man is quite witty; but intelligence is like power, one always abuses it when one has too much. One more thing, this is getting too spirited to be continued anonymously. Reveal your names, or I will stop writing. That is my last word.

De La Tour to Rousseau, October 28, 1761.

This time, monsieur, you will write to me *by name,* or not at all. At least, I presume that you will not be so eager to harm me that you will respond to Claire when it is I who am writing to you. My agreeable friend has allowed me this final resource; and she has for a time suppressed the resentment that you excite in her by attacking her sincerity: for in our relationship, as with your heroines, it is Claire who is useful to Julie.

In whatever class your imagination places me, you see me in the most disadvantageous light: I seem to you to be an imprudent woman, or an impertinent man: the alternatives are certainly not flattering: and the mood that leaps out from your letter proves well that whoever I am, I am not what it takes to obtain something from you. I admit that I am wrong: but is it for you to complain? Whom have I harmed by acting so gauchely, that I have aroused your suspicion? Certainly myself: for my clumsiness has earned me almost rough treatment from you. Do not believe, however, that I think I merit such treatment: no, very innocent intentions have led me to a behavior that I also believe to be innocent: they have produced effects that I could never have anticipated: you have caused all the harm, and it has fallen on me. However shocking your conduct with regard to me, I would rather be able to scold you than to excuse you by the sadness of your situation. However, I am perhaps the only one for whom it may serve as an excuse: for ultimately, the malaise that causes objects to seem disagreeable or insipid to you does not change their nature: even when suffering, one has a duty to be just, and this obligation is all the more pressing for you than for any other, if we owe in proportion to what we promise. What! you are not susceptible to persuasion? You do not want either to believe me or to write to me? The soul that shows itself in your works, is it not your own? Have I accorded my truest esteem only to false appearances? Was my cult only an idolatry? And how could a soul that seems made for honest feelings be insensitive to the respectful interest that you have inspired in me? To want neither to believe me, nor to write to me! . . . But what have you found in what I have sent you that is so superior to the idea that you have of women that you persist in doubting that I am one? Can women not recognize merit, cherish it, seek it out? Must the obstacles placed in their way limit their intelligence and their feelings? Or if permitted to perceive the good, are they not permitted also to love it? In a word, does the tyranny of prejudice extend as far as the most precious faculties of the soul? You have taught me that my taste for great talent may be unfortunate, but nothing will persuade me that it is condemnable. I am a woman, monsieur. In spite of that, I sacrifice my self-esteem in favor of that of the men who have most mistreated it: your state affects me even more than your injustices have wounded me; I am going to prove that to you. You seem to have the greatest desire to know who I am: if you will agree to the proposition that I am going to make you, I swear to you, that the joy of having served you will remove the mask that hides me from your eyes; and, what seems to be of yet more interest to you, my Claire will make herself known as well. To gain these two advantages, the first of which is important in itself, the other for the price that you put on it, you will only have to agree to see a man of whom I hope for the best with regard to your health. He has performed, to my knowledge, more astonishing cures than your own would be: I am certain of his skill, his prudence, and his lack of greed; but it is not with regard to you that I boast of this last quality: there is not a man in the world who would not believe his zeal, and his pains, sufficiently compensated by the sole pleasure of having been useful to you. I beg you, monsieur, consent to see him: you risk nothing: he is as far removed from the dangerous enterprises of charlatans as from the too servile observation of rules; and if he does not judge that his art will heal you, he will say so with all the frankness that your strength of character merits. My proposition is revolting to you; I believe I see that; and I sigh. But what convincing reasons do you have to resist me? If you are disillusioned with doctors, are you also disillusioned with that tender acquiescence to the desires of others that must be the habitual state of a good heart? Forget for a moment your repugnance, your illness even; and your constancy in suffering: think only of me: look on the consent I am asking of you as an act of kindness that is absolutely indifferent to you; and that will dissipate the worries of a woman far more worthy (whatever you may think) of your deferential esteem, than of the suspicions you heap upon her. I am saying nothing that Claire does not think, and that she would have said to you as well, if she had not generously ceded her rights to me. What I am soliciting as a grace, you perhaps owe to me as a reparation: and, I must tell you, your fate is in your hands, relative to myself: never will you hear me spoken of; you will never learn who took a sincere interest in your sufferings, if, neglecting to merit this knowledge, you end this exchange by a refusal more painful to me than all the others, because it will do you harm. Farewell, monsieur, send me your response, as you have already done, by Mme de Solar, and remember that this answer will give me the greatest pleasure; or the greatest suffering. No, I cannot accept that you doubted my sex, and accused me, in good faith. I am a woman; and either I am telling the truth, or I am a monster. Never has the plan of duping you entered the head of an intelligent man. I must repeat that I have no *witty abuses* to regret. Can you say the same for yourself?

Rousseau to de La Tour, October 30, 1761.
To Julie
I would add an epithet, if I knew one that could add anything to that word.

Yes, madame, you are a woman, I am persuaded of it; if I persisted in doubting because of signs to the contrary, which I will reveal to you when you wish, I would be harming only myself. That said, I feel that I must make up in your regard for all the offenses one can commit against a person whom one knows only through her mind, but this duty does not frighten me, and you would have to be quite inexorable if my willingness to humiliate myself before you was not enough to calm you. Moreover, you are quite mistaken if you believe your pride to have been offended by my doubts; the fear I felt that they would be justified is vengeance enough for you, and did you think it meant so little, when you dared to take the name of Julie, that you would not have to fight for it?

The condition you place on agreeing to satisfy the desire I have to know who you are confirms to me that it is worthy of you. I am thus doing you justice; but you are not returning it when you suppose me to be more curious than sensitive. No, madame, that which I would not do to please you, I would not do to know you, and I would not sell a favor that you wish to do me by requiring a greater one against your will. I suppose that the man you wish me to see is Brother Côme, of whom you have spoken to me before; if the thing were doable, I would obey and you would remain unknown: but friendship has preceded humanity. M. le maréchal de Luxembourg asked me to see him last summer, I obeyed and had him come twice. Brother Côme did what none of his profession had been able to do before him; I saw nothing that was not in conformity with his reputation and with your opinion of him; in the end, he delivered me from a nasty error by verifying that my illness was not what I had thought. But the illness I do have is no less mysterious or incurable, and I do not suffer less than before his visits; thus, all human attentions serve only to torment me. It is surely not your intention that they have this effect.

You reproach me for the abuse of wit that, because I supposed you to be a man, I believed I saw in your letters. I do not know if this criticism is valid; but I never thought that I had enough wit to abuse it; and I do not care enough about it to want to do so. But it is true that the type of correspondence that it has pleased you to establish with me may have caused me to have recourse to bad jokes that do not suit me and that I cannot make work. It is up to you, madame, and your delightful friend, to learn that my heart and my pen have a different language, and that the language of esteem and confidence are not absolutely foreign to me. But you who are talking, you are far from excused yourself in this matter, and I warn you that this complaint is not so slight in my opinion that it does not merit being first discussed, then thoroughly removed from an ongoing correspondence.

After folding my letter, I realized that the writing was legible through the paper, thus I put it in an envelope.

De La Tour to Rousseau, November 5, 1761.

No, monsieur, it is not of Brother Côme that I wish to speak to you: he is too famous for me to think that of all the worthy persons who take an interest in you, none would have required of your friendship that you consult with him. The man I would like you to see, although less famous, will be much more so if you put yourself in his care; and his reputation, which is however not my concern, would be all the more flattering if it rested on public opinion. My hopes in this regard are not without a justifiable basis: M. Sarbourg has operated more than one cure that Brother Côme would not take on. You see then, monsieur, that I am not going to back down; that nothing excuses you from ceding to my demands; and that you were quite mistaken if you believed that you could pretend to submit without accepting the consequences. I would go so far as to say that your belief that I was speaking of Brother Côme has led you further than you would otherwise have gone; but it is clear in your letter that you recognize having contracted an engagement; and that you are agreeing to yet another. Admit that the number of offenses for which you must make amends means that you are required to do as I say as reparation, and that, after having assured me that you would see Brother Côme at my request, if you had not seen him, to refuse to see the man whom I am proposing would be to go back on your word in an unworthy fashion. Thus, monsieur, you are not yet released; you will consent to see M. Sarbourg, you will write to me about it, and I will send him to you: or, I will forever remain in the shadows, from which you may draw me out with one word. In truth, if I were of a mind to laugh at my threats, I would, even while making them. It really matters to you, who care for so few things, who are not curious, and who cannot be *sensitive,* up to a point, to the feeling that you inspire in everyone; it really matters to you, I say, to find out who I am! Besides, however determined I am to fulfill the conditions of our agreement, it does not seem all that easy to me. For if, in the end, my husband does not have the honor of being known to you, which may well be the case in spite of what I had thought, I might be able to name myself while remaining anonymous.

I did not *dare to take* the name of Julie, monsieur (on this topic no equivocation is possible), I told you, it was my friend who gave it to me. Friendship has its blind spots as do other emotions: but they are always pardonable; and never dangerous, when they are as visible as this one is. Dare to take the name of Julie! that would be to no longer merit it. While I do not lack self-esteem, I would never compare myself to a woman for whom you reserve all your affection; or, whose character it pleased you to imagine.

You will oblige me infinitely by telling me by what signs, flattering or not, you took me to be a man; and why you were afraid that your doubts were well founded. You have made me too hopeful; for I wish to know all that you think of me: from which I will find encouragement, and lessons, that my opinion of you will make quite useful. Oh! I will eternally regret having written to you three times, without a response. However energetic one may be, one does not respond in the limits of an ordinary letter to all that ten pages not dictated by wit contain of meritorious topics. I am now, I believe, absolved of the charge of abusing my wit; and even of having any: unless you wish to go on according it to me, in order to contest that which I value a hundred times more, and do possess, the habit of telling the truth. Assuredly, if I possessed wit, if I cared about it, if I believed it merited consideration, or that one should even pay attention to it in a person who had much more; it would be to you that I would have wanted to show it; and I would not say to you that you received from me *ten pages not dictated by wit.* Farewell, monsieur. I would have had the honor of writing to you sooner if not for a tragic family event that recently occurred; and that demanded my attention, and had to be given preference over my pleasures. That is still true; all that I have said to you is true, and will be. Do not believe that Claire, who knows how to gain pardon for possessing infinite wit, wants to deprive herself forever of the charms of an exchange with you. She consents to letting me finish my project; but when you have agreed, we will both write to you; and I will be pleased, because you say things for me that are more satisfying than what you say to me.

As always by Mme de Solar.

I beg you to let me pay the postage for this letter; I have been assured that in that way they arrive more safely.

Rousseau to de La Tour, November 10, 1761.
I believe that you have guessed correctly, madame, and that I would not have gone so far with regard to the man in question if, in spite of what your friend wrote to me, I had believed that it was not Brother Côme; not, it seems to me, out of a desire to pretend to be willing to do something that I had no intention of doing, but because before seeing Brother Côme, there was still a last sacrifice that you would no doubt have obtained, although I knew it to be disagreeable, and useless; now that it is done, this sacrifice puts an end to my benevolence, and I will do nothing else in this regard other than what I promised. I do not remember my letter, but you can be the judge of this agreement yourself. If I am held to nothing I will give nothing: if you believe me to have given my word, send M. Sarbourg; he will be pleased with my docility. But as for the rest, however this interview goes, it will be of only intellectual interest to me. For should he dare take on my cure, I would not be foolish enough to join in this enterprise, and I am quite sure that I never promised any such thing. I felt in my childhood the first effects of the illness

that consumes me, it has its source in some deformity born with me; the most incredulous dupes of medical practice were never so incredulous as to think that it could cure such things. Medicine has its usefulness, I agree; it serves to give the spirit vain hope, but my spirit is no longer susceptible to poultices of that type.

As for the conditional promise of revealing yourself, I thank you but I absolve you, whatever you decide concerning M. Sarbourg. In reflecting further I have changed my mind; if you interpret that once again as disobliging indifference, I will not accuse you in that case of possessing too much wit. My pressing desire to know who you are came from my suspicions concerning your sex; they no longer exist, I believe that you are a woman, I have no doubt about it, and that is why I no longer wish to know who you are; you would have nothing to gain by it, and I would have too much to lose.

Do not believe, furthermore, that I ever took you for a man, there is nothing more contradictory than the two ideas that tormented me; I only thought that your letters were written out by a man; I believed this because of the writing, that was as well linked and formed as that of man, because of the regular spelling, because of the punctuation, more exact than that of a printer's assistant, because of an order that women do not commonly put in their letters, and which prevented me from trusting the delicacy that they put there, but that some men also exhibit, finally because of the Italian citations, which were the most confusing for me. The era of women such as Bouillon, La Suze, and La Fayette is over, of French women who read and loved Italian poetry. Today their ears, hardened at your opera, have lost all finesse, all sensitivity; this taste is dead forever among them,

> *Neppiù il vestigio appar, ne dir Si può*
> *Egli quì fue.*

> *[There remains no trace of him, and one cannot even say*
> *Who he was.]*

Add to all of that a certain little character bracketed by two dots at the end of all your letters, the most decisive factor, in spite of my particular doubts. Where for goodness sake did you dig up that damned character produced only in offices, and that caused me such despair? Charming Claire, carefully examine your friend's pretty hand; I would bet that her fingers could not make such a character without getting a callus. But that is not all; you wish to know why I was afraid that your letter was not written by a man. It is because Claire had given you life, and this man had killed you.

It is true, madame, that I did not respond to your ten pages and that I will not respond with a hundred pages. But whether you count pages, things, letters, I will always be behind, and if you require as much as you give I do not accept an exchange that is beyond my force. I do not know by what miracle I have so far been more exact with you, whom I do not know, than I have ever been in my life with my most intimate friends. I wish to conserve my freedom even in my close relationships, I want a correspondence to be a pleasure and not a duty, I even carry this independence into the realm of friendship; I want to love my friends freely for the pleasure it gives me; but as soon as they put favors in the place of feelings and as soon as gratitude is imposed on me, the attachment suffers and I no longer do with pleasure that which I am forced to do. Remember that when you send me M. Sarbourg. I understand that you will not demand anything, that is precisely why I owe you more and why I will all the more badly repay you. These tendencies do not reflect well on me, no doubt; but possessing them in spite of myself, all that I can do is to declare them openly; that is what I am. To return then to your letters, be persuaded that I will always receive them and those of your friend with something more than pleasure, that they are capable of erasing my ills and embellishing my solitude; but that when I have received ten in a row without responding, and finally write to you, instead of answering each point, I will only follow the feeling that caused me to pick up my pen, I will do nothing that I have not promised to do, and that is what you should expect.

The same is more or less the case with regard to the tone of my letters. I am not polite, madame; I feel in my heart an excuse for not being so, and much will have changed if I ever become so with you. See what interpretation your kindness can give to that, for I cannot explain it better. Furthermore, I write with great difficulty when I wish to take care with my style: I am sick to death of the profession of author, the constraint that it imposes is one of the reasons why I am renouncing it. With effort and care I am able to find the right phrase and the proper word; but I do not wish to use effort and care in writing my letters, I seek in them a relief from being constantly in the public eye, and when I write with pleasure, I want to write with ease. If my content and style are off, what does it matter? Do I not know that my friends will always understand me, and that they will interpret my speech by my character, not my character by my speech, and that if by mischance I write something objectionable to them they will be certain that they have not understood me until they have found a meaning that is unobjectionable? You will say that not all those who write to me are my friends, or know me. Excuse me, madame; I do not have nor do I wish to have simple acquaintances, I do not know nor do I want to know how to write to such people. It is possible that I am valuing my correspondence at too high a price, but I do not wish to lower anything, especially with you, although I do not know you. For I assume that it is easier for me to love you without knowing you than to know you without loving you. In any case, take this as a given: do not expect any exactitude from me, and stop analyzing what I say. I may not write to you regularly, or in the proper manner, but I am writing to you, that says it all and makes up for all the rest. These are my explanations and my conditions; accept or refuse them, but do not try to modify them; that would be pointless.

I see by your remarks and the color of your seal that you have suffered some loss, and I have heard from your friend that you are not happy: perhaps I owe to these things your commiseration and the interest you have deigned to take in me. Misfortune softens the soul, happy people are always hard. Madame, the more your attentions matter to me, the more I find them too dearly bought.

I will tell you another time what I think of your having paid the postage for your letter and of the bad reason that you give for it. In the meantime, I ask you for the same reason not to continue paying the postage; that is the real way to cause letters to be lost. I am at present very rich and will be so, I hope, for a long time; everything that I refuse to spend on vanity, I spend on true pleasures.

De La Tour to Bernardoni, November 13, 1761.
It is from my bed, and after having my foot bled twice for a terrible sore throat accompanied by a high fever and a violent headache that I have received Saint-Preux's answer, my dear friend. I hasten to send it to you. I believe that you will conclude as I have that it is useless to appeal to him to see M. Sarbourg. How sadly impotent one feels when one tries to do good to those one cares about! We have to admit it, however, in spite of ourselves. Write to him, tell him whatever you wish; and send him this note: it will explain and excuse my silence. Farewell, I cannot say more, for I am perpetually surrounded by my family who, as you know, are not in on my secret.

Would he rather know who I am or remain ignorant? Do as you think he desires on this subject.

Bernardoni to Rousseau, November 14, 1761.
Barbarian, give me back my Julie: the only cause of her sickness is your contrariness, that has inflamed her blood. Julie loves you, monsieur

> *Not of a love born in the tumult of the senses,*
> *Which the soul applauds without consulting itself,*
> *And that, knowing only blind desires,*
> *Languishes in hope, and dies in pleasure.*
> *Her passion for you, generous and solid,*
> *Has virtue for a soul and reason for a guide,*
> *Merit as an object, etc.*

If Julie were an empress and free, the rest of this speech, surely known to you, would be as appropriate as the beginning. Start from there when deciding whether or not to contribute to the reestablishment of her health; by working on your own. I am not going to examine whether or not you gave your word. Julie is sick, can I reflect and see clearly about anything? Moreover, if you had given your word, or any other, I would give it back to you, if you were capable of taking it back. I will thus not discuss here any promises that you have imprudently made, or adroitly evaded. I will instead treat the question of whether you will come to our aid, by going to your own. When I proposed Brother Côme to you it was because, judging from public talk, you had not wanted to see anyone up until that point, and it seemed better to propose to you a man who was universally known, than one known only to a few. I have seen the latter however perform miraculous cures, but because they were not publicized, they did not bring him out of the type of obscurity one only leaves by working at the Court or in high finance. It is not out of stubbornness that you refuse to consult anyone; it is not out of stubbornness that I still insist on sending him to you. Will you permit me, however confused my head may be, to reason with you on this topic? Could it be that Brother Côme, however famous he may be for relieving the sufferings of human nature, knew nothing about your own, which may be of a rarer type; and that, finding it beyond the scope of his knowledge, he decided for the honor of his art to say that it derived from a birth defect and was thus incurable? If this is the case, would it be impossible for Sarbourg, because of his more detailed knowledge, or by luck, or by chance, to be able to see more clearly and remedy it? What is certain is that, even if he sees nothing, he thinks in a manner too superior to others of his profession to play games with you. In spite of all the good and the merit that I would accord him, I sacrificed his glory to your advantage by proposing Brother Côme first. He failed: do not refuse to listen to Sarbourg. One of his cures was that of a man abandoned by the medical faculty and wounded unto death, they were saying, by a surgeon who had pierced his bladder. On another occasion he operated successfully, against the advice of a famous doctor and of a popular birthing specialist, whose names I am hiding to preserve their reputations; operated in the face of the opposition of the entire family, that had come to him when all the saints had failed: finally, it was because of a perfect knowledge of his talents, his prudence, and his activities that M. Moreau, head surgeon of the Hôtel-Dieu, where Sarbourg had worked for quite some time, just gave him to M. de Montmartel, with whom he is living, and by whom he is adored. After all of that, if you do not consent to see him it is, as my friend says, fairly useless to insist. But if you deign to listen to him, you will comfort Julie; and if he succeeds in healing you, he will achieve two cures at once. I do not fear, in thus speaking to you, to compromise my friend. If she were capable or even culpable of an emotion condemned by both human and divine law, perhaps I would know it, but you would not. There is a feeling stronger than friendship, more pure, more reasonable than that of love, superior to both, unknown to the vulgar, or contested by them. I have always believed in it; you are made to believe in it; to applaud it; to inspire it; to feel it yourself. That is what you have inspired in her! What does such a feeling not require from a man such as yourself, with regard to a woman such as she is? She desires that you meet Sarbourg; consult with him, then, in good faith, whether you have promised to do so or not. Of all your promises, we hold you only to that of possessing the *heart of a thousand Saint-Preux in one.* Give it to us, we will know how to keep from profaning it, and to share it between us without tearing it. You will write to us only when you wish, we feel in your heart, as do you, something that excuses you from politeness; and we are thrilled that you have reassured us on this point. I have said to Julie, although not as well as you, all that you say in a thousand points in your letter. I am fairly proud of having had the advantage over her of figuring out better what you were feeling: I had ceded all other advantages to her some

time ago, and I love her none the less for it. You will find that she
writes well: if you were to hear her talk, you would say that she writes
badly. She was wrong, nevertheless, to tell you that I am able to gain
pardon for possessing infinite wit: I would have been more flattered
had she said, as she should have said, that I am able to forgive her
for having infinitely more wit than myself. I have for example no
better idea than she whether or not you want to know who she is.
And so, in spite of her permission, I will still say nothing on that
subject for now. Speak to me clearly, in French, and I will answer the
same way.

It was a brother-in-law that she lost.

Rousseau to Bernardoni, November 16, 1761.
Ah those damnable doctors, they will kill her with their bloodlet-
ting! Madame, I have often suffered from sore throats, and bleeding
always turned them in my case into horrible illnesses. When, instead
of allowing myself to be bled, I merely gargled and soaked my feet
in hot water, the sore throat was gone by the next day. But unfortunately it is too late, once the bleeding is begun, it must be continued
or one risks suffocation. News of her, and quickly, I beg you; I cannot
at present respond to your letter, and I myself am less well than I
normally feel. I will only add, on the subject of your anonymity: that
it is hardly surprising that you are unable to guess my wishes; for in
truth: I do not myself know what I want. I will admit however that all
these envelopes and addresses seem rather inconvenient to me: and
I do not see any disadvantage to ridding ourselves of them.

I have not shown your letters to anyone; if you decide to name
yourselves, I highly approve the idea of keeping our correspondence
secret.

Bernardoni to Rousseau, November 18, 1761.
No, no, they will not kill her; she is feeling much better: I do not
approve any more than do you of the course that they took. Obviously it was not Sarbourg. He would have done what you indicated,
to which he adds, when the inflammation is serious, a preparation
of water lily. In the end our prayers, chance, or rather a God who
watches over his most beautiful creation, will preserve her for us.
You will learn nothing else today. You wish for quick news: I received
your letter at eight in the evening; I answered at one minute after
eight. If I had not guessed before now that you desired to know
Julie, I at least suspected that all these complicated indirect mes-

sages were bothering you. Indeed I suspected everything that you want me to have suspected; and if I did not satisfy you with my last letter, it was because I suspected that you would suspect that that was not possible in that letter. It might have gotten lost. I cannot satisfy you in this letter for the same reason. You will receive another soon after, in which you will find what you want to know: if it goes astray, or falls into hands other than your own, it will appear to be only relaying a story. I do not have the pleasure of living with Julie, or even near her; one of us lives in the neighborhood of the Palais-Royal, the other in the Marais; you understand that I am the Lady of the Marais. That will not stop me from flying to her side tomorrow after I get up: I will carry her your letter, and my answer: I will add to this letter whatever she likes, if she does not write to you herself. Will you see Sarbourg? You will perhaps ask me why he is not her surgeon. Why? Because she had one before meeting him; and because she spends her life sacrificing everything to her fear of mortifying someone.

P. S. The 19th, at Julie's home

She is completely better. They purged her yesterday for the first time. If you had written to her, she would have answered you. However late it might have been last night, I would have come to her, if that would have advanced the departure of my letter. To spare you envelopes, until we work out something better, you may address your letters to M., etc.

Bernardoni to Rousseau, November 21, 1761.

You desire, monsieur, to know a woman whose character I have praised in some of my letters. It is easier to tell you who she is, than what she is. I am capable of knowing her and loving her: but I am not able to paint her. You will be able to figure out in part what she is worth, by some of the traits spread throughout this narrative. Perhaps it would suffice merely to name her to you; her virtues, her merit, her talents, have spread her reputation quite widely, as it reached all the way to yourself. But I promised you details; and I will keep my word all the more willingly in that I never speak of her enough, or long enough, for my tastes. Prepare yourself for a long epistle. I am not excusing myself. The subject is interesting enough for you to forgive my stylistic faults. My heroine is . . .

. . . such are the attributes of my divine friend. I could cite a thousand others that immortalize her in the eyes of her husband, her parents, her relations, her friends, her acquaintances, and strangers.

I could also cite a thousand examples of ingratitude on the part of those who never tire of accumulating them; but I know that you must be tired of seeing so many virtues so badly rewarded. I will thus say only one more thing, about a phrase from one of your letters. Seek nowhere other than in the most beautiful soul that ever existed the source of the tender sensitivity that you attribute to her misfortunes. During the happiest moments of her life, the unfortunate have always had sacred rights over her heart.

Given that, in spite of her wishes, I publicly proclaim all of the infinite obligations I have toward her, some of that may reach you and render my enthusiasm suspect. Ah! do not think such a thing! Long before I owed her anything, I was as devoted to her as I am today. Gratitude might cause me, no doubt, to gloss over or attenuate her faults, if I had seen any; but not to attribute to her qualities that she does not have. As a guarantee that I did not flatter her, there are all those who know her somewhat well; and whose lowly envy does not prevent them from doing her justice.

How are you? I would have begun there, if it would have helped me to get an answer sooner. My God! Consult Sarbourg!

Your letters still to . . . until new orders.

Bernardoni to Rousseau, November 23, 1761.

We do not require you, monsieur, to write often or regularly; that is established; we will not appeal it. But we cannot allow you to leave us in anxiety as to your state, after having told us that you were feeling worse. *News, and quickly, I beg you.* Nothing else, as you wish: unless it be to acknowledge receipt of the bulletins of the 18th and 19th, and of an in-folio on the 21st; but news, above all. Eh well! Sarbourg? Is it to be that we do all you want, and you nothing that we want? Once, twice, three times, news, even secondhand, to Mme . . .

Rousseau to de La Tour, November 24, 1761.

You will be little surprised, madame, and perhaps less flattered, when I tell you that your friend's account touched me to the point of tears. You are such as to cause them to flow and to make them delicious; there is nothing new or exceptional in all that for you. But what is without doubt more rare is that your mind and your soul did all without your face entering into it, and in truth I am happy to get to know you without having seen you so that I can steal away your heart, and love you in a manner different from those who approach you. Immortal Providence! there is thus still virtue on this earth? in women? in France, in Paris, in the neighborhood of the Palais-Royal? That is assuredly not where I would have gone looking for it. Madame, there is nothing more touching than you; and yet despite all of your misfortunes, I do not pity you. An honest and noble soul may suffer; but it has compensations unknown to all others, and I am every day more persuaded that there is no more delicious pleasure than that of a heart content with itself.

Excuse me this moment of enthusiasm. You are beyond praise; praise profanes true merit, and I promise that you will never receive it from me. But on the other hand, expect frequent reproaches, you do not perhaps yet know that the more you inspire esteem in me, the more you make me difficult and exacting, oh I warn you that you are doing everything possible, you and your friend, to arrange it so that I am never satisfied with you. For example, what was that affectation, after you were better, of not writing to me because I had not written to you? Eh my God! that is precisely why you should have written, out of fear that the exchange languish on both sides. Had you then forgotten our agreement, or is that how you fulfill its conditions? What! madame, you are thus going to count my letters by number, one two three, to know when you should write to me and when you should not. Make such a calculation one or two more times and I may adore you forever but I will never write to you again in my life.

And the other who just stupidly wrote to me that she has no intelligence! I am thus a fool, I who find her to possess as much as you? Is that not obliging? Lovable Claire, pardon my frankness; I cannot stop myself from telling you that men of wit always admit to their talents, and that modesty is in them always falseness.

But if she gave me some cause for complaint in speaking of herself, how much praise does she not wring from me by speaking of you? With what pleasure does her heart expand on this charming text? With what zeal, what energy she describes the sufferings and virtues of her friend? Twenty times while reading her last letter I would have kissed at least her hand, if we had been at the harpsichord. If only that were my greatest problem! But no: the worst of it is that I must admit this to you as if it were a crime that I am obliged to confess to you.

Farewell, beautiful Julie, I will not write to you for six weeks, that is resolved; we will see what you do during that time. I would speak to you of myself if I had something consoling to say: but, ah! hurting more than usual, overwhelmed with troubles and worries of all

kinds, my illness is the least of my sufferings. This is not the time for
M. Sarbourg; I have not forgotten this topic, to which your friend so
obstinately returns; I will treat it in my next letter.

De La Tour to Rousseau, November 24, 1761.
You are quite lucky, monsieur, that your last letter found me so
weakened by my illness and its cures that I was unable to act on the
anger that it inspired in me. I was annoyed to the last degree by the
air of independence it contains; and that is in such dramatically sul-
len contrast with the *willingness* with which, several days earlier, you
claimed *to humiliate yourself before me. Accept or refuse; but do not negotiate: that would be pointless. No more discussion:* and, what else? *My patience is at an end.* What submission, my God! what a tone! I would
find it too absolute coming from the mouth of my master. Eh! who
spoke to you of *gratitude,* that you should forbid me to have any? You
have not wanted me to inspire any; your inflexibility was stronger
than my appeals. I think, however, that we should count our obligations less according to the services that others have rendered us,
than by those that others have wished to do us: but I require nothing
of you: no, not even *gratitude.* You believe that you have thought of
everything by declaring that you are not polite: as if one fault could
repair another; you say with quite unphilosophical ostentation, *I feel
in my heart an excuse for not being polite.* Eh well! monsieur, I find in
mine, and I am not boasting, the capacity to be polite without effort.
The tenderness that I feel when I think of the suffering of any sensitive creature; the wish to contribute to the satisfaction of anyone
who approaches me; the fear of being disobliging; and finally, the
character of my soul, make me affectionate in manner: and that is
politeness; although this name is commonly given to a boring collection of ceremonious falsehoods. I know how to suppress a bow, a
compliment, etc. and I believe myself all the more polite in doing
so; because I try to replace these nothings with kindnesses more satisfying both to others and to myself.

It was a wise choice of strategy for you to attribute the defects in
our women's taste to our opera, when speaking to myself, whom you
supposed touched by the beauties of Italian poetry and music; and
who know no other opera than our own. Can the ears be incapable
of receiving impressions, as long as the heart is susceptible? You will
object in vain that it is for the ears to pass sounds and words on to
the heart. Independently of the fact that poetry has a harmony that,
if I am permitted to say so, affects the eyes; this objection is not solid

except with regard to the deaf: if it is true that one cannot feel that which one is unable to hear at all; it is none the less true that each time the ears carry either speech or a succession of sounds to the heart; it is up to the qualities of the heart to give to the one or the other the charm that must agreeably affect the ears. Monsieur, the greatest merit of any observation is to be well placed. But you never waste the opportunity to let loose against our music and our women. As for music, I leave that to you: one does not choose how one responds. As for your attacks on my sex, I find a refutation of your view, and of those of many men, in a source from which you claim women do not draw. An Italian poet, struck by the ferocity of men, said:

> *Tutti gli altri animai che sono in terra*
> *O che vivon quieti, e stanno in pace,*
> *O se vengono a rissa, e si fan guerra,*
> *A la femina, il maschio non la face.*
>
> *[All animals existing on earth*
> *Either live tranquilly and in peace*
> *Or fight each other,*
> *But when they make war,*
> *The males do not attack the females.]*

Conclude from this, monsieur, conclude, that it is a shame that the influence of our opera has not been as nefarious to me as to all other French women! I would not have challenged, with the help of a foreign language, the insults that you heap on us so skillfully in your own. But let us stop speaking of music; you have done so much in that domain that it is not for me to discuss it . . . Pardon, monsieur, pardon, you have been scolded enough to be wounded by a woman, if you are delicate; and if you are not, I will not repent having thought you to be so. An overly positive opinion of a man of merit never degrades the soul that conceives it. Let us go back to *the little character bracketed by two dots, which ends all of my letters*: I forget everything, as soon as there is talk of teaching me. One can be a woman, understand Italian, know how to spell, punctuate correctly, and write coherently; and be ignorant of a great many things: no one knows this better than I. This character that caused you such *despair*, is it ridiculous everywhere other than in an office? I do not know where I *dug it up*, nor why I make it. I think, though, that this habit came to me because I like things to be well finished. If it is better that I lose it, please, tell me that seriously. It is necessary to speak clearly to me; I warned you of that; I possess no cleverness, and I always hesitate when interpretation is required.

You showed me a touching sign of interest when you wrote to Claire about my sickness. Never was a laconic style more eloquent. I believe I can best thank you by assuring you that I felt it. Farewell, monsieur, place, I beg of you, at the top of all the letters that you address to me, TO JULIE. I was tempted to send back the last one because these words were not there (so that you would put them there, of course), I want to have only this name with regard to you. When I see it traced by your hand, that made such precious use of it, I experience a momentary illusion that I would not perhaps exchange for many things commonly viewed as real goods. Finally, you have given this name to me, for you have not taken it away; and it would be the same as taking it away, if you do not continue to give it to me.

Take care, please, with the little bit of paper contained in this letter.

De La Tour to Rousseau, November 27, 1761.
We are seriously worried, monsieur: why have you not written a word to us? We are not counting with you, nor do we wish to place any constraints on you. We would suffer your inexactitude without complaint, if you had not alarmed us about your health by writing, *I myself am less well than I normally feel.* Your negligence is a bad response to the care Claire took to give you news of me; and well proves that this news was not necessary to you: for in the end, if you had taken the least interest in me, you would still feel it; what have I done to weaken it? And if you are still interested, would you abandon me to a situation the bitterness and dangers of which I believed you to be familiar with, given your concern in a similar case. After the portrait that was just made of me for you; after the way I have acted toward you, much less suspect than the brush strokes of friendship; can you doubt that I am sensitive? and can you believe me so, and leave me in the most profound ignorance as to your fate? Ah! I am no doubt wrong, to establish such a link between us: you are just like other men; always ready to seize a moment of pleasure; and incapable of lasting attention. Saint-Preux, Saint-Preux, how little your author resembles you! You did not need to love in order to want good, to do good: and he who pretends to feel attached to me as much as one can be to a woman he knows only through her mind

and name, needs only to say one word in order to do me a service, and does not say it. Monsieur, among all the conjectures that your silence authorizes, here are the two I choose: either our exchange is no longer agreeable to you; or you are unable to write. In the first case, you owe us too little to hesitate to tell us: in the second, you are not to be forgiven for not having informed us of your state through one of the people around you. You will in vain refer to the need for prudence: the inconvenience that you avoid is not comparable to that into which you fall; and furthermore, one is less blameworthy in permitting such an indiscretion than in performing the smallest of cruel actions. Small, if it be so in the eyes of humanity.

Bernardoni to Rousseau, November 28, 1761.
The infinitely small Claire, to Saint-Preux
What does it mean, please, monsieur? *You are doing everything possible, you and your friend, to arrange it so that I am never satisfied with you.* You, and your friend! As if it were my fault, mine, that Julie, the most delicate of women, took it into her head once in her life to be mistaken out of true delicacy. I am not mistaken, myself, unworthy one; I indeed felt that it was because you were so occupied with her that you wrote only to me, supposing me to be in a better state to give *news, quickly,* as she was in her bed and I, standing on my legs. In vain did I use all of my rhetorical skills to make her see things as I do; she would not let go of her idea; and I, without renouncing my own, I wrote under her dictation all that she wished: persuaded that I had to go along with a fantasy born of sickness that would pass with the illness: it did pass, as you have seen. Up to this point, I do not quite see what my crime is. What did you mean, as well, by *the other?* And the other, is really very well said; but this other, is not me. You love to mix up all that we write, to confuse Julie and me (and that is what one might call a well-stuffed joke); it is for her to be angry, yet it is I who am so; given that her glory, as I have already told you, is dearer to me than my own. Read, monsieur, read, I say to you, and you will see that it is she who so *stupidly* writes in all of her letters that she possesses no *esprit*; and that finally disgusted with all that, I said in one or two of mine that she possesses infinitely more than myself. She has proven it; you judiciously agreed in your last letter. Why are you setting yourself up as a policeman? Oh! Do not put yourself in a position to quarrel with me over the faults of another: you will find enough matter in my own.

Really you all turn my blood. Can you tell me, for example, why I only received yesterday, the 27th, your letter dated the 24th? It made a beautiful crusade and a lot of noise: I carried it this morning to Julie, who received me with the grace of a dog. Madame, furious to have been taken to task in your letter of yesterday, and blaming you for something you did not do, had the happy thought of taking it out on me, and of retaining me for dinner, the better to devour me at her ease. I should have brought her your letter earlier; I should have brought it to her before receiving it; because I received it only yesterday evening, and hers left before noon. I did not mention in my panegyric that she was crazy; because she was not, before getting to know you. Try, I beg you, to restore to her a head that I would be angry to see her lose. Try, both of you, to put a bit of order in your exchange; or talk to each other on your own; because you are making me impatient.

She will write to you; or she will not write to you: she has not exactly made a decision about that. She has only decided no longer to trust in a countersignature, since our last lost packet. As for me, I want to try once more: let me know if I have succeeded; and I will either return to that method, or give it up forever.

Now she wants to give you my story! As I do not see the need, I have forbidden her from doing so. Although my friendship for her is not superior to her own, I was not able to say anything worthy of her, and everything she would say would be more than I deserve. Hear it from me, then, this pretty story, if you want to know it as it truly is; because she is dying for you to know it: it will not be long.

I am curious, a real gawker, the daughter of a rather good soldier, who used up in service a more than honest fortune: the wife of a man richer in probity than in revenues: a good wife . . . that is all, a good mother, to the point of weakness, a useless friend, *dixi.*

Rousseau to de La Tour, November 29, 1761.
To Julie.
Another lost letter, madame? This is becoming frequent, and it is bizarre that this misfortune happens to me only with you. In the first emotion inspired in me by your friend's account of you, I wrote to you with a heart full of tenderness and admiration, my eyes filled with tears. My letter was posted to the rue des Barres address as she had indicated. The next day I received your letter in which you complain of my lack of politeness, and I feared that my last letter would also have displeased you, for I have only one tone, madame, and I am not able to change, even for you. If my style displeases you, I

must be silent; but it seems to me that my feelings should excuse me. Farewell, madame, I am unable to speak to you now of my health, nor to write to you for some time; but be assured that whatever happens, your memory will always be dear to me.

A thousand things from me to my lovable Claire, I am sorry not to be able to write to both of you.

De La Tour to Rousseau, November 29, 1761.

Forgive me monsieur: but . . . should I not be forgiving you, you who accuse me of capriciousness, although I had written you twice before receiving your last letter, which only arrived yesterday? None of that would have happened, if not for the bizarre idea you have of only writing when you feel like it; with no regard for the coherency of our correspondence, which you interrupt constantly by the perpetual crossing of our letters. As a result they perfectly resemble those conversations in which everyone speaks at once, and no one is able to hear. You love independence, you require it everywhere: myself, I love order: that is my freedom; and I propose that you love it for me; for I will surely not give it up for you. I do not hold much for agreements as frivolous as the one you claim I have broken: but when I have agreed to something precise and useful to others, I remember and follow through. For example, I owe you Claire's story; and I will tell it to you, with all the more pleasure in that doing so will make me truly interesting. I have many more beautiful things to tell you about her, than she was able to tell you of me: and I hope that you will kiss my hand also: at least if you think a feeling deserves a caress. You will no doubt judge badly as to the worth of the feeling that animates me: for it is so strong, that I will not be able to capture it. I have already been foolish in calling a "story" an account of what Claire should be, is, appears to be. This term does not fit: there are in her life no striking events that bring one's efforts into the public eye and thus make them less difficult. A hundred times more rare and estimable than my own, her merit consists in the constant practice of a thousand virtues that horrible circumstances have left in obscurity; and it will never be asked of her whether she is more inviolably attached to good itself or to the glory that comes with it. This adorable woman, who in my opinion has a firm right to the respect of good people, is on both sides linked to the highest nobility: she is the daughter of Colonel Bernard who was attached to the Dauphin's regiment, and has been dead for several years; after having ruined his fortune in a manner that makes indigence seem honorable.

Raised by an attentive mother (Mlle de Saint-Just) who loved her a great deal, but who put herself first in all things (Claire must either forbid me from speaking, or allow me to be sincere); after a great number of obstacles, caused by two types of attachments; she was married to M. Bernardoni [. . . .]

Farewell, monsieur; why do you write *beautiful Julie*? I preferred that phrase that was more characteristic of you: *To Julie, I would add an epithet, if I knew one that could add anything to that word.*

Eh! what sort of chagrin can a philosopher feel who has nothing to reproach himself for? Farewell, once more: I declare to you in my turn, that I will not write you again until you have responded to this letter; even if you had written to me an hour before receiving it. We will see what you do about that.

Rousseau to de La Tour, December 19, 1761.

I would like to continue writing to you, madame, to you and your worthy friend, but I cannot; and I cannot bear your attributing to negligence or to indifference a silence that I count among the miseries of my state. You require exactitude in an exchange, and that is the least I owe you, given the exchange you have deigned to engage in with me; but exactitude is not possible for me, my worsened state means I split my time between work and suffering, I have no more time to give to my pleasures. It is not natural that you be able to put yourself in my place, you have leisure and health; but do as the gods do,

Give while commanding the power to obey.

I must, in spite of myself, end a correspondence to which I cannot devote enough attention, and which with good reason you are not able to keep up on your own. If perhaps in the future . . . but . . . it is foolish to willingly blind oneself, and stupid to fight against necessity. Farewell, then, mesdames, I am forced by my state to cease writing to you, but I will not stop thinking of you.

I have just discovered that all of your letters were going to Beaumont before reaching me. You only need to put *Montmorency* on the address, without referring to the road to Beaumont.

De La Tour to Bernardoni, December 20, 1761.

Here, Claire, is a letter I just received. I most certainly do not have to have it before me in order to answer. Answer it yourself as well, and send it back to me Tuesday by your sister, to whom I will give my answer providing that she brings me yours. Goodbye.

De La Tour to Rousseau, January 9, 1762.
For God's sake, madame, you who can perform miracles, tolerate the indiscretion of my prayer; I ask you on my knees to change this man back into a woman: abuse me, lie to me; but please, make of him, as you are able to do, another Julie, and I will give to you both the hearts of a thousand Saint-Preux in one. In this manner, on October 19, did *Jean-Jacques Rousseau, citizen of Geneva,* express himself concerning Claire and Julie. One might imagine that a man of his character would not go so far unless he had every reason to believe that he would not turn back. To the contrary: these same women, who under the veil of anonymity appeared so interesting to him, no longer attract his attention: they have lost all by making themselves known, even though, having painted each other, they showed nothing that contradicted the idea he had of them. Such a sudden and complete change offers ample matter for sad reflection to the rational mind: how it reduces humanity! Where can one hope to find lasting feeling, when one seeks it in vain from you? Fortunately for myself, as I cherish your glory, your conduct toward me is almost completely secret: this fact will seem unimportant to you; I know that, and I fear that by being insensitive to the opinion others have of you; you run the risk of deserving this opinion. Claire, her lovable sister, her worthy husband, the only witnesses to the disagreeable treatment I am receiving, are ready to accuse you of capriciousness: and also, unable to believe that you find in your own self the force to resist an emotion that so few people inspire; and that no one can pretend does not exist; they suspect those who surround you; and believe that the change in you is the fruit of some disadvantageous comments made about me. To that I answer, would Saint-Preux risk doing an injustice by deserting someone in order to mortify her, after having heard bad things about her? Can rumor affect a heart such as his? Is he even capable of listening to such things? Such is the ascendancy of the favorable impression that you have made on me, monsieur: even though appearances work against you, I am unable to believe you guilty: I think, I say, that you may have motives that I cannot penetrate; and that would rehabilitate you in our group: truly, you owe me an explanation; and you cannot refuse me without hurting yourself: for in the end, although there is no apparent danger in mistreating me, a soul such as yours will not escape punishment for its misdeeds. A

soul such as yours . . . yes, I still admire it: the author of *Héloïse*, must be the best or the most false of all men: and how to believe that you are not the best? . . . I have just now received a note from a man who greatly admires you: this note is in response to an invitation as modest as invitations must be, when one has little merit and little fortune. I think I will copy it for you; it seems unusual to me; here it is.

There is no engagement that I would not sacrifice for a tête-à-tête with such beautiful women: with all the more reason, when one of the beautiful women is also honest and wise. Tuesday, M. de . . . will have the honor of going to the house of Mme de . . . For you, this lady is named Julie. Boredom will not be one of our party. M. de . . . is to make a visit that day to a serious man of the Church: he will take care to leave this god in all his greatness. It is for madame to bring wit, reason, and grace to the party.

This is an exact copy, the character, the two points, all is as you see it . . . The poor man! What doe he know of *wit, reason, grace*: would Saint-Preux be silent, if I possessed all of that! In truth, I am rather mad: but you want me to write to you, and I cannot respond to what you have written, so I speak of what others write to me: if I wrote of what I felt, I would always be scolding you. Farewell, maddening Saint-Preux; do not be shocked by my wild babbling: if I were reasonable, I would not write you.

December 20, December 30, these are the dates of my last two letters. Did you receive them? At least let me know that.

Rousseau to de La Tour, January 11, 1762.
Saint-Preux was thirty years old, healthy, and concerned only with his pleasures; nothing less resembles Saint-Preux than J.-J. Rousseau. On receiving a letter like my last, Julie would be less offended by my silence than alarmed by my state; she would not in such a case entertain herself with counting letters and underlining words; nothing resembles Julie less than Mme de La Tour. You have much intelligence, madame, and you are pleased to show it, and you want only letters from me. You are more the product of your neighborhood than I believed.
J.-J. Rousseau

Bernardoni to de La Tour, January 15, 1762.
It is, no doubt, my Julie, because Molière consulted his servant, that you wish to have my opinion of your letter to Jean-Jacques. Well then! Here it is: it is delicious, with as much dignity as delicacy, and as much wit. I would rather have written it than the Héloïse novel. I

cannot express to you, on the other hand, nor do I understand myself, all that I feel in reading the letter from your bear. If I had only seen capriciousness in it, that would not have astonished me: but in recalling his earlier letters, I find it overall to be contradictory, false, impertinent, etc. I gave myself three good blows on the chest for having begun the exchange between the two of you. Socrates said that he would look in the mirror, if he wanted to see a madman: send this recipe to our animal, to spare him the trouble of leaving his den when he feels the same curiosity. Truly, if Diogenes were still alive, he would burn more than one candle. As you said yourself one day, my Julie, the esteem that God apportioned to you will not be wasted. You may add to your own what you will take from many others. My esteem for you is always increasing, and is still the least of the feelings I have for you. My husband, who will be visiting you on Thursday, claims that Jean-Jacques should be buried alongside his dog. I find, myself, that this would be doing him too great an honor.

Notes

Introduction

1. References to the Rousseau-de La Tour exchange are given by the letter's date, after the edition of the correspondence edited by Georges May, *Jean-Jacques Rousseau/Madame de La Tour: Correspondance* (Arles: Actes Sud, 1998). References to other letters by, to, or concerning Rousseau will be given by volume and letter number (*CC*, vol:letter), after R. A. Leigh's *Correspondance complète* (Oxford: The Voltaire Foundation, 1965–1998); references to Rousseau's *Oeuvres complètes* (Paris: Gallimard, 1959–69) will be by volume and page number (*OC*, vol:pgs). All translations from works in French are my own, unless otherwise indicated.

2. For an exploration of the eighteenth-century letter as ideally mimicking conversation, see Bruce Redford's *The Converse of the Pen: Acts of Intimacy in the Eighteenth-Century Familiar Letter* (Chicago: University of Chicago Press, 1986). Redford is concerned not with intention per se but rather with epistolary style: "How does the eighteenth-century letter-writer—committed to 'prattling upon paper,' in Johnson's phrase—capture the artful spontaneity of conversation? How does he make himself fully present to his absent interlocutor?" (5).

3. Janet Altman, "The Letter Book as a Literary Institution 1539–1789: Toward a Cultural History of Published Correspondences in France," *Yale French Studies* 71 (1986): 49–50. Altman argues that the casual tone of Sévigné's letters caused her to be largely ignored in France until 1725, the date of the first separate publication of her correspondence. For Altman, this renewed attention to Sévigné's letters some thirty years after her death signals the appearance of a new type of letter book, characterized by chronological arrangement and designed to communicate a personal narrative rather than to highlight letters as crafted objects. Altman also connects Sévigné's rise to prominence to a desire by publishers to please readers whose expectations and interests had been profoundly altered by developments in narrative forms between 1670 and 1735, including the rise of the novel.

4. The issue of authentic emotion was so insignificant in seventeenth-century letter manuals that editors lumped together real and apocryphal letters with abandon; see Louise K. Horowitz, "The Correspondence of Madame de Sévigné: Letters or Belles-lettres?," *French Forum* 6.1 (January 1981): 25.

5. The debate is played out primarily in Roger Duchêne, "Réalité vécue et réussite littéraire: le statut particulier de la lettre," *Revue d'Histoire Littéraire de la France* 71 (1971): 177–94, and Bernard Bray, "Quelques Aspects du système épistolaire de Mme de Sévigné," *Revue d'Histoire Littéraire de la France* 69 (1969): 494–500. For an analysis of the debate, see Altman, "The Letter Book as a Literary Institution," 29–32. See also Horowitz, "The Correspondence of Madame de Sévigné."

6. See Roger Duchêne, "Le Lecteur de lettres," *Revue d'Histoire Littéraire de la France* 78 (1978): 977–90.

7. Duchêne, "Réalité vécue et réussite littéraire," 185.

8. See Catherine Montfort-Howard, "Les Fortunes de Mme de Sévigné au XVIIIe siècle," *Etudes littéraires françaises* 18, Tübingen: Gunter Narr, 1982, especially pp. 72–78. Montfort-Howard's thesis—that in a period of growing animosity toward elegance and nobility, one might well expect Sévigné's letters to meet with overall opposition—is convincing, and is supported by the infrequency with which Sévigné is mentioned in *Encyclopédie* articles on the letter form (I discuss these articles at length in chapter 4). The issue is complicated by Sévigné's growing fame at the time; Marie-Claire Grassi argues against Montfort-Howard's reading by noting how often Sévigné is cited as a model in eighteenth-century letter manuals ("Naissance d'un nouveau modèle: l'apparition de Madame de Sévigné dans les manuels épistolaires," *Revue d'Histoire Littéraire de la France* 96 [1996]: 446–60). As Grassi herself points out, however, Montfort-Howard considers such manuals to be of little importance to her argument. She is interested instead in the reception of Sévigné among the influential philosophes, and she finds their pointed neglect of the marquise to be characteristic of their values in general; Sévigné's cult of royalty and her overall social conservatism were unlikely to attract the attention of men such as Diderot, however eager the average letter writer may have been to emulate her style. For Sévigné's recuperation as "sincere" and "natural" in the nineteenth century, see Emmanuel Bury, "Madame de Sévigné face aux critiques du XIXe siècle," *Revue d'Histoire Littéraire de la France* 96 (1996): 446–60.

9. Michel Foucault, "What is an Author?," in *The Foucault Reader*, edited by Paul Rabinow (New York: Pantheon, 1984), pp. 107–8.

10. English Showalter, "Authorial Self-Consciousness in the Familiar Letter," *Yale French Studies* 71 (1986): 123.

11. Altman, "The Letter Book as Literary Institution," 61.

12. Horowitz proposes a limited version of allowing the author's consciousness to enter into an analysis: "May not the critic explore an approach that stresses the closed nature of the text, but that, nevertheless, accepts the very real emotional drive that engendered and supported it?" ("The Correspondence of Madame de Sévigné," 18).

13. Mireille Bossis argues for an increased awareness that a real correspondence is a joint endeavor in which meaning is the product of collaboration ("Methodological Journeys through Correspondences," *Yale French Studies* 71 [1986]: 63–75). Bossis, interested in the textual effects of this epistolary collaboration, refers to this aspect of the performative function of the letter as the "return effect," characterized by an inevitable displacement in time.

14. Fritz Nies, "Un Genre féminin?," *Revue d'Histoire Littéraire de la France* 78 (1978): 999–1000. Nies concludes that the attributes associated with the letter were more a factor of nobility than of gender: "It was people of quality who were, according to Molière, supposed to speak on every topic 'without ever have learned anything' . . . Effort and work were proper to the bourgeoisie and the people" (1002).

15. Judith P. Stanton, "Statistical Profile of Women Writing in English from 1660 to 1800," in *Eighteenth-Century Women and the Arts*, edited by Frederick M. Keener and Susan E. Lorsch (New York: Greenwood Press, 1988), pp. 248–49.

16. For a refutation and analysis of this assumption, see Aurora Wolfgang, "Falla-

cies of Literary History: The Myth of Authenticity in the Reception of *Fanni Butlerd*," *Studies on Voltaire and the Eighteenth Century* 304 (1992): 735–39.

17. Carla Hesse, "Female Authorship and Revolutionary Law," *Eighteenth-Century Studies* 22.3 (Spring 1989): 477.

18. Showalter, "Authorial Self-Consciousness," 124–25.

19. Faith Beasley, "Altering the Fabric of History: Women's Participation in the Classical Age," in *A History of Women's Writing in France*, edited by Sonya Stephens (Cambridge: Cambridge University Press, 2000), p. 64.

20. Joan Landes, *Women and the Public Sphere* (Ithaca: Cornell University Press, 1988), p. 2. Landes is principally concerned in this study with proving that modern feminism was born of the repression that came with the rise of bourgeois law, the rise, that is, of the Habermasian bourgeois public sphere: "I relate the genesis of feminism to the fall of the politically influential women of the absolutist court and salon of Old Regime France" (1). For a critique of this view of women and the public sphere, see Lawrence E. Klein, "Gender and the Public/Private Distinction in the Eighteenth Century: Some Questions about Evidence and Analytic Procedure," *Eighteenth-Century Studies* 29.1 (1995): 97–109.

21. Landes, *Women and the Public Sphere*, 59. For more on this topic see Nina Gelbart, *Feminine and Opposition Journalism in Old Regime France: Le Journal des dames* (Berkeley: University of California Press, 1978).

22. Martin Hall, "Eighteenth-Century Women Novelists: Genre and Gender," in *A History of Women's Writing in France*, edited by Sonya Stephens (Cambridge: Cambridge University Press, 2000), p. 102.

23. Stanton, "Statistical Profile," 249.

24. The Bibliothèque Nationale also lists as one of de La Tour's publications a work that is attributed to her nowhere else: "L'Anti-Grelot, Par Mme de ***." This short piece (twenty-three pages), an attack on a novel entitled the *Grelot*, appeared in 1754. De La Tour would have been twenty-four years old. While the library's catalogue attributes this work to her, there is no indication on the work itself, or anywhere else, that she wrote it.

25. In a letter to Rousseau of October 24, 1761, Bernardoni does make a reference to de La Tour's having almost died in childbirth, as part of her effort to convince Rousseau that de La Tour is indeed a woman.

26. May, *Jean-Jacques Rousseau/Madame de La Tour*, 9.

27. Sonya Stephens, *A History of Women's Writing in France* (Cambridge: Cambridge University Press, 2000), p. 3.

28. Janet Altman comments: "The woman who receives a letter and responds, be she Crébillon's marquise, Mme Riccoboni's Fanni Butlerd, Dorat's Syrcé, or countless others, is taking a first step along a fatal path" (*Epistolarity: Approaches to a Form* [Columbus: Ohio State University Press, 1982], p. 61). Ruth Perry points out that merely receiving a letter was almost as suspect as responding to one: "By the time of Fanny Burney's *Evelina*, just one unsolicited and familiar letter from even a favorite suitor was enough to damn the man in the eyes of the pristine heroine" (*Women, Letters, and the Novel* [New York: AMS, 1980], p. 133). See also Françoise Meltzer, "Laclos' Purloined Letter," *Critical Inquiry* 8 (Spring 1982): 515–29.

29. See Rufus Reiberg, "James Boswell's Personal Correspondence: The Dramatized Quest for Identity," in *The Familiar Letter in the Eighteenth Century*, edited by Howard Anderson, Philip B. Daghlian, and Irvin Ehrenpreis (Lawrence: University of Kansas Press, 1966).

CHAPTER 1. CLAIRE AND JULIE

1. Louise d'Epinay's *Histoire de Madame de Montbrillant*, often referred to as the *Contre-Confessions*, was first published in 1818. Now classified as a novel, the work is best viewed as a roman à clef in which she recounts her troubled relationship with Rousseau and contradicts his autobiographical version of the same events.

2. For an overview of readers' responses to *Julie*, see Claude Labrosse, *Lire au XVIIIe siècle: La Nouvelle Héloïse et ses lecteurs* (Lyons: Presses Universitaires de Lyons, 1985), and Anna Attridge, "The Reception of *La Nouvelle Héloïse*," *Studies on Voltaire and the Eighteenth Century* 120 (1974): 227–67.

3. In *The Great Cat Massacre and Other Episodes in French Cultural History* (New York: Vintage, 1985), Robert Darnton quotes this instance of sexual crowing just before he makes a passing reference to de La Tour: "Women threw themselves at [Rousseau], in letters and in pilgrimages to his retreat at Montmorency. Marie-Anne Alissan de La Tour cast herself as Julie, while her friend Marie-Madeleine Bernardoni took the role of Claire, and together they deluged Rousseau with letters so artfully turned that soon he was playing Saint-Preux to them in a correspondence that lasted several years" (245–46). The main subject of this chapter of Darnton's study, however ("Readers Respond to Rousseau"), is not de La Tour, but rather the Swiss merchant Jean Ranson, who wrote to a friend about his efforts to apply his readings of Rousseau to his life. Darnton is arguing for a particular relationship of the reader to the printed word; such evidence if far less complexly coded when the author of the works in question is not also the recipient of the reader's letters.

4. Bossis, "Methodological Journeys," 74.

5. *CC*, n. to 9:1513.

6. For an account of the origins of *La Nouvelle Héloïse* and of Rousseau's passion for d'Houdetot, see book 9 of the *Confessions, OC,* 1:437–80. Future references will be given in the text. For a review of opinions on Rousseau's account of the origins of his novel, see Susan Klem Jackson, "Redressing Passion: Sophie d'Houdetot and the Origins of *Julie, or La Nouvelle Héloïse*," *Studies in Eighteenth-Century Culture* 17 (1987): 271–87.

7. The unlikely courier for Rousseau's correspondence with d'Houdetot was his current "governess" and future wife, Thérèse Levasseur. He pronounces Thérèse shocked by only one aspect of the correspondence: Mme d'Epinay's efforts to spy on the goings-on between Rousseau and her sister-in-law d'Houdetot by obliging Thérèse to hand over the letters before delivering them. According to this account, d'Epinay would read and then carefully reseal them (*OC*, 1:449).

8. Saint-Lambert also played a role in the correspondence of two of the most famous intellectuals of the French Enlightenment. After her ten-year liaison with Voltaire, Emilie du Chatêlet became involved with Saint-Lambert; she died giving birth to their child in September 1749. In his biography of Voltaire, Theodore Besterman remarks: "The destruction of the correspondence between these two remarkable people was Saint-Lambert's greatest crime" (*Voltaire* [New York: Harcourt, Brace & World, 1969], p. 186).

9. Rousseau does not mention in this context the six letters to d'Houdetot that would become known as the *Lettres morales*, or *Lettres à Sophie*. Written during the winter of 1757–58, these letters discuss the quest for virtue and happiness. Sophie is urged to trust her innermost feelings and cautioned to avoid the curse of her

class, idleness. Published in two parts in 1861 and 1888, these letters were expressly written for publication.

10. Rousseau, *Lettre à M. d'Alembert sur les spectacles* (Paris: Garnier-Flammarion, 1967), pp. 199–200.

11. For the argument demonstrating Guilleragues's authorship, see the introductory material to *Lettres portugaises, Valentins et autres oeuvres de Guilleragues*, edited by Frédéric Deloffre and Jacques Rougeot (Paris: Garnier, 1962).

12. Maurice Cranston comments: "It is some indication of Rousseau's wretched condition that he agreed to see [de La Tour's] surgeon" (*The Noble Savage: Jean-Jacques Rousseau, 1754–62* [London: Penguin Press, 1991], p. 314).

13. Howard Anderson and Philip Daghlian discuss the influence of the development of the postal service on the letter in the concluding essay to *The Familiar Letter in the Eighteenth Century* (Lawrence: University of Kansas Press, 1966). They point out, for example, that writers "were perhaps the more likely to take care that their letters should be long and worth reading because throughout the century the recipient had to pay the post, and might be inclined to judge rather critically what he had paid for" (270).

14. Vera Lee argues that Julie is first among her virtuous fictional contemporaries; see "The Edifying Examples," in *French Women and the Age of Enlightenment*, edited by Samia I. Spencer (Bloomington: Indiana University Press, 1984).

15. "The fallacy of realistic fiction seems to have blinded us to the figural abstraction invited by the neo-medieval title, although it should be obvious in a work in which 'characters' have little more human individuality than the theological virtues, the five senses, or the parts of the body" (Paul de Man, *Allegories of Reading: Figural Language in Rousseau, Nietzsche, Rilke, and Proust* [New Haven: Yale University Press, 1979], p.189). As I discuss further in chapter three, the characters' lack of verisimilitude is an important theme of the "Préface dialoguée" to *La Nouvelle Héloïse*, which begins with a debate as to what their otherworldly nature indicates about the letters' authenticity.

16. "Esprit" is an elusive concept, and difficult to translate; I have used "wit" or "intelligence," according to the nuance of usage in these letters.

17. Given in *CC*, 10:1698. The flood of readers' letters had subsided to a trickle by March 1762, although attacks against the novel in the periodicals of the day had just intensified.

18. That *esprit* and authorship combine to deadly effect goes a long way to explaining Rousseau's condemnation of the novel as a genre. He addresses the obvious contradiction of his having created Julie in his "Préface dialoguée": "Remember that I was thinking of publishing these letters while I was writing against the theater, and that the thought of justifying one of these works did not cause me to alter the truth in the other. I accused myself in advance more strongly perhaps than anyone else was to accuse me. One who chooses truth over glory may hope to choose it over his life. You want people to be always constant; I doubt that such is possible for man; but what is possible for him is to be always true" (*OC*, 2:27).

19. *Encyclopédie*, vol. 5 [1755], 973–74.

20. Such suspicion was hardly unusual for the time. Patricia Meyer Spacks points to a general eighteenth-century fear of the amorphousness of words, quoting Locke as to the freedom everyone enjoys to speak as he pleases (*Imagining a Self: Autobiog-*

raphy and Novel in Eighteenth-Century England [Cambridge: Harvard University Press, 1976], p. 22); but as Jean Starobinski has famously observed, in Rousseau's writings language becomes an insurmountable obstacle to the expression of truth (*Jean-Jacques Rousseau: la transparence et l'obstacle, suivi de sept essais sur Rousseau* [Paris: Gallimard, 1971], especially chapter 6, "Le Pouvoir des signes").

21. The *Essais* is cited as an authoritative text: "Montaigne's father, a man no less scrupulous and true than strong of constitution, swore that he was a virgin when he married at thirty-three . . . and one can see in the writings of his son what vigor and gaiety the father retained at over sixty years of age. Certainly the contrary opinion arises more from our mores and prejudices than from a knowledge of the general species" (*OC*, 4:640).

22. Once in Paris, even Saint-Preux, although armed with his simple ways and his love for Julie, succumbs to the one infidelity of his life, brought on by too much white wine inadvertently consumed. The repentant lover explains to Julie that he believed himself to have been drinking only water; his companions fooled him in this way into consuming copious quantities of alcohol. To his horror, he woke up the next morning in bed with a woman of ill repute, with the sinking feeling that he was "as guilty as it was possible for me to be" (*OC*, 2:297)

23. The editor Bernard Guyon notes of this letter: "[Rousseau] gives us the elements of a true *Discourse on Style*. Its principles are clear. The refusal of *bel esprit*, of *esprit* period, this 'French mania' that serves only to lie; the call to truth and simplicity" (*OC*, 2:1482).

24. A related project, one Rousseau apparently never completed, was to be entitled *Essai sur les événements importants dont les femmes ont été la cause secrète* (*OC*, 2:1257–69). Rousseau's readers are of course not always implied as male, but in making a moral point, he often identifies one sex or the other as the intended recipient of his advice or pleas. See for example Sarah Herbold, "Rousseau's Dance of Veils: The *Confessions* and the Imagined Woman Reader," *Eighteenth-Century Studies* 32.3 (Spring 1999): 333–53.

25. Letter to Caspar Hess, Oct. 12, 1762 (*CC*, 13).

26. Rousseau, *Lettre à d'Alembert*, 114.

27. Ibid., 200.

28. This "one little thing" will torment de La Tour, but by the time Rousseau responds to her question as to what this "little thing" might be, he claims to have forgotten it, declaring that there is nothing that bothers him about her (letter of July 17, 1763).

29. The work is included in the "Catalogue of Works by Women Over the Last Few Years" produced by the *Journal des Dames* in June 1764 (see *CC*, 20:3328).

30. Markus F. Motsch emphasizes the popularity of this form in eighteenth-century Germany, with references to England as well. Citing some of the many subjects treated in such works, Motsch comments: "All this and much more is reflected in poetic epistles, which provide an intimate picture of the diversity of German intellectual life in the eighteenth century—a picture which frequently does not correspond with present day concepts of that era" ("The Forgotten Genre: The Poetic Epistle in Eighteenth-Century German Literature," *Studies in Eighteenth-Century Culture*, vol. 4, edited by Harold E. Pagliaro [Madison: University of Wisconsin Press, 1975], p. 124).

31. *Encyclopédie*, 5:821. The current definition of *épître* given by the *Petit Robert*

reflects how foreign the notion of a "verse letter" has become: "2. In antiquity, Missive letter . . . by extension. Ironically V. Letter. 'a long epistle.' "

32. In a note to letter 1:24 of *La Nouvelle Héloïse*, the "editor" feels obliged to excuse Saint-Preux's rhetorical prowess (whatever its relation to his true feelings) as youthful folly, and to blame the mother for throwing the young couple together: "And if his extreme youth did not excuse him, with his fine words [Saint-Preux] would be only a villain. The two lovers are to be pitied; only the mother is unpardonable" (*OC*, 2:85).

33. Bernardoni was also somehow indebted to de La Tour. When de La Tour later refers to her ex-friend as "a woman who would lower herself not to elevate me" (Apr. 16, 1763), Leigh remarks in a note: "Mme Alissan de La Tour makes it understood here that she had been the benefactress of Mme Bernardoni" (*CC*, n. to 16:2627).

34. May, *Jean-Jacques Rousseau/Madame de La Tour*, n. to 95.

35. See Leigh, *CC*, n. to 10:1631; also May, n. to Bernardoni's letter of Nov. 18, 1761.

36. May, *Jean-Jacques Rousseau/Madame de La Tour*, n. to 71.

37. See *CC*, n. to 9:1496. In addition to her own portrait by Bernardoni, de La Tour chose not to include in her edited version of the exchange a letter in which she relates her friend's life story in detail (Nov. 29, 1761).

38. De La Tour returned Rousseau's originals but kept copies of all of his letters. Rousseau's originals, along with most of de La Tour's originals to Rousseau, copies of her remaining letters (Rousseau did not preserve all of her originals), and copies of Bernardoni's letters, are in the Bibliothèque de Neuchâtel. The edited copy of the exchange as a whole, made by de La Tour in 1770 with the aim of publishing the correspondence, is in the Palais-Bourbon in Paris (this version was used by the 1803 editors).

Chapter 2. Going Public

1. Raymond Trousson, *Jean-Jacques Rousseau* (Paris: Tallandier, 1988–89), p. 2:221.

2. Georges May includes a detailed "Dossier" to de La Tour's publishing career as "Mme de ***" in his edition of the letters (325–49).

3. This response, as Leigh notes (*CC*, n. to 11:1816), is not dated nor does it exhibit postal marks, as it would have been handed over to de La Tour's waiting messenger.

4. *OC*, 1:601–2. In *La Nouvelle Héloïse*, the presence of a male participant is said to the contrary to constrain such female "babbling" among Swiss women: "Our Swiss women like to gather with each other . . . and although they apparently do not hate being with men, the presence of a man certainly injects a sort of constraint into this little gynecocracy. In Paris, quite to the contrary, women love to live with men alone . . . That is how women there learn to speak, act, and think like men" (Saint-Preux to Julie, *OC*, 2:269).

5. See de La Tour's letter of Jan. 13, 1763, and May's n. 1 to p. 160.

6. On both the epistolary and the amorous levels, de La Tour could have found disturbing information as to the fidelity of her correspondent in an editor's foot-

note to *La Nouvelle Héloïse,* directed at female readers of the work: "You are quite mad, you women, to believe that an emotion as frivolous and fleeting as love can be constant. Everything in nature changes, all is in continual flux and you try to inspire lasting passion! And by what right do you claim to be loved today because you were yesterday! . . . to change constantly, and to expect to be loved always, is to expect that at each moment one ceases to love you; that is not to seek constant hearts, but to seek hearts as changeable as yourselves" (*OC,* 2:509–10).

7. It is unclear why de La Tour's first name, legally "Marie-Anne," becomes Marianne in the exchange. In the extant letters, Rousseau is the first to write "Marianne," in the citation just given in the text. Her next letter is the first signed "Marianne"; perhaps in the missing piece of correspondence in which "Claire" and "Julie" reveal their true names, de La Tour had written her first name with this spelling. In any case, de La Tour is not yet ready to give up on her claim to incarnate Rousseau's feminine ideal: "If one must be as happy as Julie in order to claim the honor of bearing her name, I renounce it; but whatever qualities you suppose me to have, if you imagine me as different from her, how do you expect me to be happy with my fate? Did you not create her according to your own tastes?" (June 1, 1762).

8. In a note to de La Tour's letter of Oct. 8, 1763, May points out that while the *Littré* dictionary cites Rousseau's use of *peintresse* as a first occurrence of the word, he was actually repeating her previous use.

9. "In fact, it is a general impression experienced by all men, although they do not all notice it, that in the high mountains where the air is pure and subtle, one breathes more easily, feels lighter in one's body, more serene in one's mind; pleasures there are less ardent, passions more moderate" (*La Nouvelle Héloïse, OC,* 2:78).

10. The classic reference for the affair is Henri Guillemin, *"Cette affaire infernale." L'affaire J.-J. Rousseau-Hume – 1766* (Paris: Plon, 1942). The public clamor that surrounded this dispute between two famous individuals has been studied by Dena Goodman as an exemplary instance of the reading public's entrance into the authentic public sphere as defined by Habermas ("The Hume-Rousseau Affair: From Private *Querelle* to Public *Procès," Eighteenth-Century Studies* 25.2 [1991]: 171–201).

11. David Hume, *Exposé succinct de la contestation qui s'est élévée entre M. Hume et M. Rousseau avec les pièces justificatives* (London: [s.n.], 1766), p. xi.

12. Ibid., xi–xii.

13. Marie-Anne de La Tour, "Lettre à l'auteur de *la justification de M. Rousseau,*" in *Précis pour M. J. J. Rousseau, en réponse à 'l'exposé succinct de M. Hume': suivi d'une lettre de Madame de *** à l'auteur de la justification de M. Rousseau* (N.p., 1767), p. 2. Future references by page number in the text.

14. For an alternative view, see Gita May, "Rousseau's 'Antifeminism' Reconsidered," in *French Women and the Age of Enlightenment,* edited by Samia I. Spencer (Bloomington: Indiana University Press, 1984). See also the subtle placing of Rousseau with regard to misogyny in chapter 3 of Landes, *Women and the Public Sphere.*

15. Georges May notes: "Another posthumous edition of Rousseau's *Works,* that of 1793, also reprinted in volume 27 the 'Lettre à l'auteur de *la justification de M. Rousseau*' (p. 141–159)" (333). This edition, edited by Mercier, Brizard, and d'Aulnaye, was in thirty-seven volumes; volume 27 includes a number of pieces related to the Hume affair.

16. De La Tour's knowledge from afar of Rousseau's life astonishes Leigh at

times, especially in its attention to the details of his relations with others. Consider his note b to letter 37:6632: "But how did Mme de La Tour learn so quickly about this important matter?" (it should be noted that Leigh is using "important matter" ironically, for de La Tour has referred jealously to Rousseau's sending some of his writings to M. de Villepatour).

17. See Lecercle, "Rousseau critique littéraire: 'le coeur' et 'la plume'," in *Reappraisals of Rousseau: Studies in Honor of R. A. Leigh,* edited by Simon Harvey, Marian Hobson, David Kelley, and Samuel S.B. Taylor (Manchester: Manchester University Press, 1980), p. 222.

18. R. A. Leigh, note c to *CC,* 37:6589: "Mme de La Tour did not know that this engraving displeased JJ, and that he would transfer his aversion to the portrait itself, that he probably never saw in its finished state . . . Whatever the case, this passage of Mme de La Tour's letter raised the ever vigilant JJ's suspicion, as their remaining letters demonstrate." May notes of the same letter: "Marianne could not have suspected that JJR hated this portrait, and that he had accused Hume of having it made in order to attack him, as he explained later in the second of his *Dialogues.* One must see in this an essential reason for the epistolary silence that he will break only after receiving letter n° 165 [Sept. 4, 1770]" (note 1 to letter of July 9, 1769).

19. See May, *Jean-Jacques Rousseau/Madame de La Tour,* n. to 231.

20. May, who points out that Rousseau did at this time visit a much younger epistolary rival of de La Tour, the countess Rose de Berthier, asks: "Is it a coincidence that during their nine-month correspondence Marianne was suffering through Jean-Jacques's persistent silence?" (*Jean-Jacques Rousseau/Madame de La Tour,* 18).

21. De La Tour's reference to "your verse, your hieroglyphic date" refers to Rousseau's habit at the time of heading his letters as follows:

	Poor blind creatures that we are!	
	Heaven, unmask the imposters	4
Paris	And force their barbarian hearts	17—70
	To open themselves to the sight of men.	9.

22. Trousson, *Rousseau,* 2:406.

23. See *CC,* n. b to 39:6931.

24. The strange tale of the allegorical King Phénix and Queen Fantasque, their twins Prince Raison and Princesse Caprice, along with "The Discreet Fairy whose sex and name contrasted amusingly at times with her character," had first been published in 1758 without Rousseau's consent as an example of the dangerous writings of the "Cacouacs" or philosophes.

25. May, *Jean-Jacques Rousseau/Madame de La Tour,* 320.

26. Leigh notes: "Mme de La Tour had received a copy of the reprinting ordered by JJ" (*CC,* 23:4066).

27. Bronislaw Baczko, "Brûler Diderot," in *Rousseau visité, Rousseau visiteur: les dernières années (1770–1778),* edited by Jacques Berchtold and Michel Porret (Geneva: Droz, 1999), p. 351.

28. Elie Fréron, famous for his opposition to Voltaire, edited the journal from 1754–1776; Louis Stanislas from 1776–1789. With the coming of the Revolution, the latter abandoned the *Année littéraire* and started a newspaper, *L'Orateur du peuple.*

29. Published in the *Mercure de France* Oct. 5, 1778:7–28 (*CC*, 42:7314). Corancez's rebuttal appeared in the *Journal de Paris* no. 303:1213–15 (*CC*, 42:7335).

30. *Année littéraire* 7 (1778): 307–19.

31. See *CC*, 41:7196, 7197.

32. *Année littéraire* 8 (1778): 274–85.

33. See *CC*, 43:7436.

34. *Année littéraire* 5 (1779): 53–62.

35. Dena Goodman, *The Republic of Letters* (Ithaca: Cornell University Press, 1994), p. 138.

36. Marie-Anne de de La Tour, *Jean Jaques Rousseau vangé [sic] par son amie, ou morale practico-philosophico-encyclopédique des coryphées de la secte* (Paris: Au Temple de la vérité, 1779), pp. i–ii. Future references by page number in the text.

37. The *Collection des oeuvres de J.-J. Rousseau* was intended to benefit Rousseau's widow. The presence in the *Confessions* of a rather unflattering portrait of Du Peyrou (*OC*, 1:602–3) makes this publishing endeavor all the more impressive. While the Hume affair had brought de La Tour closer to Rousseau, Du Peyrou's resistance to thinking badly of "the good David" caused Rousseau to question his devotion. For a history of the relationship between Rousseau and Du Peyrou, see Charly Guyot, *Un Ami et défenseur de Rousseau: Pierre-Alexandre Du Peyrou* (Neuchâtel: Ides et Calendes, 1958); for the details surrounding the publication of the *Collection des oeuvres de J.-J. Rousseau*, see Raymond Birn, *Forging Rousseau: Print, commerce, and cultural manipulation in the late Enlightenment* (Oxford: SVEC, 2001:08). Birn dismisses de La Tour with a few words: "There is little doubt that the lady was thoroughly infatuated with Rousseau" (190).

38. Marie-Anne de La Tour, *La Vertu vengée par l'amitié ou Recueil de lettres sur J. J. Rousseau par Madame de ****, vol. vi of *Supplément à la Collection des oeuvres de J.-J. Rousseau* or vol. xxx:52–90 of *Collection des oeuvres*, 33 vols., edited by Alexandre Du Peyrou (Geneva: 1782), p. 149. Future references by page number in the text.

39. Not all the pieces included in the *Vertu vengée* are serious; take for example the "Anonymous Response, to the Anonymous Author, of the Response to the Response Made by Anonymous, to the Letter that M. d'Alembert Sent by Way of the *Mercure*, to the Friends of J.-J. Rousseau, Who Deserve a Response" (235–62; de La Tour is careful to point out that her title is a joke).

40. Denis Diderot, *Oeuvres* (Paris: Gallimard, 1951), p. 1029.

41. De La Tour's defense of the publication of these letters is supported by their relative lack of scandalous content. The publication of the second part of the *Confessions* would in 1789 reveal to the world that Warens had been Rousseau's lover as well as his protector; the issue in 1779 was simply the publication of letters exchanged by Rousseau and Warens without their permission.

42. Jean-François de La Harpe, Dec. 15, 1778, cited by Leigh (*CC*, 42:7402).

Chapter 3. The Sanctity of Response

1. Louis Fauche-Borel printed an edition of the second part of the *Confessions* in 1790, under Du Peyrou's direction. As reported by the *Journal de Paris*, this edition was superior to that of 1789 in two ways: it was faithful to the original manuscript, and was "enriched by pieces related to the *Confessions*, published for the first

time, and by a large number of interesting letters that had never before been printed" (Pierre-Paul Plan, *Jean-Jacques Rousseau raconté par les gazettes de son temps* [Paris: Mercure de France, 1912], p. 302).

2. Quoted in the 1803 Giguet and Michaud edition, *Correspondance originale et inédite de J.-J. Rousseau avec Mme Latour de Franqueville et M. Du Peyrou* (Paris: Giguet and Michaud, 1803), p. 6. The reference to the well-known epistolary novelist Isabelle de Charrière (1740–1805) is an indication of the importance Du Peyrou attached to the de La Tour-Rousseau exchange; such unusual letters were obviously in his view deserving of an editor possessed of a sensitive literary mind. In addition to her merits as a novelist, Isabelle de Charrière had collaborated with Du Peyrou on his edition of the *Confessions.*

3. On the evolution of the novel, see Ian Watt's classic *The Rise of the Novel: Studies in Defoe, Richardson, and Fielding* (Berkeley: University of California Press, 1957). Georges May traces the birth of the eighteenth-century novel's relationship to Truth to the end of the seventeenth century in "L'Histoire a-t-elle engendré le roman?," *Revue d'Histoire Littéraire de la France* 55 (1955): 155–76.

4. It is common today in both French and English to refer to private letters as *familières,* as well as *missives;* the loss of the distinction made in the *Encyclopédie* illustrates yet again the much more complex eighteenth-century relationship to the epistolary genre.

5. Goodman, *Republic of Letters,* 137.

6. *Encyclopédie,* 9:426. Exceptions to the prohibition against handing over the letters of one's correspondents are given, as when a missive letter must enter the juridical realm as evidence of a debt. A missive will, however, is declared nonvalid.

7. Perry, *Women, Letters, and the Novel,* 71. For more on Pope's letters, see Stephen Brown, "Alexander Pope's Correspondence as Fiction," *Studies on Voltaire and the Eighteenth Century* 304 (1992): 925–28.

8. Perry, *Women, Letters, and the Novel,* 70.

9. *Encyclopédie,* 9:411.

10. Ibid., 9:413.

11. For additional analysis of Servan's writings on letters and publication, see Dena Goodman, "Epistolary Property: Michel de Servan and the Plight of Letters on the Eve of the French Revolution," in *Early Modern Conceptions of Property,* edited by John Brewer and Susan Stave (New York: Routledge, 1995).

12. Autobiography may well have been defined in relation to the missive letter, given that it was a new genre. Rousseau's *Confessions* is considered the first autobiography in the modern sense; the word itself entered the French language through its English coinage in 1771.

13. Michel de Servan, *Réflexions sur les* Confessions *de J.-J. Rousseau* (Paris: Les Libraires qui vendent les nouveautés, 1783), p. 4. Future references by page number in the text.

14. The danger of letter writing is stressed in a 1751 manual by Eleazar de Mauvillon, for whom a letter "is a witness who may testify for or against its Author" (*General Treatise on Style, with a Particular Treatise on Epistolary Style,* p. 255; quoted by Teresa Sousa de Almeida, "Pour une théorie de la lettre au dix-huitième siècle," *Studies on Voltaire and the Eighteenth Century* 304 [1992]: 864). Such manuals do not interest me here per se, as I am far more interested in theoretical considerations of the epistolary genre, rather than practical advice on how to write letters. It is never-

theless important to note that Mauvillon follows his peers in insisting on the letter's style as "natural" and as an imitation of conversation.

15. The question of the author's sincerity in revealing "truth" is now debated most fiercely with regard to autobiography. Current arguments as to the value of autobiography—fiction or truth? literary or not?—mirror in interesting ways eighteenth-century preoccupations with the letter form.

16. De La Tour, *Correspondance originale et inédite*, 9.

17. The anti-Rousseau rhetoric is heightened in a review of these published letters by (probably the same) Michaud, signed "M . . . . . . d" and entitled "Quelques remarques sur le caractère de J.-J. Rousseau, à l'occasion de sa *Correspondance avec Mad. de Franqueville et M. Dupeyrou*," in *Le Spectateur français au XIX.ᵐᵉ siècle, ou Variétés morales politiques et littéraires, recueillies des meilleurs écrits périodiques*, vol. 2 (Paris: Société Typographique, 1805): 399–405. He repeats the assertions of the preface as to the value of the Rousseau-de La Tour exchange (albeit in a less effusive tone), then describes the second part of the work: "The second part of this collection contains several letters written by Rousseau during his stay in England and his return to France" (400). After ironically asking why, if Rousseau truly wanted to be happy, he did not stay with the animals in the forest, Michaud adds: "No, happiness is not that loud, it is not that ostentatious; it may increase in the presence of natural beauty, but it does not contain as a precept the exaltation of a poet or a mystic" (403).

18. See May, *Le Dilemme du roman au XVIIIᵉ siècle: Etude sur les rapports du roman et de la critique*, 1715–1761 (Paris: Presses Universitaires de France, 1963).

19. Terry Eagleton makes an important and related point concerning how another paradigmatic eighteenth-century female character was viewed/used by readers, and by her creator: "[Richardson's] calculated hesitancy between fact and fiction is more than a generic muddle; it belongs to a fruitful crisis in the whole problem of literary representation. The term *fiction*, let alone the contemptible *novel*, is ideologically impermissible—not because of some puritan neurosis about lying, but because it would seem merely to devalue the reality of the issues at stake . . . . It is true that Clarissa Harlowe never existed, but not important. As the fruit of certain dialogues and source of certain effects, Clarissa is, as it were, real enough to be going on with" (*The Rape of Clarissa* [Minneapolis: University of Minnesota Press, 1982], p. 16).

20. See *OC*, 2:9–30, 1344–55.

21. De Man, *Allegories of Reading*, p. 206.

22. Rousseau, *Lettre à d'Alembert*, 199–200.

23. The "Préface-Postface" is reproduced in Diderot, *Oeuvres*, 1383–1404. Croismare makes a cameo appearance in the Rousseau-de La Tour exchange when she proposes that he was the man with whom she had a discussion about Rousseau in a theater. Rousseau responds that Croismare was a person "to whom I surely never gave advice" (Dec. 18, 1762).

24. Diderot, *Oeuvres*, 1386.

25. Ibid., 1404.

26. Jane Tompkins describes this aspect of eighteenth-century aesthetics as echoing a classical concern with oratorical efficacy, albeit with a new emphasis on explaining effect as linked to technique, that is, to exploring mental functioning rather than guiding behavior. See "The Reader in History: The Changing Shape of

Literary Response," in *Reader-Response Criticism: From Formalism to Post-Structuralism*, edited by Jane P. Tompkins (Baltimore: Johns Hopkins University Press, 1980), p. 213. Elizabeth J. MacArthur also analyzes this lack of interest in *Extravagant Narratives: Closure and Dynamics in the Epistolary Form* (Princeton: Princeton University Press, 1990), pp. 100–101.

27. Charles Augustin de Sainte-Beuve, "Madame de La Tour-Franqueville et Jean-Jacques Rousseau," *Causeries du lundi* (Paris: Garnier Frères, 1858), p. 2:63. Future references by page number in the text. For an analysis of Sainte-Beuve's essay, see Roger Fayolle, *Sainte-Beuve et le XVIII*ᵉ *siècle ou comment les révolutions arrivent* (Paris: Armand Colin, 1972), pp. 92–107. Fayolle castigates Sainte-Beuve for misreading de La Tour, who for him is a sentimental heroine, however insignificant: "Uniquely concerned with demonstrating that her passion was false, [Sainte-Beuve] does not notice the patience and humility demonstrated by Jean-Jacques's correspondent" (94).

28. Michaud makes a similar comment in his review, although it is far from the central point of his remarks, being relegated to a note. Unlike Sainte-Beuve, he is aiming to mock rather than to understand Rousseau: "One may judge Rousseau's character by that of his most fervent partisans; they are always women or young men who have not acquired much real knowledge, or who are in an exalted state of mind. But when one reaches maturity, when one has embraced a particular party, whether one remains religious or has become a real philosophe, one still admires the eloquent writer; but one is no longer of the cult of Rousseau" ("Quelques remarques," n. to p. 405).

29. For an analysis of Sainte-Beuve on eighteenth-century women writers, see Mary Trouille, "Eighteenth-Century Women Writers Through the Eyes of Sainte-Beuve: Gender Ideology and the Politics of Literary History," *Romance Notes* 37.1 (Fall 1996):3–16. See also Roxana M. Verona's examination of the relationship between women's virtue and their exclusion from the canon in the writings of Sainte-Beuve, "*Au bonheur des dames*: Sainte-Beuve's Literary Agency," *French Forum* 19.3 (Sept. 1994): 279–94.

30. As a child, Mlle Aïssé was purchased at a slave auction by the French ambassador to Constantinople; she received a convent education in France, and lived an eventful life in Paris. Sainte-Beuve devotes one of his *Literary Portraits* to her letters (1787). Mme de Coulanges figures among Mme de Sévigné's correspondents.

31. Charles Augustin de Sainte-Beuve, "Madame de Sévigné," in *Oeuvres* (Paris: Gallimard, 1951), p. 2:1006. Bury explores Sainte-Beuve's reading of Sévigné in "Madame de Sévigné face aux critiques du XIX*ᵉ* siècle."

32. *Encyclopédie*, 5:816.

33. Fontette de Sommery, *Lettres de Madame la Comtesse de L*** à Monsieur le comte de R**** (Paris: Barrois l'Aîné, 1785), p. ij.

34. Bernard Bray, "Madame de Sévigné personnage de roman: les *Lettres de Madame la Comtesse de L*** à Monsieur le Comte de R**** de Mlle Fontette de Sommery (1785)," in *Correspondances: Mélanges offerts à Roger Duchêne*, edited by Wolfgang Leiner and Pierre Ronzeaud (Tübingen: Narr, 1992), p. 435.

35. Ibid., 435; quoting Sommery, *Doutes sur différentes opinions reçues dans la société*, 153.

36. See, as referenced in the introduction, Grassi, "Naissance d'un nouveau modèle," and Montfort-Howard, "Les Fortunes de Mme de Sévigné au XVIII*ᵉ* siècle."

37. Gabriel-Henri Gaillard, review of *Lettres de Mme la Comtesse de L*** à M. le Comte de R****, by Mlle Fontette de Sommery [review unsigned], *Mercure de France* January 1786: 159. Future references by page number in the text.

38. Trousson, *Rousseau*, 2:137.

Chapter 4. Authenticity Devalued

1. Quoted by Susan Read Baker, "The Rhetoric of Self-Presentation in Saint-Evremond," *French Literature Series: Strategies of Rhetoric* 19 (1992): 19.

2. I take these principles from Claudine Gothot-Mersch, "Sur le renouvellement des études de correspondances littéraires: l'exemple de Flaubert," *Romantisme* 72 (1991): 5–30.

3. Pierre Riberette, "On Editing Chateaubriand's Correspondence," *Yale French Studies* 71 (1986): 135.

4. Ibid., 145.

5. Sainte-Beuve, "Madame de La Tour-Franqueville," *Causeries du lundi*, 2:81.

6. Bossis, "Methodological Journeys Through Correspondences," 63.

7. Alexandre Deleyre (1726–97) collaborated on the *Encyclopédie* ("Fanaticism"), edited a journal, and wrote some romances put to music by Rousseau, before becoming a private librarian. In the *Confessions* Rousseau accuses Diderot of turning Deleyre against him (*OC*, 4:428–29). After visiting Montmorency with an uninvited woman friend, which greatly upset Rousseau, Deleyre informed his host that he had not only promised to marry the woman in question but had signed the document attesting to this promise in blood. Rousseau's careful positioning of himself vis-à-vis friendship and love in his response of November 10, 1759, is noteworthy: "Dear Deleyre, without being your friend, I feel friendship toward you, and am alarmed by your state. Ah please remember that love is only an illusion, that we see nothing as it is when we are in love; if you retain one spark of reason, do nothing without the consent of your parents" (*CC*, 6:884).

8. Vincent Kaufmann, *L'Equivoque épistolaire* (Paris: Minuit, 1990), p. 8.

9. Sainte-Beuve, *Oeuvres*, 2:1163. See Gita May's discussion of Roland's epistolary style in *De Jean-Jacques Rousseau à Mme Roland: essai sur la sensibilité préromantique et révolutionnaire* (Geneva: Droz, 1964), p. 29–34.

10. Kaufmann, *L'Equivoque épistolaire*, 8.

11. Gothot-Mersch, "Sur le renouvellement des études de correspondances littéraires," 5.

12. See my account of Deloffre and Rougeot's successful attempt to prove Guilleragues's authorship in "Poststructuralist Feminism and the Imaginary Woman Writer: The *Lettres portugaises*," *Romantic Review* 90.1 (January 2000): 27–44.

13. Gabriel Joseph de Lavergne de Guilleragues, *Correspondance*, edited by Frédéric Deloffre and Jacques Rougeot (Geneva: Droz, 1976), p. vii.

14. Marie-Claire Grassi, *L'Art de la lettre au temps de La Nouvelle Héloïse et du romantisme* (Geneva: Slatkine, 1994), p. 211.

15. Ibid., 222.

16. De La Tour was perhaps fortunate not to receive a more biting response to her attempt to engage Rousseau in a discussion of his *Emile*, given that the tutor makes quite clear in book 4 that women are not to meddle in such matters: "Since

[women] established themselves as the arbiters of literature, since they began to judge books and to do so with all their force, they no longer know anything. Authors who consult learned women about their works are sure to be always misadvised" (*OC,* 4:673).

17. Labrosse, *Lire au XVIIIe siècle,* 11. Future references by page number in the text.

18. Trousson, *Jean-Jacques Rousseau,* 2:38.

19. See *CC,* n. to 9:1502, for what is known of de La Tour's marriage.

20. Samuel Richardson's productive exchanges with his readers illustrates that authors could even be open to participation in the composition of their novels. See Eagleton, *The Rape of Clarissa,* 7–17.

21. Naomi Schor, "For a Restricted Thematics: Writing, Speech, and Difference in *Madame Bovary,*" in *The Future of Difference,* edited by Hester Eisenstein and Alice Jardine (Boston: G. K. Hall and Co., 1980), p. 177.

22. May, *Jean-Jacques Rousseau/Madame de La Tour,* 8. Future references by page number in the text.

23. For another example of a woman whose letters were consistently misread in this way, despite what I view as obvious authorial desire, see my forthcoming article in *Comparative Literature:* "Goethe's Number-One Fan: A Neo-Feminist Reading of Bettina Brentano-von Arnim, with Balzac and Kundera."

24. May came across this question when he consulted my original treatment of de La Tour's letters in my dissertation, "Rhetoric, Genre and Gender in Eighteenth-Century France," to which he refers; I consider similar issues in a 1997 article, "Julie Responds to St. Preux: Marie-Anne de La Tour's Letters to Rousseau," *Women in French Studies* 5 (1997): 135–48.

Chapter 5. Postscript

1. For an important exception, see Lorely French, *German Women as Letter Writers: 1750–1850* (Madison: Fairleigh Dickinson Press, 1996).

2. On the phenomenon of men writing fictional letters by women to great effect and fame, see for example Madeleine Kahn, *Narrative Transvestism* (Ithaca, Cornell University Press, 1991); and especially Nancy K. Miller, "'I's' in Drag: The Sex of Recollection," *The Eighteenth Century* 22.1 (Winter 1982): 47–57.

3. Choderlos de Laclos, review of *Cecilia ou les Mémoires d'une héritière,* in *Oeuvres complètes* (Paris: Gallimard, 1979), p. 450.

4. See "Lafayette's Ellipses," *PMLA* 99 (1984): 884–902, Joan DeJean's important contribution to this issue, in which she reads Mme de Lafayette's anonymous publication of *La Princesse de Clèves* (1678) as a strategy of simultaneous self-defense and self-promotion.

5. Servan, *Réflexions,* 111–12.

6. Jean Bloch, "The Eighteenth Century: Women Writing, Women Learning," in *A History of Women's Writing in France,* edited by Sonya Stephens (Cambridge: Cambridge University Press, 2000), n. to p. 100.

7. See my article, "Historical Autobiography: The *Mémoires de Mme Roland,*" *Romance Quarterly* 47.1 (Winter 2000): 3–17.

8. Beasley, "Altering the Fabric of History," 80.

9. Bloch, "The Eighteenth Century," 86.

10. Dena Goodman, "Suzanne Necker's *Mélanges*: Gender, Writing, and Publicity," in *Going Public: Women and Publishing in Early Modern France*, edited by Elizabeth C. Goldsmith and Dena Goodman (Ithaca: Cornell University Press, 1995), p. 223.

11. Ibid., 215.

12. Dena Goodman, "Julie de Lespinasse: A Mirror for the Enlightenment," in *Eighteenth-Century Women and the Arts*, edited by Frederick M. Keener and Susan E. Lorsch (New York: Greenwood Press, 1988).

13. Goodman, "Suzanne Necker's *Mélanges*," 214, quoting from *Mélanges extraits des manuscrits de Mme Necker* (Paris: C. Pougens, 1798), 3:382.

14. Elizabeth Goldsmith, *Writing the Female Voice: Essays on Epistolary Literature*, edited by Elizabeth C. Goldsmith (Boston: Northeastern University Press, 1989), p. vii.

15. For a history of the debate, see *Conflicts in Feminism*, edited by Marianne Hirsch and Evelyn Fox Keller (New York: Routledge, 1990), pp. 105–20. For an expansion of the argument I am making here, see my article "Poststructuralist Feminism."

16. See Gabrielle Verdier, "Gender and Rhetoric in Some Seventeenth-Century Love Letters," *L'Esprit Créateur* 23.2 (Summer 1983): 45–57.

17. Miller, " 'I's' in Drag," 56.

18. Ibid., 70.

19. Ibid., 72 (her emphasis).

20. Goldsmith, "Authority, Authenticity, and the Publication of Letters by Women," in *Writing the Female Voice: Essays on Epistolary Literature*, edited by Elizabeth C. Goldsmith (Boston: Northeastern University Press, 1989), p. 56.

21. *Année littéraire* 8 (1778): 274–85.

22. Patricia Meyer Spacks has studied the rhetoric of Boswell's *Journals* in comparison to autobiographical writing by eighteenth-century women, and concluded that "unlike his female counterparts, [Boswell] demonstrates no paramount need to defend against the opinion of others, although his concern with appearances yields to none in its intensity" (*Imagining a Self*, 16).

23. Reiberg, "James Boswell's Personal Correspondence," 252.

24. For more information on Henriette's letters and attempts to identify her, see Leigh's notes to *CC*, 19:3192.

25. For a stylistic analysis of the exchange, see Anna Jaubert, *Etude stylistique de la correspondance entre Henriette *** et J.-J. Rousseau* (Paris: Champion, 1987).

26. His suspicions were nonetheless known to Curchod herself. In a letter of June 7, 1764, Julie von Bondeli, whose style Rousseau had admired for its androgynous quality, wrote to Curchod that she would defend her if she were herself still in contact with Rousseau. The terms of her own break with Rousseau are obvious in Bondeli's letter: "I suspect that he will no longer write me, I will let him do so, he is wrong to accuse me of having wanted to praise him at Voltaire's expense, I never thought of doing so. However if he writes me again, I will certainly defend you" (*CC*, 20:3329).

27. *J.-J. Rousseau et Henriette, jeune Parisienne inconnue*, edited by Hippolyte Buffenoir (Paris: Leclerc, 1902), p. 36.

28. Ibid., 37.

29. Ibid., iv.

30. Mary Trouille, *Sexual Politics in the Enlightenment: Women Writers Read Rousseau* (Albany: SUNY Press, 1997), n. 46 to p. 335.

31. Ibid., 79.

32. Ibid., 91.

33. Nancy K. Miller, "Women's Autobiography in France: For a Dialectics of Identification," in *Women and Language in Literature and Society*, edited by Sally Mc-Connell-Ginet, Ruth Borker, and Nelly Furman (New York: Praeger, 1980), p. 58; Birgitte Szymanek, "French Women's Revolutionary Writings: Madame Roland or the Pleasures of the Mask," *Tulsa Studies in Women's Literature* 15.1 (Spring 1996): 113.

34. Sidonie Smith, *A Poetics of Women's Autobiography: Marginality and the Fictions of Self-Representation* (Bloomington: Indiana University Press, 1987), p. 176.

35. Although Szymanek's study was published in 1996, the year after *Women's Words* appeared in French, it might have served as exhibit A for the type of treatment of Roland that Ozouf is denouncing. Ozouf herself cites next to no examples. Mona Ozouf, *Les Mots des femmes: Essai sur la singularité française* (Paris: Fayard, 1995); *Women's Words: Essay on French Singularity*, translated by Jane Marie Todd (Chicago: University of Chicago Press, 1997).

36. Virginia Woolf, *A Room of One's Own* (New York: Harcourt, Brace & World, n.d. [first published 1929]), p. 77.

37. Ibid, 103.

38. In *What Is a Woman? and Other Essays* (Oxford: Oxford University Press, 1999), Toril Moi has convincingly argued that we should break free of the theoretical trap of constructionism by adapting Simone de Beauvoir's radical philosophy of individual freedom to the current needs of feminism; but in doing so, Moi goes around rather than through the roadblock that poststructuralist thought represents for any such insistence on the notion of individual autonomy. Moi's study, while a powerful redemption of Beauvoir's status as an existentialist philosopher in the face of poststructuralist attacks, is at the same time not entirely free of poststructuralism in its own right. Moi is well aware of this conundrum; the whole of her preface (vii-xvi) is devoted to this issue, particularly important to Moi as a thinker given the influence of her *Sexual/Textual Politics* (1985): "My new work is an attempt to work my way out from under poststructuralism (particularly in Chapter 1), and to see what happens when one goes elsewhere (particularly in Chapter 2)" (xii).

Bibliography

Altman, Janet Gurkin. *Epistolarity: Approaches to a Form.* Columbus: Ohio State University Press, 1982.

———. "The Letter Book as a Literary Institution 1539–1789: Toward a Cultural History of Published Correspondences in France." *Yale French Studies* 71 (1986): 17–62.

———. "Women's Letters in the Public Sphere." In *Going Public: Women and Publishing in Early Modern France*, edited by Elizabeth C. Goldsmith and Dena Goodman. Ithaca, NY: Cornell University Press, 1995.

Année Littéraire [Literary Year]. Geneva: Slatkine Reprints, 1966.

Attridge, Anna. "The Reception of *La Nouvelle Héloïse*." *Studies on Voltaire and the Eighteenth Century* 120 (1974): 227–67.

Baczko, Bronislaw. "Brûler Diderot" (Burn Diderot). In *Rousseau visité, Rousseau visiteur: les dernières années (1770–1778)*, edited by Jacques Berchtold and Michel Porret. Geneva: Droz, 1999.

Badinter, Elisabeth. *Emilie, Emilie: l'ambition féminine au XVIIIe siècle* (Emilie, Emilie: Feminine Ambition in the Eighteenth Century). Paris: Flammarion, 1983.

Baker, Susan Read. "The Rhetoric of Self-Presentation in Saint-Evremond." *French Literature Series: Strategies of Rhetoric* 19 (1992): 19–27.

Beasley, Faith. "Altering the Fabric of History: Women's Participation in the Classical Age." In *A History of Women's Writing in France*, edited by Sonya Stephens. Cambridge: Cambridge University Press, 2000.

Besterman, Theodore. *Voltaire.* New York: Harcourt, Brace & World, 1969.

Birn, Raymond. *Forging Rousseau: Print, Commerce, and Cultural Manipulation in the Late Enlightenment.* Oxford: SVEC, 2001.

Bloch, Jean. "The Eighteenth Century: Women Writing, Women Learning." In *A History of Women's Writing in France*, edited by Sonya Stephens. Cambridge: Cambridge University Press, 2000.

Bossis, Mireille. "Methodological Journeys through Correspondences." *Yale French Studies* 71 (1986): 63–75.

Bray, Bernard. "Madame de Sévigné personnage de roman: les *Lettres de Madame la Comtesse de L*** à Monsieur le Comte de R*** de Mlle Fontette de Sommery (1785)*" (Madame de Sévigné as a Character in a Novel: The *Letters of Madame la Comtesse de L*** to Monsieur le Comte de R*** by Mlle Fontette de Sommery, 1785). In *Correspondances: Mélanges offerts à Roger Duchêne*, edited by Wolfgang Leiner and Pierre Ronzeaud. Tübingen: Narr, 1992.

———. "Quelques Aspects du système épistolaire de Mme de Sévigné" (Some Aspects of the Epistolary System of Mme de Sévigné). *Revue d'Histoire Littéraire de la France* 69 (1969): 494–500.

Brown, Stephen. "Alexander Pope's Correspondence as Fiction." *Studies on Voltaire and the Eighteenth Century* 304 (1992): 925–28.

Bruss, Elizabeth. *Autobiographical Acts: The Changing Situation of a Literary Genre.* Baltimore: Johns Hopkins University Press, 1975.

Bury, Emmanuel. "Madame de Sévigné face aux critiques du XIXe siècle" (Madame de Sévigné According to the Critics of the Nineteenth Century). *Revue d'Histoire Littéraire de la France* 96 (1996): 446–60.

Conflicts in Feminism. Edited by Marianne Hirsch and Evelyn Fox Keller. New York: Routledge, 1990.

Cranston, Maurice. *The Noble Savage: Jean-Jacques Rousseau, 1754–62.* London: Penguin Press, 1991.

Darnton, Robert. "Readers Respond to Rousseau." In *The Great Cat Massacre and Other Episodes in French Cultural History.* New York: Vintage, 1985.

DeJean, Joan. "Lafayette's Ellipses: The Privileges of Anonymity." *PMLA* 99 (1984): 884–902.

De Man, Paul. *Allegories of Reading: Figural Language in Rousseau, Nietzsche, Rilke, and Proust.* New Haven, CT: Yale University Press, 1979.

Diderot, Denis. *Oeuvres* (Works). Paris: Gallimard, 1951.

Duchêne, Roger. "Du Destinataire au public, ou les métamorphoses d'une correspondance privée" (From the Recipient to the Public, or the Metamorphoses of a Private Correspondence). *Revue d'Histoire Littéraire de la France* 76 (1976): 29–46.

———. "Le Lecteur de lettres" (The Reader of Letters). *Revue d'Histoire Littéraire de la France* 78 (1978): 977–90.

———. "Réalité vécue et réussite littéraire: le statut particulier de la lettre" (Lived Reality and Literary Success: The Particular Status of the Letter). *Revue d'Histoire Littéraire de la France* 71 (1971): 177–94.

Eagleton, Terry. *The Rape of Clarissa.* Minneapolis: University of Minnesota Press, 1982.

Encyclopédie. Edited by Denis Diderot and Jean d'Alembert. Paris: Briasson [etc.], 1751–65.

Faguet, Emile. *Les Amies de Rousseau* (Rousseau's Women Friends). Paris: Société Française d'Imprimerie et de Librairie, 1910.

The Familiar Letter in the Eighteenth Century. Edited by Howard Anderson, Philip Daghlian, and Irvin Ehrenpreis. Lawrence: University of Kansas Press, 1966.

Fayolle, Roger. *Sainte-Beuve et le XVIIIe siècle ou comment les révolutions arrivent* (Sainte-Beuve and the Eighteenth-Century or How Revolutions Occur). Paris: Armand Colin, 1972.

Femmes en toutes lettres: Les épistolières du XVIIIe siècle (Women of Letters: The Women Letter Writers of the Eighteenth Century). Edited by Marie-France Silver and Marie-Laure Girou Swiderski. Oxford: SVEC, 2000.

Fergus, Jan, and Janice Farrar Thaddeus. "Women, Publishers, and Money, 1790–1820." *Studies in Eighteenth-Century Culture* 17 (1987): 191–207.

Fontanier, Pierre. *Les Figures du discours* (Figures of Discourse). Paris: Flammarion, 1977.

Foucault, Michel. "What is an Author?" In *The Foucault Reader*, edited by Paul Rabinow. New York: Pantheon, 1984.

French, Lorely. *German Women as Letter Writers: 1750–1850.* Madison, NJ: Fairleigh Dickinson Press, 1996.

Gaillard, Gabriel-Henri. Review of *Lettres de Mme la Comtesse de L*** à M. le Comte de R****, by Mlle Fontette de Sommery. [Review unsigned]. *Mercure de France,* January 1786, 159–78.

Gelbart, Nina Rattner. *Feminine and Opposition Journalism in Old Regime France: Le Journal des dames.* Berkeley: University of California Press, 1978.

Going Public: Women and Publishing in Early Modern France. Edited by Elizabeth C. Goldsmith and Dena Goodman. Ithaca, NY: Cornell University Press, 1995.

Goldsmith, Elizabeth C. "Authority, Authenticity, and the Publication of Letters by Women." In *Writing the Female Voice: Essays on Epistolary Literature*, edited by Elizabeth C. Goldsmith. Boston: Northeastern University Press, 1989.

Goodman, Dena. "Epistolary Property: Michel de Servan and the Plight of Letters on the Eve of the French Revolution." In *Early Modern Conceptions of Property*, edited by John Brewer and Susan Stave. New York: Routledge, 1995.

———. "The Hume-Rousseau Affair: From Private *Querelle* to Public *Procès*." *Eighteenth-Century Studies* 25, no. 2 (1991): 171–201.

———. "Julie de Lespinasse: A Mirror for the Enlightenment." In *Eighteenth-Century Women and the Arts*, edited by Frederick M. Keener and Susan E. Lorsch. New York: Greenwood Press, 1988.

———. *The Republic of Letters.* Ithaca, NY: Cornell University Press, 1994.

———. "Suzanne Necker's *Mélanges*: Gender, Writing, and Publicity." In *Going Public: Women and Publishing in Early Modern France*, edited by Elizabeth C. Goldsmith and Dena Goodman. Ithaca, NY: Cornell University Press, 1995.

Gothot-Mersch, Claudine. "Sur le renouvellement des études de correspondances littéraires: l'exemple de Flaubert" (On the Renewal of the Study of Literary Correspondences: The Example of Flaubert). *Romantisme* 72 (1991): 5–30.

Graffigny, Françoise de. *Letters from a Peruvian Woman.* Translated by David Kornacker. New York: MLA, 1993.

Grassi, Marie-Claire. *L'Art de la lettre au temps de* La Nouvelle Héloïse *et du romantisme* (The Art of the Letter at the Time of *The New Heloise* and Romanticism). Geneva: Slatkine, 1994.

———. "Naissance d'un nouveau modèle: l'apparition de Madame de Sévigné dans les manuels épistolaires" (Birth of a New Model: The Appearance of Madame de Sévigné in the Epistolary Manuals). *Revue d'Histoire Littéraire de la France* 96 (1996): 446–60.

Guillemin, Henri. *"Cette affaire infernale." L'affaire J.-J. Rousseau-Hume – 1766* ("That Infernal Affair." The J.-J. Rousseau-Hume Affair—1766). Paris: Plon, 1942.

Guilleragues, Gabriel Joseph de Lavergne. *Correspondance.* Edited by Frédéric Deloffre and Jacques Rougeot. Geneva: Droz, 1976.

———. *Lettres portugaises, Valentins et autres oeuvres de Guilleragues* (*The Portuguese Let-*

ters, Valentins, and Other Works by Guilleragues). Edited by Frédéric Deloffre and Jacques Rougeot. Paris: Garnier, 1962.

Guyot, Charly. *Un Ami et défenseur de Rousseau: Pierre-Alexandre Du Peyrou* (A Friend and Defender of Rousseau: Pierre-Alexandre Du Peyrou). Neuchâtel: Ides et Calendes, 1958.

Hall, Martin. "Eighteenth-Century Women Novelists: Genre and Gender." In *A History of Women's Writing in France,* edited by Sonya Stephens. Cambridge: Cambridge University Press, 2000.

Henriette ***. *J.-J. Rousseau et Henriette, jeune Parisienne inconnue, manuscrit inédit du XVIIIe siècle* (J.-J. Rousseau and Henriette, A Young Unknown Parisian, An Unpublished Manuscript from the Eighteenth Century). Edited by Hippolyte Buffenoir. Paris: Leclerc, 1902.

Herbold, Sarah. "Rousseau's Dance of Veils: The *Confessions* and the Imagined Woman Reader." *Eighteenth-Century Studies* 32, no. 3 (Spring 1999): 333–53.

Hesse, Carla. "Female Authorship and Revolutionary Law." *Eighteenth-Century Studies* 22, no. 3 (Spring 1989): 469–87.

A History of Women's Writing in France. Edited by Sonya Stephens. Cambridge: Cambridge University Press, 2000.

Horowitz, Louise K. "The Correspondence of Madame de Sévigné: Letters or Belles-lettres?" *French Forum* 6, no. 1 (January 1981): 13–27.

Hume, David. *Exposé succinct de la contestation qui s'est élévée entre M. Hume et M. Rousseau avec les pièces justificatives* (A Concise Account of the Quarrel That Arose between M. Hume and M. Rousseau, with Documents). Translated by Jean-Baptiste-Antoine Suard. London: [s.n.], 1766.

Jackson, Susan Klem. "Redressing Passion: Sophie d'Houdetot and the Origins of *Julie, ou la Nouvelle Héloïse.*" *Studies in Eighteenth-Century Culture* 17 (1987): 271–87.

James, Henry. "The Real Thing." In *Complete Stories, 1892–1898.* New York: Library of America, 1984.

Jaubert, Anna. *Etude stylistique de la correspondance entre Henriette *** et J.-J. Rousseau* (Stylistic Analysis of the Correspondence between Henriette and J.-J. Rousseau). Paris: Champion, 1987.

Kahn, Madeleine. *Narrative Transvestism.* Ithaca, NY: Cornell University Press, 1991.

Kamuf, Peggy. "Writing Like a Woman." In *Women and Language in Literature and Society,* edited by Sally McConnell-Ginet, Ruth Borker, and Nelly Furman. New York: Praeger, 1980.

Kaufmann, Vincent. *L'Equivoque épistolaire* (Epistolary Ambiguity). Paris: Minuit, 1990.

Klein, Lawrence E. "Gender and the Public/Private Distinction in the Eighteenth Century: Some Questions about Evidence and Analytic Procedure." *Eighteenth-Century Studies* 29, no. 1 (1995): 97–109.

Labrosse, Claude. *Lire au XVIIIe siècle:* La Nouvelle Héloïse *et ses lecteurs* (Reading in the Eighteenth Century: *The New Heloise* and Its Readers). Lyons: Presses Universitaires de Lyons, 1985.

Laclos, Choderlos de. *Oeuvres complètes* (Complete Works). Paris: Gallimard, 1979.

Landes, Joan B. *Women and the Public Sphere in the Age of the French Revolution.* Ithaca, NY: Cornell University Press, 1988.

La Tour [Franqueville], Marie-Anne [Marianne] de. "L'Anti-Grelot, Par Mme de ***" (The Anti-Grelot, by Mme de ***). N.p.: n.d. [1754].

————. *Correspondance originale et inédite de J.-J. Rousseau avec Mme Latour de Franqueville et M. Du Peyrou* (Original Unpublished Correspondence of J.-J. Rousseau with Mme Latour de Franqueville and M. Du Peyrou). 2 vols. Paris: Giguet and Michaud, 1803.

————. *Jean-Jacques Rousseau/Madame de La Tour: Correspondance.* Edited by Georges May. Arles: Actes Sud, 1998.

————. *Jean Jaques Rousseau vangé* [*sic*] *par son amie, ou morale practico-philosophico-encyclopédique des coryphées de la secte* (Jean Jaques Rousseau Avanged [*sic*] by his Woman Friend or Practical-Philosophical-Encyclopedic Morality of the Leaders of the Sect). Paris: Au Temple de la vérité, 1779.

————. *Précis pour M. J. J. Rousseau, en réponse à 'l'exposé succinct de M. Hume': suivi d'une lettre de Madame de *** à l'auteur de la justification de M. Rousseau* (Brief for M. J.-J. Rousseau, in Response to the Concise Account by M. Hume: Followed by a Letter by Madame D*** to the Author of the Justification of M. Rousseau). N.p., 1767.

————. *La Vertu vengée par l'amitié ou Recueil de lettres sur J. J. Rousseau par Madame de *** (Virtue Avenged by Friendship, or Collection of Letters on J. J. Rousseau by Madame de ***). Vol. 6 of *Supplément à la Collection des oeuvres de J.-J. Rousseau* [or vol. 30:52–90 of *Collection des oeuvres*, 33 vols., edited by Alexandre Du Peyrou]. Geneva, 1782.

Lecercle, Jean-Louis. "Rousseau critique littéraire: 'le coeur' et 'la plume'" (Rousseau as literary critic: "the heart" and "the pen"). In *Reappraisals of Rousseau: Studies in Honor of R. A. Leigh,* edited by Simon Harvey, Marian Hobson, David Kelley, and Samuel S. B. Taylor. Manchester: Manchester University Press, 1980.

Lee, Vera. "The Edifying Examples." In *French Women and the Age of Enlightenment,* edited by Samia I. Spencer. Bloomington: Indiana University Press, 1984.

MacArthur, Elizabeth J. *Extravagant Narratives: Closure and Dynamics in the Epistolary Form.* Princeton, NJ: Princeton University Press, 1990.

May, Georges. *Le Dilemme du roman au XVIIIᵉ siècle: Etude sur les rapports du roman et de la critique, 1715–1761)* (The Dilemma of the Novel in the Eighteenth Century: A Study of the Relationship between the Novel and Criticism, 1715–1761). Paris: Presses Universitaires de France, 1963.

————. "L'Histoire a-t-elle engendré le roman?" (Did History Give Birth to the Novel?). *Revue d'Histoire Littéraire de la France* 55 (1955): 155–76.

May, Gita. *De Jean-Jacques Rousseau à Mme Roland: essai sur la sensibilité préromantique et révolutionnaire* (From Jean-Jacques Rousseau to Mme Roland: Essay on Preromantic and Revolutionary Sensibility). Geneva: Droz, 1964.

————. "Rousseau's 'Antifeminism' Reconsidered." In *French Women and the Age of Enlightenment,* edited by Samia I. Spencer. Bloomington: Indiana Univeristy Press, 1984.

McAlpin, Mary. "Historical Autobiography: The *Mémoires de Mme Roland.*" *Romance Quarterly* 47, no.1 (Winter 2000): 3–17.

————. "Julie Responds to St. Preux: Marie-Anne de La Tour's Letters to Rousseau." *Women in French Studies* 5 (1997): 135–48.

———. "Poststructuralist Feminism and the Imaginary Woman Writer: The *Lettres portugaises*." *Romanic Review* 90, no. 1 (January 2000): 27–44.

Meltzer, Françoise. "Laclos' Purloined Letter." *Critical Inquiry* 8 (Spring 1982): 515–29.

M. . . . . .d [Michaud]. "Quelques remarques sur le caractère de J.-J. Rousseau, à l'occasion de sa *Correspondance avec Mad. de Franqueville et M. Dupeyrou*" (Some Remarks on the Character of J.-J. Rousseau, on the Occasion of his *Correspondence with Mad. de Franqueville and M. Dupeyrou*). In *Le Spectateur français au XIX.*^*me* *siècle, ou Variétés morales politiques et littéraires, recueillies des meilleurs écrits périodiques*, 2:399–405. Paris: Société Typographique, 1805. Originally *Mercure de France* 13 (1803) [messidor an 11]:111–20.

Miller, Nancy K. " 'I's' in Drag: The Sex of Recollection." *Eighteenth Century* 22, no. 1 (Winter 1982): 47–57.

———. "The Text's Heroine." In *Subject to Change: Reading Feminist Writing*. New York: Columbia University Press, 1988.

———. "Women's Autobiography in France: For a Dialectics of Identification." In *Women and Language in Literature and Society*, edited by Sally McConnell-Ginet, Ruth Borker, and Nelly Furman. New York: Praeger, 1980.

Moi, Toril. *What Is a Woman? and Other Essays*. Oxford: Oxford University Press, 1999.

Montfort-Howard, Catherine. "Les Fortunes de Mme de Sévigné au XVIIIe siècle" (The Fortunes of Mme de Sévigné in the XVIIIth Century). *Etudes littéraires françaises* 18. Tübingen: Gunter Narr, 1982.

Motsch, Markus F. "The Forgotten Genre: The Poetic Epistle in Eighteenth-Century German Literature." In *Studies in Eighteenth-Century Culture*, vol. 4, edited by Harold E. Pagliaro. Madison: University of Wisconsin Press, 1975.

Nies, Fritz. "Un genre féminin?" (A Feminine Genre?) *Revue d'Histoire Littéraire de la France* 78 (1978): 994–1003.

Ozouf, Mona. *Les Mots des femmes: Essai sur la singularité française*. Paris: Fayard, 1995. *Women's Words: Essay on French Singularity*. Translated by Jane Marie Todd. Chicago: University of Chicago Press, 1997.

Perry, Ruth. *Women, Letters, and the Novel*. New York: AMS, 1980.

Plan, Pierre-Paul. *Jean-Jacques Rousseau raconté par les gazettes de son temps* (Jean-Jacques Rousseau in the Gazettes of His Day). Paris: Mercure de France, 1912.

Redford, Bruce. *The Converse of the Pen: Acts of Intimacy in the Eighteenth-Century Familiar Letter*. Chicago: University of Chicago Press, 1986.

Reiberg, Rufus. "James Boswell's Personal Correspondence: The Dramatized Quest for Identity." In *The Familiar Letter in the Eighteenth Century*, edited by Howard Anderson, Philip B. Daghlian, and Irvin Ehrenpreis. Lawrence: University of Kansas Press, 1966.

Riberette, Pierre. "On Editing Chateaubriand's Correspondence." Translated by Charles A. Porter. *Yale French Studies* 71 (1986): 131–47.

Rousseau, Jean-Jacques. *Correspondance complète de Jean-Jacques Rousseau* (Complete Correspondence of Jean-Jacques Rousseau). Edited by R. A. Leigh. 52 vols. Oxford: Voltaire Foundation, 1965–98.

———. *Lettre à M. d'Alembert sur les spectacles* (Letter to M. d'Alembert on Theater). Paris: Garnier-Flammarion, 1967.

———. *Oeuvres complètes* (Complete Works). Edited by Bernard Gagnebin and Marcel Raymond. 4 vols. Paris: Gallimard, 1959–69.

Sainte-Beuve, Charles Augustin de. *Causeries du lundi* (Monday Chats). 16 vols. Paris: Garnier Frères, 1858.

———. *Oeuvres*. 2 vols. Paris: Gallimard, 1951.

Schor, Naomi. "For a Restricted Thematics: Writing, Speech, and Difference in *Madame Bovary*." Translated by Harriet Stone. In *The Future of Difference*, edited by Hester Eisenstein and Alice Jardine. Boston: G. K. Hall, 1980.

Servan, Joseph-Michel-Antoine de. "Réflexions sur la publication des lettres de Rousseau, et des lettres en général" (Reflections on the Publication of Rousseau's Letters, and of Letters in General). In *Réflexions sur les Confessions de J.-J. Rousseau*. Paris: Les Libraires qui vendent les nouveautés, 1783.

Showalter, English. "Authorial Self-Consciousness in the Familiar Letter: The Case of Madame de Graffigny." *Yale French Studies* 71 (1986): 113–30.

Smith, Sidonie. *A Poetics of Women's Autobiography: Marginality and the Fictions of Self-Representation*. Bloomington: Indiana University Press, 1987.

Sommery, Fontette de. *Lettres de Madame la comtesse de L*** à Monsieur le comte de R**** (Letters of Madame la comtesse de L*** to Monsieur le comte de R***). Paris: Barrois l'Aîné, 1785.

Sousa de Almeida, Teresa. "Pour une théorie de la lettre au dix-huitième siècle" (For a Theory of the Letter in the Eighteenth Century). *Studies on Voltaire and the Eighteenth Century* 304 (1992): 863–66.

Spacks, Patricia Meyer. *Imagining a Self: Autobiography and Novel in Eighteenth-Century England*. Cambridge, MA: Harvard University Press, 1976.

Stanton, Judith P. "Statistical Profile of Women Writing from 1660 to 1800." In *Eighteenth-Century Women and the Arts*, edited by Frederick M. Keener and Susan E. Lorsch. New York: Greenwood Press, 1988.

Starobinski, Jean. *Jean-Jacques Rousseau: la transparence et l'obstacle, suivi de sept essais sur Rousseau* (Jean-Jacques Rousseau: Transparency and Obstacle, Followed by Seven Essays on Rousseau). Paris: Gallimard, 1971.

Sturzer, Felicia. "Epistolary and Feminist Discourse: Julie de Lespinasse and Madame Riccoboni." *Studies on Voltaire and the Eighteenth Century* 304 (1992): 739–42.

Szymanek, Brigitte. "French Women's Revolutionary Writings: Madame Roland or the Pleasures of the Mask." *Tulsa Studies in Women's Literature* 15, no. 1 (Spring 1996): 99–122.

Tompkins, Jane P. "The Reader in History: The Changing Shape of Literary Response." In *Reader-Response Criticism: From Formalism to Post-Structuralism*, edited by Jane P. Tompkins. Baltimore: Johns Hopkins University Press, 1980.

Trouille, Mary Seidman. "Eighteenth-Century Women Writers Through the Eyes of Sainte-Beuve: Gender Ideology and the Politics of Literary History." *Romance Notes* 37, no. 1 (Fall 1996): 3–16.

———. *Sexual Politics in the Enlightenment: Women Writers Read Rousseau*. Albany: State University of New York Press, 1997.

Trousson, Raymond. *Jean-Jacques Rousseau.* 2 vols. Paris: Tallandier, 1988–89.

Verdier, Gabrielle. "Gender and Rhetoric in Some Seventeenth-Century Love Letters." *L'Esprit Créateur* 23, no. 2 (Summer 1983): 45–57.

Verona, Roxana M. "*Au bonheur des dames:* l'agence littéraire de Sainte-Beuve" (*Au bonheur des dames:* The Literary Agency of Sainte-Beuve). *French Forum* 19, no. 3 (Sept. 1994): 279–94.

Watt, Ian. *The Rise of the Novel: Studies in Defoe, Richardson, and Fielding.* Berkeley and Los Angeles: University of California Press, 1957.

Wolfgang, Aurora. "Fallacies of Literary History: The Myth of Authenticity in the Reception of *Fanni Butlerd.*" *Studies on Voltaire and the Eighteenth Century* 304 (1992): 735–39.

Woolf, Virginia. *A Room of One's Own.* New York: Harcourt, Brace & World, n.d. [first published 1929].

Writing the Female Voice: Essays on Epistolary Literature. Edited by Elizabeth C. Goldsmith. Boston: Northeastern University Press, 1989.

Index